THE PERRAULTS

THE PERRAULTS

A FAMILY OF LETTERS IN EARLY MODERN FRANCE

ODED RABINOVITCH

CORNELL UNIVERSITY PRESS
Ithaca and London

This book was published with the support of the Israel Science Foundation.

First published 2018 by Cornell University Press

Printed in the United States of America

Library of Congress Cataloging-in-Publication Data

Names: Rabinovitch, Oded, author.
Title: The Perraults : a family of letters in early modern
    France / Oded Rabinovitch.
Description: Ithaca : Cornell University Press, 2018. |
    Includes bibliographical references and index.
Identifiers: LCCN 2018019463 (print) | LCCN 2018020013
    (ebook) | ISBN 9781501730085 (e-book pdf) | ISBN
    9781501730092 (e-book epub/mobi) | ISBN
    9781501729423 | ISBN 9781501729423 (hardcover ;
    alk. paper)
Subjects: LCSH: Perrault family. | France—Intellectual life—
    17th century. | France—Civilization—17th century. |
    Families—France—History—17th century. | Social
    networks—France—History—17th century. | Perrault,
    Charles, 1628–1703. | Perrault, Claude, 1613–1688. |
    Perrault, P. (Pierre), 1611–1680.
Classification: LCC DC121.7 (ebook) | LCC DC121.7 .R33
    2018 (print) | DDC 929.20944—dc23
LC record available at https://lccn.loc.gov/2018019463

❧ Contents

❧ Figures

❧ ACKNOWLEDGMENTS

I have accumulated numerous debts of gratitude while researching and writing this book, and I am glad for the opportunity to acknowledge at least some of them. The project took shape at Brown University, under the benevolent guidance of Tara Nummedal. Ever perceptive and encouraging, Tara graciously taught me what professional history is like. Joan Richards and Caroline Castiglione patiently followed the progress of the manuscript and contributed many useful suggestions. Moshe Sluhovsky generously agreed to read this work at an early stage; going well beyond the call of duty, he has been unfailing in supporting the project ever since. At Harvard University, Ann Blair helped me to develop the book conceptually and empirically and offered an inimitable model of scholarship as a mentor. Tom Conley, Katharine Park, and Daniel Smail helped with astute advice; Patrice Higonnet generously braved a reading of the entire manuscript at a crucial moment.

In Paris, I was fortunate to find a home at the Groupe de Recherches Interdisciplinaires sur l'Histoire du Littéraire (GRIHL). The wonderful seminars opened new ways of looking at texts and contexts, and the warm hospitality made it an ideal home away from home. I thank Mathilde Bombart, Marion Brétéché, Alain Cantillon, Laurence Giavarini, Élie Haddad, Sophie Houdard, Judith Lyon-Caen, Bérengère Parmentier, Dinah Ribard, Marine Rousillon, Nicolas Schapira, Cécile Soudan, Alain Viala, and two at-large participants, Déborah Blocker and Xenia Von Tippelskirch. Special thanks go to Christian Jouhaud, who supported the project from an early stage and was always ready to share his intimate knowledge of the seventeenth century and his deep reflections on its history.

Many colleagues have discussed this work, read the manuscript (or parts of it), shared their own ideas, or helped with points of information. Giora Sternberg discussed the world of Louis XIV and early modern France with me countless times, in three continents and at all times of day and night. I am truly privileged to share a research field with a good friend. For their help and support in its many forms, I thank Danna Agmon, Clare Crowston,

Robert Descimon, Nicholas Dew, Jonathan Dewald, Marie-Claude Felton, Jorge Flores, Laurence Fontaine, Dena Goodman, Anita Guerini, Rivi Handler-Spitz, Julie Hardwick, Tim Harris, Christine Haynes, Elizabeth Hyde, Florence Hsia, Vera Keller, Virginia Krause, Evelyn Lincoln, Dániel Margócsy, Steven Mentz, Prabhu Mohapatra, Chandra Mukerji, Bérengère Parmentier, Ritika Prasad, Jeff Ravel, Amy Remensnyder, Thierry Rigogne, Meghan Roberts, David Sabean, Robert Schneider, Lewis Seifert, J. B. Shank, April Shelford, Peter Shoemaker, Otto Sibum, Jacob Soll, Alessandro Stanziani, Mary Terrall, Simon Teuscher, Geoffrey Turnovsky, Stéphane Van Damme, Liana Vardi, Jaqueline Wernimont, Kath Weston, Stephen White, Dorothee Wierling, and Abby Zanger. Maxime Martignon helped with opportune research assistance. S. R. Gilbert's unmatched linguistic skills greatly improved the phrasing and structure of this book.

I thank the staff at Cornell University Press, where Bethany Wasik and Jennifer Savran Kelly helped me through the editing and production phase. Jamie Fuller's eagle-eyed copyediting corrected numerous infelicities, and David Prout did an expert job indexing the volume. I am deeply grateful to Emily Andrew, who went out of her way to help a first-time author with invaluable feedback. Indeed, the two anonymous readers for the press have proved remarkably thorough and offered insightful feedback: any faults that remain are, of course, my own. Short sections of chapters 2 and 4 have appeared as "Stratégies familiales, carrières littéraires, et capitalisme de cour dans la famille Perrault," *XVIIᵉ siècle* 264 (2014): 403–15; an early version of chapter 5 appeared as "Versailles as a Family Enterprise: The Perraults, 1660–1700," *French Historical Studies* 36 (2013): 385–416 (Copyright, 2013, the Society of French Historical Studies. All rights reserved. Republished by permission of the copyrightholder, and the present publisher, Duke University Press. www.dukeupress.edu).

Tel Aviv University played an extraordinary role in my training, and I am fortunate to have returned to it as a teacher. The first seeds of this project were sown here, and this is where I completed the manuscript. I would like to thank the community of early modernists in the Department of History, who inspired me as teachers and have more recently sustained me as colleague: Benjamin Arbel, Élie Barnavi, Miriam Eliav-Feldon, Tamar Herzig, David Katz, Nadine Kuperty-Tsur, and Joseph Mali. Gadi Algazi deserves special thanks for introducing me to the social history of early modern scholars, for his remarkable breadth of knowledge, and for his incisive insights. When I was a first-year student at Tel Aviv's Interdisciplinary Program, Raz Chen-Morris—perhaps unwittingly—set me on this wandering path; many thanks! I have been learning a great deal from my students, and I would especially like to thank those whose theses taught me about the intellectual life of early modern France: Rachel Ben David, Netta Green, and Yoni Yedidya.

Numerous friends shared their intellectual enthusiasm and encouraged my work in so many ways. I thank Naor Ben-Yehoyada, Naama Cohen-Hanegbi, Daniel Hershenzon, Ayelet Even Ezra, Shaul Katzir, Noam Maggor, Tali and Sagi Schaefer, Amir Teicher, and Ittai Weinrib for innumerable conversations at Tel Aviv. Other friends helped me get to graduate school, to survive it, or both: Boaz Keren-Zur, Derek Seidman, Yuval Ramot, Raanan Schul, Yannay Spitzer, Julia Timpe, Eyal Tzur, Roy Vilozny, Adam Webster; Chris Barthel and Mo Moulton were true friends in need when I had to deal with the exotic way of life in the United States. Shay Rojanski did much the same in France and helped with designing the genealogies.

Librarians and archivists at the Archives de l'Académie des sciences, the Archives nationales, the Bibliothèque de l'Arsenal, the Bibliothèque Mazarine, the Bibliothèque nationale de France, and the Bibliothèque du château de Chantilly provided assistance in tracing the Perraults across the seventeenth century. I owe special thanks to Marie-Françoise Limon-Bonnet from the Minutier Central for going out of her way in making documents accessible. At Brown, I thank the staff of the Rockefeller and John Hay libraries, and especially Dominique Coulombe. At Harvard, I thank the staff of the Houghton and Weidner libraries. I am grateful for generous financial support from Brown University; the Fulbright program; the French government in the form of a Bourse Chateaubriand; the Program in Renaissance and Early Modern Studies and the Cogut Center for the Humanities at Brown University; the Zvi Yavetz Graduate School of Historical Studies at Tel Aviv University for a Thomas Arthur Arnold Postdoctoral Fellowship; the Israel Science Foundation, which supported this publication; and an invitation to spend a crucial month as a *Professeur invité* at the Université de Paris-Est (Marne-la-Vallée).

It is only fitting for this book to conclude with deep thanks to my own family: my brother, parents, and grandparents encouraged, supported, and sustained me throughout in innumerable ways, for which I am profoundly indebted. I cannot imagine a better partner in these academic and "real life" peregrinations than Inna. Romi and Ilay teach us every day about the challenges and opportunities of kinship.

❧ Abbreviations

Annales: E.S.C.	*Annales: Économies, sociétés, civilisations*
AAS	Archives de l'Académie des Sciences
AN	Archives nationales
BL	British Library
BN	Bibliothèque nationale de France
FF	Fond Français
MC	Minutier central des notaires de Paris
PV	Registre des procès-verbaux des séances

❧ CAST OF CHARACTERS

The Perrault Brothers

Pierre Perrault (1611–80[?]): A barrister by training, Pierre became a high-level functionary in the French monarchy's financial system until he was disgraced in the early 1660s. While he played host to sociable gatherings as a financier, he developed literary and scholarly ambitions after his disgrace. He composed a critique of *Don Quixote* and a scientific treatise on the origin of fountains.

Charles Perrault (1628–1703): Also trained as a barrister, he chose not to practice but invested himself in the career of his brother Pierre. Charles became a cultural advisor to Colbert and held formal commissions in the Royal Buildings. A writer with a keen sense of irony and wit, he was elected to the literary Académie française. Late in his career, he played a major role in the "quarrel of the ancients and the moderns" and composed toward the end of his career the canonical versions of *Mother Goose Tales*.

Claude Perrault (1613–88): A physician by training, he developed an unremarkable career until he was chosen as a founding member of the Parisian Academy of Sciences. He then invested himself in scientific and architectural projects, such as the design of the eastern façade of the Louvre and the translation in French of Vitruvius's classical work on architecture from the original Latin. Diligent and hardworking, he nonetheless probably owned his appointments to the influence his brother Charles had under Colbert.

Nicolas Perrault (1624–62): Trained as a theologian, he gained notoriety after defending Antoine Arnauld as the Jansenist crisis erupted at the Sorbonne. While he published vehemently anti-Jesuit works and was known for his piety, he also had a talent for mathematics and displayed a playful personality in composing a burlesque work with his brothers.

Jean Perrault (?–1669): He pursued the same legal career as his father had and did not collaborate to a significant extent with his brothers. Tragically, when

he traveled to Bordeaux with Claude in 1669, he became ill and was acciden-
tally bled to death by Claude and the local physicians.

Other Family Members and Noteworthy Characters

Catherine Lormier: Daughter of an officer in the *Cour des aides*, a Parisian tax
court, she married Pierre Perrault after she became a widow. Her personal
wealth, as well as her ability to play a role in the family's social life, was instrumental in Pierre's financial career.

Pierre Perrault (?–1652): Born to a royal embroiderer from Tours, he arrived
in Paris in the early seventeenth century and developed a career as a barrister
(*avocat*) in the city.

Paquette Le Clerc (?–1657): Daughter of a prosperous Parisian bourgeois, she
had networks that were probably instrumental in the family's early rise to
notability in the parish of Saint-Étienne-du-Mont. Pierre and Paquette married in Paris and guided the education of the generation of brothers that is
the focus of this book.

Christiaan Huygens (1629–95): One of the greatest scientific giants of the
seventeenth century, he was imported as a star to the Parisian Academy of Sciences and became a close friend of the Perrault family. A brilliant mathematician prone to bouts of depression, he also indulged himself in gambling and
the high society life around the Perraults' Parisian and countryside houses.

Jean-Baptiste Colbert (1619–83): Born to a mercantile family from Reims, Colbert rose to become a powerful minister in charge of finance, of the king's
buildings, and of the navy under the young Louis XIV. Assiduous, austere,
and ambitious, he became responsible for numerous cultural ventures of the
monarchy and developed the formal academy system that would characterize
the French cultural sphere until the Revolution.

Jean Chapelain (1595–1674): The son of a notary, he rose to fame on the basis
of his work as translator, poet, and critic, though his long-anticipated epic
poem on Jean d'Arc was greeted with derision. Under Richelieu, Chapelain
became an influential cultural broker who mediated the relations between the
monarchy and the world of letters, a role much more important than his pen
in establishing him as an influential Parisian author.

THE PERRAULTS

Introduction

A staple of children's literature for the better part of the last two centuries, Charles Perrault's "Cinderella" has been adapted and retold countless times. Bruno Bettelheim claimed in *The Uses of Enchantment*, his classic study of the psychological aspects of fairy tales, "By all accounts, 'Cinderella' is the best-known fairy tale, and probably also the best-liked."[1] Bettelheim explained this popularity through a reading that centered on the individual child and Oedipal feelings of guilt. But Perrault's "Cinderella" is at its core a story about the family and kinship. Charles Perrault and his readers took for granted the powerful embedding of individuals in networks of kinship, which played a considerable role in the fate not only of Cinderella but of every member of early modern society, from kings and queens to the most humble peasants.[2] This is obvious in the very opening sentences of the story:

> Once upon a time, there was a gentleman who married—it was his second marriage—the most condescending and arrogant woman ever seen. She had two daughters who resembled her in every way, including her unpleasant ways. On his side, the husband had a young daughter whose kindness and good nature were beyond compare. She had inherited them from her mother, who was the best person in the whole wide world. As soon as the wedding ceremony was over, the stepmother unleashed her bad temper. She could not tolerate the good qualities of this girl, who made her own daughters appear even more despicable.[3]

The first sentence of the tale presents not the protagonist but the marriage of her presumably widowed father to a second wife. As the story's other characters are introduced, their personal traits do not stem from an idiosyncratic and individualistic sense of self but from their lineage. Just like Cinderella, her stepsisters have inherited their mother's nature. The division of labor within the household is mirrored by the rooms the characters occupy. Cinderella, a drudge always slaving to keep the place clean, lives in the attic and sleeps on an "awful mattress," while her stepsisters have fashionable beds and large mirrors. Familial power dynamics shape the fabric of everyday life.

Cinderella's plight changes only through a familial intervention: the misery of being left behind when her stepsisters set off for the prince's ball triggers an intervention by her godmother. Significantly, Perrault presented this figure as godmother first and fairy second: during a previous conversation, he offered no hint about any supernatural powers. Only when they became relevant did he write, "Her godmother, who was a fairy, said, 'You want, more than anything, to dance at the ball, don't you?'"[4]

The resolution of the story, too, does not take place simply in individual terms. After the glass slipper is fitted to Cinderella's foot and she has produced its partner, her two stepsisters are stunned. Her godmother steps in to transform Cinderella's everyday rags into magnificent clothes. In a moral appended to the story, Perrault makes the point about family networks even plainer: no matter how fine one's talents and qualities, he explained, without godparents to publicize these qualities, one would never get ahead. The stepsisters understand this very well and throw themselves at her feet. After Cinderella marries the prince, she accordingly brings her stepsisters to the palace, where she "had them married that very day to two great lords from the court." Cinderella lived happily ever after only in the company of her formerly abusive kin. Even this kind of a happy conclusion did not imagine her as an untethered individual who broke free from her family.[5]

This book takes the family as a point of entry into a complex and rapidly changing world. Kinship networks played a crucial yet seldom examined role in the cultural and intellectual ferment of seventeenth-century France, even as culture in its turn shaped kinship. Just as Charles Perrault placed Cinderella in the context of kinship dynamics, so I place Charles in the web of his own family (see appendix for genealogies), whose kinship ties structured the careers and writing projects of its members.

Too often these ties are neglected, in spite of their importance. Since modern Western identity is heavily invested in notions of individuality, recent chapters in the history of the family emphasize the contraction or even

FIGURE 0.1. In Henri Testelin's depiction of Colbert presenting to Louis XIV the members of the newly created Royal Academy of Sciences, Charles Perrault stands immediately behind Colbert, carrying documents; above the monarch is an image of the Royal Observatory, whose design was widely attributed to Claude Perrault. Photo © Château de Versailles, Dist. RMN-Grand Palais / Christophe Fouin.

disappearance of kinship ties, culminating in the nuclear family. "Within this framework," write David Sabean and Simon Teuscher, "kinship is the functional predecessor of almost everything, but never a constructive factor in the emergence of anything."[6] Yet family and kinship were precisely "constructive factors" in the creation of the new cultural and intellectual forms of the seventeenth century. The careers of four Perrault brothers—Pierre, Claude, Nicolas, and Charles—overlapped and connected. Together, they take us straight into the heart of the problem of explaining cultural and intellectual change in early modern Europe. They wrote in vernacular French rather than Latin, and they laid claim to new forms of knowledge and new aesthetic forms. They spearheaded the scientific revolution and the newest trends in the world of vernacular literature. And, like Cinderella, they did so through the savvy use of networks and new institutions.

Pierre Perrault Sr., a barrister (*avocat*), moved to Paris from Tours in the first decade of the seventeenth century and married Paquette Le Clerc, daughter of a Parisian bourgeois. The couple had five children who survived to adulthood—Pierre, Jean, Claude, Nicolas, and Charles—and two who did not: a son, Charles's twin brother, who died at the age of six months, and a daughter named Marie who passed away at the age of thirteen. Starting in the 1660s, they ingratiated themselves with those at the pinnacle of power. Charles—a witty author with a knack for appealing to literary fashion but also a dedicated aide to his patrons—advised Colbert, Louis XIV's powerful minister, on the cultural politics of the monarchy, a role nicely documented in figure 0.1; with his brother Claude and his son, he worked on various courtly projects as well. Charles and Pierre both hosted sociable gatherings that brought together scientific luminaries, such as the Dutch Christiaan Huygens, as well as visual artists and aspiring writers. Their lives connect such cultural and intellectual interests, which today we associate with the scientific revolution and the rise of national literatures, to the histories of the family, of social mobility, of the role of networks in the creation of institutions. By looking at their lives as a whole, this book thus provides an integrative approach, finely articulating the connections among the institutional changes that defined early modern literature, science, and society.[7]

This discussion of the Perrault family combines the advantages of institutional and biographical approaches, taking account of the Perraults' broad range of interests as biographies do while aiming to avoid the biographical pitfalls of overestimating the influence of their subjects in the broader culture and underestimating the impact of institutions on individuals.[8] I have exploited a new corpus of sources, notarial documents that make possible an in-depth reconstruction of the Perraults' family strategies, updating scholarship that was conscious of the connections among family members but rarely focused on these kinship ties and on their broader implications.[9] I have treated the family as an institution crucial for the cultural and intellectual life of the seventeenth century, like long-recognized courts and academies. Kinship ties mattered just as much as other institutions, and any attempt to map social and cultural institutions in early modern France cannot ignore the family. Further, the complex networks that the Perraults wove offer new vantage points on the court, royal academies, and salons. Historians have stressed the formal regulation and inner mechanisms of such institutions, which come to appear as rigid entities that embody or define such concepts as Cartesianism, empiricism, or the purity of the French language.[10] By contrast, the Perraults' maneuvers reveal these institutions as nodes that connect actors, intellectual projects, family strategies, and practices of writing.

The result is a new and different understanding of the "genius" in the "century of genius."[11] There has been much debate on the "rise of the modern self," or the transformation of Europeans, previously defined by collectives such as the family, the local community, and the church, into introspective individuals, aware of their own distinctive emotions and their unique place in the world. Yet it is clear that the middle of the seventeenth century was a watershed moment, at least for intellectual definitions of the self.[12] It is equally clear that even the Enlightenment, when new forms of genius were consecrated, was shot through with anti-individualistic trends.[13] Understanding how these apparently contradictory cultural forms could interrelate becomes a crucial task. Many institutional forms consecrated writers and scientists like the Perraults as "individual geniuses," from publications in print bearing their names to biographical entries in dictionaries and prestigious seats in royal academies. This book uncovers the role of the family in the production of putatively isolated individuals and the multilayered interplay between the effective fiction of the solitary writer and the networks that made it possible. The newly gained autonomy of the individual was not a clean-cut switch between an "antiquated" identity based in collective terms and a new form of a reflective, individual self. Instead, it was predicated on forms of community, with the family taking a major place among them.[14]

Over the course of the seventeenth century, the Perraults developed from a family of lawyers new to Paris into a "family of letters" able to capitalize on new forms of scholarly and literary identity. Historians have used the concept of "family strategy" to deal with the tension between discussions of a family as a whole and of its individual members. Thinking in terms of strategies helps account for the choices made by family members in terms of the overall goals of the family. Scholars have recognized the usefulness of this concept, but they have also questioned the degree of conscious planning it implies and raised doubts about its tendency to occlude the decisions made by individuals.[15] Two additional ways of conceiving of family strategies, which do not rely on the need to view them as the results of conscious planning, are useful for studying the Perraults.

The Perraults' family strategy was an aggregate of the actions taken by a loosely connected group of actors with interlocking goals and behaviors. Changes in a family strategy are measured in terms of the actors taking center stage (hence not neglecting the importance of individuals), changing goals, and techniques used to achieve these goals.[16] So, for example, Charles embarked upon his literary career when he served as an aide to his brother, Pierre, who was involved in finances. Pierre, certainly ambitious and career-oriented, also kept up with the literary and intellectual pursuits of his brothers: he provided Charles with a library, and together they hosted Parisian notables in social events that served to circulate Charles's poetry. Claude abandoned the life of a physician and regent at the Faculty of Medicine to become a diligent member of the Academy of Sciences; he won the appointment and architectural commissions when his brother, Charles, was in a position to influence the decisions of Colbert, the minister in charge of such projects. These were concrete measures for helping one's siblings in reaction to changing circumstances, not necessarily the results of long-term planning.

Such examples of mutual help relate the Perraults' story to the second way of thinking about strategies, namely, as socially viable ways of achieving goals. Strategies, understood as ways of doing rather than as simple planning, are in fact one of the elements that show the constructed and historically specific form of intellectual life in the seventeenth century. Just like ideas or cultural forms, strategies changed over time, and forms of writing and publishing intermingled with considerations of patronage, politics, or kinship in ways that were highly contingent. This definition therefore highlights the fact that regardless of one's goals, there are only few career paths that lead to them.

At times individual members of the Perrault family probably made conscious strategic decisions, but I believe that only some of their actions were carefully considered; many were nothing but timely reactions to changing circumstances. In other words—and this is the third way for thinking about strategies—the history of the Perraults includes both strategic action, based on the ability to plan ahead from a position of strength, and tactical actions, attempts to deal with changing circumstances through improvisation.[17]

The Perraults were nothing if not ambitious. Pierre, Nicolas, Claude, and Charles (yet not Jean) were persistent in the pursuit of their ambitions, and when they floundered in finance, they took up the pen. But their personalities were much richer (see cast of characters). Charles had an acute sense of irony and combined wit with dry observation. Nicolas was indeed pious, as was becoming for a theologian, but he also participated in writing a humorous *burlesque* with his brothers. Claude epitomized the hard-working scholar after he was drawn at a relatively advanced stage in the career of a physician to the service of the monarchy's cultural projects. Pierre enjoyed playing the host to a variety of guests, but this apparently light-hearted nature did not stop him from composing a lengthy critique of *Don Quixote* or publishing on the nature of fountains.

The Perraults were praised or ignored by their contemporaries on the basis of common perceptions of authorship, as chapter 1 shows. While modern studies of authorship stress the emergence of the individual author through the relatively narrow frame of aesthetic categories and legal regulation based on censorship and copyright, here I show that in the seventeenth century people turned to new sources to understand who authors were; an author's persona was defined through novel biographical dictionaries and journals. These sources highlighted the family as a key element of authorship in the seventeenth and early eighteenth centuries and placed it in direct relation to other issues such as patronage and membership in formal institutions.

Chapter 2 analyzes the social and financial aspects of the Perrault family strategy from the early seventeenth century up to about 1660. Initially, the family had no obvious connections to literature. The status of barrister, the profession of Pierre Sr., did not offer promising enough prospects, and the couple's sons chose careers that diversified the family's educational and professional investments. Claude became a doctor and regent at the Paris Faculty of Medicine, and Nicolas became a doctor of theology at the Sorbonne. Most significantly, Pierre Jr. developed a career in the monarchy's financial administration. This was a burgeoning field, since in the seventeenth century the French monarchy relied more and more on increased taxation and on loans. The financiers who responded to these needs became prominent—though often derided—members of society. This was the milieu Pierre gradually entered. His marriage to a member of a family of officeholders in a tax court allowed him to purchase a financial office. Responding to the monarchy's thirst for cash, financiers played a high-stakes game: while they could go bankrupt, they also stood to make immense profits from dealing in the king's money. This chapter analyzes the social and economic implications of this first phase of the family's strategy and demonstrates the importance of "court capitalism" and office holding for a family that would later be known primarily as authors.

The relations between this phase of the family strategy and literary sociability form the core of chapter 3. Always in need of credit, financiers had to project an image of wealth, and the world of letters provided the means. Charles went to work as Pierre's aide and began to circulate poetry that propagated their renown. The brothers entertained notables and men of letters in their country house at Viry, producing poems that described their sumptuous dinners. The Perraults also conducted scientific experiments at Viry in collaboration with Huygens, himself a progeny of a brilliant intellectual family, who became a close friend of the family.

In this phase of the family's strategy, literary life bolstered Pierre's career in finance. Charles's entry into the world of letters was motivated by the need to augment the reputation of Pierre, whose career in finance peaked in the late 1650s and early 1660s. The Perraults' country house offers a new view of the contested concept of the salon. Rather than a well-bounded institution operating under the refined norms of polite conversation, the salon was a powerful image that contemporaries could draw on in attempts to distinguish themselves socially; this image was connected not merely to literary activities but to conventions of hospitality and the image of aristocratic affluence.

In the early 1660s things changed rapidly and dramatically for the Perraults. With the beginning of Louis XIV's personal reign, a new and powerful minister, Jean-Baptiste Colbert, assumed control of the monarchy's financial and cultural endeavors. One result was Pierre's disgrace, part of the general purge of the financiers that Colbert orchestrated. Nevertheless, Charles profited from this change. Thanks to the literary reputation that he had already acquired, he became one of Colbert's trusted cultural advisers. This enabled him to assist his brother Claude in becoming one of the founding members of the Parisian Academy of Sciences, while Pierre himself cultivated literary and scientific endeavors in an effort to join one of the royal academies. As chapter 4 shows, in this period writing became the most important avenue for social mobility left to the family members, though economically it could not begin to be compared to the career in finance that Pierre had previously pursued with Charles's help. This chapter follows the transformations of the Perrault family's economic and social networks, defining the ways in which literature shaped its fortunes in the second half of the seventeenth century.

Charles's work for Colbert offered the family new ways to act in the social world. Chapter 5 offers a new view on the cultural politics of absolutism by concentrating on the ways the Perraults drew upon their access to Versailles in a variety of settings, from the dissections of exotic animals in the Academy of Sciences to their literary sociability. In fact, the palace's reputation grew through the scientific, cultural, and artistic appropriations of men of letters: while they promoted the king's glory, the Perraults benefited by association.

The sixth and final chapter considers the impact of the family on scientific inquiry from the perspective of the individual. Focusing on Claude's *Of the Mechanics of Animals* (*De la mécanique des animaux*), this chapter shows how the project depended on a unique set of skills Claude possessed, from drawing to knowledge of mechanics. These skills, in turn, depended on his place in the family network. The *Mechanics of Animals* project shows how the Academy of Sciences functioned in practice as a node in a broader network that connected scholars, royal resources, and projects that ranged from art and writing to anatomy and medicine.

The epilogue follows Charles's children as they drifted away from the life of letters and into the court during the latter part of the reign of Louis XIV. As contemporaries understood, the publication of the fairy tales was itself a family endeavor. Charles sought to assist his son in the pursuit of a military career, which required connections at court facilitated by the fairy tales, which were dedicated to a high-ranking princess residing in Versailles. Charles used his publications to consolidate his brothers' reputations as well. For him, literature was both a way to act in the social world and a crucial component of his family's identity. For the Perraults, he almost became a fairy-tale godfather.

This book takes on two broad issues, the history of the scholarly family and the institutional transformation of seventeenth-century intellectual culture, linking them through a sustained consideration of the importance of kinship networks. Over the past fifteen years, scholars have begun to address the intellectual family as a historical phenomenon, yet as Caroline Sherman argues, "the role of the European family in the manufacturing of knowledge has largely escaped modern-day scrutiny."[18] These scholars have examined how the household, viewed as both a gendered space and a social unit, served as the organizing framework for the life of the mind. Sherman's own work on the Godefroy family showed how intellectual skills, habits, and techniques were transmitted over three centuries by a family of scholars specializing in legal and historical questions.

This approach builds on the work done by Gadi Algazi, who argued that a new scholarly way of life emerged during the fifteenth and sixteenth centuries. As universities created salaried posts, which replaced church benefices and the celibate lifestyle they imposed, scholars began to form families and households. As the household became the main locus of intellectual work, scholars had to develop and codify ways to treat their families, or the spaces they were working in. The result was the emergence of a new scholarly way of life.[19]

Indeed, recent studies examine how such gendered models of behavior determined the use of rooms in the scholarly household, how they served to model the intellectual self, and how they sustained and subverted patriarchal discourses.[20] In a study of the sixteenth-century mathematician and mystic John Dee, Deborah Harkness has pointed out that the domestic sphere served as an important stop in the movement of European philosophical production from universities to scientific academies. Jane Dee, John's wife, had to negotiate the traditional duties of a wife running a household as well as the tasks imposed by marriage to a natural philosopher, such as maintaining privacy in a household where alchemy was practiced and conversations with angels regularly occurred.[21] Paula Findlen has shown how, in sixteenth-century Italy, the collecting of natural specimens and family life could interpenetrate. Building on the observation that museums were usually located within the household, Findlen explored the way discussions of nature built on familial models. As "controlling space became a primary means of asserting patriarchal authority," women were barred from Ulisse Aldrovandi's public studio, his country villa, and his household museum.[22] In Renaissance England and Italy, Sarah Ross has demonstrated, the "virtuous learned lady" depended on her father for both an education and routine subversions of the language of domesticity; the creation of a new discourse of femininity lent itself to declarations of equality, as did the rise of a vernacular literature that stood apart from Latin models and their attendant sexism.[23] Meghan Roberts has traced the rise of a new "domestic philosopher" in eighteenth-century France, highlighting cases in which affectionate marriages were also intellectually productive.[24] And Dániel Margócsy has shown that most Dutch science of the seventeenth century was based on the household.[25]

The story of the Perraults advances the discussion in several significant ways. It takes us to seventeenth-century Paris, the most important crucible for the institutions that would dominate European cultural and intellectual life for two hundred years. More important, this book reconnects the family to other intellectual institutions. Previous studies that argued for the importance of the scholarly family as an institution have too often failed to acknowledge its relations to other, formal and informal, institutions.[26] The reconstruction of the Perraults' networks and their impact on august institutions such as the Parisian Academy of Sciences and the royal court at Versailles link the family with other agents of change.[27]

This argument builds on a renewed understanding of the history of the family. In the 1960s and 1970s, the family became an object of sustained historical study through a focus on the structure of households. Scholars working in the field tried to reconstruct the emergence of the "nuclear family," supposedly a hallmark of modern industrial society, by recovering forms of household formation and rules for the transmission of property. In French history, regional variations in family forms and the relations between families and the state gained much attention.[28] Foundational studies showed, for example, that the family developed a symbiotic relationship with the French monarchy in the sixteenth and seventeenth centuries, strengthening the authority of the monarch and of the heads of households among elites.[29]

Other studies of kinship, however, conceptualize family ties in a different way. Rather than focusing on the household, they see kinship ties as based on sets of values and obligations that relate to the reproductive roles of the family but that are deployed in a wide range of economic, social, and cultural spheres. In this view, kinship served as an idiom used to conceptualize broad ranges of interactions and transactions.[30] The painstaking reconstruction of the broad uses of kinship led to a revision of the historical role of the European family. The transition from the Middle Ages to the early modern period, this work has shown, was accompanied by the stabilization of kin groups. More clearly defined than their relatively fluid medieval predecessors, these groups came to use more elaborate family strategies and more consistent control of resources. Early modern families played a larger role in the division of patrimonies, access to formal offices, and the distribution of political power than did medieval families. This work challenges previous views on family structures in relation to society and politics. Rather than a transition from medieval structured kin groups and weak state institutions to more rigid state institutions that dominated powerful kin groups in the early modern period, state formation and family formation went hand in hand. Protobureaucratic state institutions reinforced tighter conceptions of kin organization rather than undermining them. In this world, kinship signified more than blood ties or the household. It was a supple set of cultural options that shaped social worlds through alliances, the control and circulation of property, and the management of emotions. Viewed this way, the history of the familial household is but one element in a broader history of kin relations, with wide cultural, social, and political ramifications; indeed, even authorship and plagiarism have been cast through kinship metaphors.[31]

A close observation of the Perraults shows kinship as a form of culture in action, as the brothers shaped one another's social and cultural practices. This facilitated social mobility, with stunning successes as well as spectacular failures. This is a remarkable story in which family strategies interacted with formal and informal institutions, the professional identities they provided, the social geography of seventeenth-century Paris, and changes in royal policies. Limiting the study of intellectual families to households and to the transmission of skills and values risks neglecting a great deal, particularly how many components came together to create distinctly early modern forms of science, literature, and authorship.

The seventeenth century saw a broad transformation in the production of knowledge, literature, and art, whose contours—geographical, social, and political—can be made tangible by contrasting the situation in the late sixteenth century with the one in the early eighteenth century. Over the course of the seventeenth century, Paris became the epicenter of French cultural life. Around 1600, provincial centers still possessed their own luminaries. As Peter Miller claimed in his study of the erudite Nicolas-Claude Fabri de Peiresc, "Peiresc's 'out of the way,' provincial headquarters was not a liability in an age just before the emergence of modern capitals like Paris and London made the term 'provincial intellectual' an oxymoron."[32] By 1700, the cultural vitality of the provinces had declined, along with their print industries.[33] This means that Parisian society played a crucial role in the careers of its authors. Indeed, the Perraults were happily and hopelessly entangled in a complex and stratified urban society. At the time, Paris was one of the largest cities in western Europe, with a population reaching perhaps half a million. The groups that struggled for dominance or mere survival ranged from aspiring nobles of the robe to artisans and beggars.[34] In this hierarchical world, the pursuit of wealth and status was legitimate and widely accepted, and men of letters competed for wealth and status as fiercely as ambitious merchants and financiers. This contrasts with the Romantics' idea, of which we are the heirs, of incessant opposition between artists and bourgeois society.[35] In the early modern period, struggles over status, property, and patronage formed an integral part of intellectual careers.[36] In such an environment, leaving out the gritty details of this complex world can only distort the intellectual projects undertaken by men of letters.[37]

The relations of patronage between aristocrats and writers shaped the world of letters. Nobles provided protégés more than lodgings, prestige, and material support, shaping their working conditions and inflecting the aesthetic of their works. Studies that explore the multifaceted ways patronage could operate demonstrate that many powerful actors—including but not limited to the monarch—took part in the creation of culture and knowledge. Bearing such links in mind helps us appreciate the dynamic interplay between cultural and political change: the fortunes of the Condé princes shaped their relations with philosophers and men of letters such as the Abbé Bourdelot, the leader of a circle of natural philosophers.[38]

While patronage relations remained a constant during the period, the seventeenth century was a novel age of academies. Dozens of learned circles met on a regular basis to discuss literature, science, or art in informal settings. The French monarchy supported or created eight royal academies, assigning each a particular responsibility over topics such as literature, architecture, and science. For instance, the Académie française, founded in 1635, was charged with creating a dictionary of the French language. Through the academy and similar ventures, the French monarchy attempted a powerful intervention in the cultural sphere.[39]

Studies of such institutions and the new social and material infrastructure they provided for the pursuit of cultural activities ascribe to them changes in the categories of "literature" and "science." There is no mistaking the importance of the material support, as well as the prestige, that came from royal patronage. One scholar even argues that "for literary history, the decisive event in the seventeenth century is the creation of the Académie française."[40] Studies of the Parisian Academy of Sciences emphasize the unreliability of the networks the "new philosophy" relied on before the material resources of the monarchy were committed.[41] Literary salons led to the "refinement" of French literature under the guidance of elite women.[42] The French court itself, especially after it moved to Versailles in 1682, drove new currents in taste, absorbing the creative output of many, from the playwright Molière to the composer Jean-Baptiste Lully.[43]

France produced the first "literary field," to use the term coined by Pierre Bourdieu. Bourdieu had in mind a system of relations of production, circulation, and consumption of symbolic goods that defined the social space of literature.[44] And while the field did not assume its mature shape until the nineteenth century, crucial components developed earlier, in the seventeenth century. Most notably, academies and private circles established new forms of literary sociability; the economic and judicial status of authors changed, reflecting a growing awareness of the importance of state patronage and regulation; and a larger and more stratified reading public allowed authors to experiment with new literary forms, notably the novel and the theatrical tragedy. Therefore, if the culture of the late sixteenth century was the product of scholars, lawyers, physicians, and theologians, who wrote for a similar audiences, by Louis XIV's death in 1715, literary authors had gained a measure of social autonomy, the importance of the university had declined in relative terms, and the reading public had grown more complex and variegated, including a substantial number of female readers.[45]

Ultimately neither patronage nor institutions, narrowly conceived, are sufficient for understanding the ways cultural careers intersected with society. While studies of patronage focus on a single type of social relation and institutional studies address a single cultural domain, most writers and scholars in early modern Europe wandered among a range of activities and relations, adopting and shedding institutional affiliations. This is where a focus on networks and family strategies bears fruit.

Network analysis puts ties and connections at its center. The crucial issue is not what constitutes the nodes in such networks but rather how they relate to each other. This approach assumes that actors are dependent; that the relations among them play an important role in channeling information, resources, or affect among them; and that the patterns of these relations serve as the foundation of social structures and institutions.[46]

In the case of the Perraults, relations with patrons, neighbors, and extended kin constituted the family of letters as a node in their networks.[47] The analysis of the Perraults' networks highlights the specific connections that held their world together, phenomena too often neglected by those who consider only personal attributes, such as class or gender. For example, if the Perraults' relations to Colbert had been seen simply in class terms or simply in terms of clients and their patron, Pierre's efforts to gain recognition from members of the Academy of Sciences, a body formally sponsored by Colbert, after losing his position as a financier because of Colbert's policies, would have appeared senseless. To follow the story, I intend to account for a range of connections, based on personal recognition and patronage but also on offices, political changes, and intellectual trajectories. In Pierre's case, Charles's role as a cultural adviser and Claude's position in the Academy of Sciences proved to be crucial to his attempts to rebuild his career. Such connections among brothers cannot simply be captured by the categories of class and patronage relations or by family histories that focus on the transmission of property and see siblings as either collaborators or competitors. Kinship ties had multiple uses and forms that shifted during the early modern period, and the seventeenth century in fact saw a culmination of the importance of lineage for sibling relations.[48]

This book enriches the field of network studies in several respects. It deals with early modern scientific and literary networks, which often stress long-distance networks at the expense of the local context, the focus of this book.[49] It strikes a balance between the structures the Perraults navigated and their own agency.[50] Since the story stretches across the better part of a century, I have been able to document changes in the Perraults' networks instead of the usual static image. Most significant, in contrast to studies that aggregate various categories of links and refer to the result as a single network—thereby homogenizing different types of connections and neglecting the history of the actors—the virtual laboratory provided by the Perraults has allowed me to distinguish between different types of connections and the uses to which the family put them.[51]

In each chapter, the careers and identities of the Perraults are linked to the history of their households and the opportunities kinship offered. In this society, physical proximity and a sense of living together took on a value of their own.[52] Yet families were also held together by legal obligations, mutual expectations, and broader norms, all components of a complex identity.[53] When we see the Perraults as actors in multifaceted networks, we are less prone to treat the family as a group whose coherence is assumed in advance. The ultimate goal of this book is to clarify the relations among formal institutions, socially recognized ways of doing things, and the ties that bind individuals in groups in the world of early modern culture. An issue that lies at the intersection of all three is the subject of the first chapter: What was an early modern author?

CHAPTER ONE

Representing a Family of Letters

Images of Authorship (1650–1750)

Puss in Boots knew quite well that names and appearances matter. He triumphed thanks to his ability to fabricate an image for his owner, the third son of a miller, whose livelihood appeared uncertain since he did not inherit his father's mill or the donkey. Pretending to serve the Marquis de Carabas, Puss in Boots sent gifts to the king and ultimately faked a drowning scene to present his master to the king as the marquis. The cat even threatened peasants into telling the king that the lands they were cultivating belonged to the miller's son, obtained a castle for him, and sealed the marriage deal between his owner and the princess. By bestowing a new name and identity on his master, the cat effectively transformed a miller's son into a member of the royal family.[1]

The most significant strand in the story of the Perrault family is their acquisition of a literary identity. Such was the literary acclaim bestowed on the family that, although they were not nobles, Charles and three of his brothers won places in the Cabinet d'Hozier—the royal genealogical collection, which even highlighted Charles and Claude, the more prominent authors among the brothers.[2] Adrien Baillet, the author of a voluminous and learned work assessing a wide range of authors, started his entry on Charles Perrault by claiming that "even if M. Perrault had plausible excuses for not standing out from the crowd of French poets, I do not think that posterity could ever accept them, in light of his family's distinction among so many learned houses in Paris that make letters their profession."[3]

Building on approaches from the history of the book, this chapter argues that in the seventeenth century—and probably throughout the early modern period—the family provided a crucial framework for establishing authorship.[4] The Perraults represent a richly documented and emblematic case: acquiring a literary identity was *the* central process the family underwent after 1640. Until that year, the lineage had produced undistinguished lawyers and doctors without any literary aspirations or reputation; by the end of the seventeenth century—as Baillet indicated—they were recognized by contemporaries as a literary house.[5]

For too long, ideas about authorship have suffered because of the failure to consider the part played by kinship and its relation to a range of categories, from informal patronage ties to office holding and membership in formal institutions. Indeed, Michel Foucault's influential suggestion that texts were constitutive of their authors might have prompted studies of the different types of discourses that defined the relations between authors and their works. But in a somewhat ironic development, scholars focused instead on the disciplinary institutions dear to Foucault himself: censorship and copyright, the legal regulation of authorship.[6] But as David Saunders and Ian Hunter have argued, no single logic ever defined authorship and an "authorial subject." Instead, shifting interactions among cultural, legal, technological, economic, and ethical factors determined who was assigned authorship of what. Saunders and Hunter saw authorial personae as "positive forms of social being distributed unevenly across individuals and institutions in a variety of ways and according to a variety of cultural, legal, technological, economic, and ethical imperatives. The expressive author represents a particular configuration of this shifting distribution."[7]

Seventeenth-century French authors certainly had to respond to "shifting distributions" of cultural forms that were in dynamic and productive interaction with one another. Even a powerful model such as *galanterie* (the gallant style associated with refined courtly behavior), which defined a form of life and not merely a literary style, could not claim exclusive control over the world of literary authorship.[8] Therefore, as Nick Wilding has argued, we need to understand textual relations as embodying complex social relations, without simply reducing authors to the personae generated by institutions.[9] So instead of focusing on disciplinary institutions and the way they shaped the relations between authors and texts, in this chapter I look at the problem from the perspective of the readers and the information they had on authors, focusing on the Perraults but adding other examples: the Perraults provide a remarkable prism for studying authorship, and such comparisons only deepen the story of authorship told in this chapter.

By 1703, the year that Charles Perrault died, readers interested in learning about him or his brothers could choose from a number of biographical texts in different genres; for simplicity's sake I shall refer to all of these works as "biographies." This was a common phenomenon: as the wars of religion tore Europe apart, scholars joined saints, generals, and statesmen as worthy biographical subjects.[10] The seventeenth century, especially its second half, saw a dramatic increase in the publication of journals and dictionaries devoted to scholarly and literary themes, propagating these biographies to new audiences. Although scholars usually focus in this context on "erudite" authors active in the republic of letters, this period saw a massive new wave of encyclopedias and dictionaries covering a range of topics and authors.[11]

In addition to erudite publications such as Daniel Morhof's *Polyhistor* and the new genre of *ana* literature, collecting anecdotes and saying of famous scholars, men of letters began using the vernacular to cultivate a broader audience.[12] As the case of the Perraults shows, such writers were featured in the new biographical dictionaries, learned journals, and published eulogies. Wherever French books were read, this development picked up with the inaugural publication in 1665 of *Journal des sçavans*, devoted to philosophical and scholarly works, followed seven years later by *Mercure galant*, a literary journal. These periodicals were quickly emulated: Pierre Bayle's *Nouvelles de la république des lettres* began publication in 1684.[13]

Louis Moréri's *Grand dictionnaire historique* provided the model for brief biographies, becoming enormously successful. First published in Lyon in 1674, it quickly went through numerous editions; by 1759, it had reached its twenty-fourth. Bayle's renowned *Dictionnaire historique et critique* (1697) followed Moréri's model while correcting many errors and famously adding a wealth of information and documentation in footnotes. Entries in these dictionaries quickly became a means for claiming status. Noble families had to advertise and defend their status; some even used Moréri's dictionary as a means for advertising their genealogies, deflecting royal attempts to weed the nobility of so-called usurpers.[14] Certain erudite scholars even tracked down the authors of anonymous and pseudonymous publications.[15] Recently created royal academies, such as the Académie française and the Royal Academy of Sciences, emerged as foci for the production of biographical discourses, since members' posthumous eulogies were widely circulated.[16]

The new learned journals were destined for a broad scholarly audience that wanted to stay up-to-date on recent developments without having to buy great heaps of books. Thanks to such specialized publications, an unprecedented volume of information on authors and their works was published; scholars certainly felt overwhelmed by this "information overload."[17] From antiquity to the sixteenth century, collections such as Diogenes Laertius's *Lives of Eminent Philosophers* and Étienne Pasquier's epigrams on his literary and intellectual circle fulfilled this function.[18] Yet the new journals and dictionaries circulated more widely and provided readers with more information and broader coverage. They also tended to be more affordable and accessible.[19] The growing popularity of biography can be seen, for example, in the extraction of such material from Jacques-Auguste de Thou's renowned universal history, published in Latin, so that it could be presented in French in two stand-alone volumes in 1683.[20]

The Perraults' reputations took shape in this new discursive environment, and their lives were presented in a range of forms. These included obituaries in literary and learned journals, sketches of their lives in prefaces to posthumous publications, eulogies in collections of academic discourses and in works on the lives of learned men, entries in Moréri's popular biographical dictionary,[21] and articles in literary histories.

In spite of the wide range of genres and authors involved in crafting the Perraults' lives, the details remain surprisingly stable. Biographers did not hesitate to borrow liberally from lives published in other genres. Briefer sketches were often copied word for word into longer texts. The author of the obituary for Charles that appeared in *Journal des sçavans* freely admitted that he had merely summarized Abbé Tallemant's eulogy delivered at the Académie française.[22] Even Charles's biography of his brother Claude, which appeared in *Hommes illustres*, his collection of biographies, was composed largely of passages from obituaries published in *Journal des sçavans* and *Histoire des ouvrages des savants*; only the final section included original information.[23] After that revelation, it is hardly surprising to learn that Charles based his life of his patron Colbert on an entry in the 1694 edition of Moréri.[24] The need for easy copy apparently trumped other considerations.

The derivative nature of these accounts and their authors' awareness of the other texts mean that they provide a credible overview of the information and images that were available to broad readership on the Perraults. The free flow of long passages from one publication to another, regardless of differences in genre, suggests that information was not constrained by generic conventions. By analyzing all such texts as a single corpus, I hope to present the Perraults' reputations as a holistic phenomenon; I shall use other authors as examples to demonstrate the broad relevance of these authorial categories.

While the lives of the Perrault brothers were presented in works that fall into several different genres, the categories around which the narratives were organized were relatively stable, with the family playing a prominent role. In most of these works, the authors mentioned (1) the institutional affiliations or the formal appointments held by the Perraults, (2) the works they were known for, (3) their kinship connections, (4) their place in relations of patronage, and finally (5) their moral virtues and noteworthy deeds.

In this first section I focus on formal offices and membership in academies and recognized corporate bodies. These were prominent markers that placed one within Old Regime hierarchies. Indeed, according to the jurist Charles Loyseau's famous dictum (1610), an office was "a dignity with a public function," and officeholders shared the king's authority by delegation; the offices bestowed honor and were much more than what are simply called "jobs" today.[25] Charles Perrault was identified as *commis des bâtiments* (aide for buildings) and later *contrôleur général* (comptroller general) of the Royal Buildings—the department in charge of the monarchy's palaces, patronage of the arts, and royal manufacturing sites, such as the Gobelins—as well as a member in the Académie française. Pierre's position as *receveur général* (receiver-general) was always noted, as was Nicolas's membership in the Sorbonne—the way authors used to describe the Parisian Faculty of Theology—and Claude's position in the Paris Faculty of Medicine and at the Academy of Sciences. The inclusion of these positions—even when they had no evident connection to the literary works or deeds of the Perraults—proved their importance as markers of status.

While Claude was indeed a member of the Paris Faculty of Medicine, as his biographies never failed to mention, his reputation rested on his work in architecture and natural science; writers did not draw a connection between his training as a doctor and his intellectual production. Even his work at the Academy of Sciences seemed in the eyes of his biographers to express a talent for mechanics and machines rather than skill related to medicine.[26] Above all, Claude's fame rested on his career as a man of letters—even his medical colleagues thought so. As Charles Perrault noted in *Hommes illustres*, when the Faculty of Medicine commissioned him to produce a portrait of his brother, the Latin register made upon its acquisition praised Claude's work on "physics," his translation of Vitruvius, and his skills in mathematics, architecture, drawing, and music—nothing directly related to medicine.[27] And when Dom Clemencet, the author of a Jansenist literary history, described Nicolas's brothers as having "enriched the Republic of Letters with the production of their pens," he mentioned that Pierre was a receiver-general without mentioning what he had written.[28]

Similarly, those who wrote about Nicolas cited his institutional position as a theologian to demonstrate his authority in matters of religion and his motivation for writing. Further, his position at the Faculty of Theology precluded the need to hold a post at court or benefit from cultural patronage. It was agreed that other members of the faculty esteemed Nicolas as a brilliant theologian.[29] The Faculty of Theology provided the setting for his most noteworthy action, mounting a defense in 1656 of the Jansenist theologian Antoine Arnauld, whom some wished to expel after the publication of his polemical letters.[30] This intervention brought him much renown in Jansenist circles, and it was highlighted in reports of his life. Robert Arnauld d'Andilly, Antoine Arnauld's older brother, even translated Nicolas's Latin peroration into French and circulated it in manuscript.[31]

Official roles and membership in institutions served all writers as the first means for placing authors in society, even in texts of completely different genres. As we will see in the following chapters, notarial documents, and particularly marriage contracts, afforded all members of Parisian society, including authors, opportunities to display their status. Claude was identified as a "Doctor of medicine from the Paris Faculty" on a lease for a house on the rue Saint-Jacques; the playwright Philippe Quinault, already widely published by the time of his marriage in 1660, signed the contract as barrister in the Parlement.[32] Charles Perrault, who had no interest in practicing law and did so only for a few years in the 1650s, was identified in 1698, by which date he was a well-established author, as a barrister in the Parlement and a former comptroller general.[33]

Possibly less frequently mentioned in legal contracts of the day was membership in academies. The affiliation is mentioned by signatories who reckoned it would improve their status, as was the case with Guillaume Amonton, a lowly student (elève) who was identified as "from the Royal Academy of Sciences" in his marriage contract.[34] France's most distinguished astronomer, Giovanni Domenico Cassini, another member of that celebrated academy, did not feel the need to mention this affiliation when his marriage was documented. The contract mentioned instead that his letters of naturalization had been signed by Louis XIV and Colbert, both of whom signed the marriage contract itself.[35] Important as membership in academies might be for an author to present professional credentials, the right elite connections trumped institutional affiliations. Still, neither of these considerations had much to do with literary qualities: instead they defined one's place in an intricate social hierarchy, built on a range of offices, academies, and corporate bodies.

Seventeenth- and eighteenth-century definitions of authorship connected individuals to the world of print, in contrast to the putatively bygone mode of circulating manuscripts. In his 1690 dictionary, Antoine Furetière defined "author" as follows: "In literature, said about all those who have published a book. Today, said only of those who have brought it to print."[36] And indeed, biographies of men of letters served a crucial role in establishing their status as authors, since they discussed and listed their published works. Moréri's dictionary even appended such lists at the ends of entries.[37] But simply referring to one's printed works could not satisfy readers whose notion of talent combined capacity with an innate disposition toward particular paths.[38]

While biographers surveyed the Perraults' works, they also paid careful attention to other aspects of the brothers' creative work. For example, they identified Claude as an architect responsible for the eastern façade of the Louvre; this work of architecture became so celebrated that quarrels broke out about its paternity before the end of the seventeenth century. In his guide to Paris, Germain Brice assigned all credit to the architects Louis Le Vau and François d'Orbay, "in spite of all that has been published to the contrary," that is, in support of Claude.[39] As for Charles Perrault, his reputation in the world of letters rested on his work as a cultural broker for Colbert as much as on his books. Biographers described how Charles spent his nights writing not his own books but the briefs that served as a basis for a renaissance of the arts and sciences under Colbert, including the establishment of several academies, and they credited him for moving the Académie française's assemblies to the Louvre. The Perraults' creative activity was not reduced to their works in print, nor was print the only source of eulogies. Their biographies devoted space to discussions of manuscripts: the list of Nicolas's works included manuscripts he left, and manuscript drawings helped to bolster Claude's status as an architect even more than fifty years after his death.[40]

Charles's biographies usually mentioned his published works in detail but according to a certain hierarchy of renown. A prominent place was reserved for *Le Siècle de Louis Le Grand* (the Age of Louis the Great), the poem that ignited a new phase in the "quarrel of the ancients and the moderns," and the four volumes of *Parallèle des anciens et des modernes* (Parallels between the ancients and the moderns); both works represented the modern position. Also highlighted were three other poems: one on the life of Saint Paulinus, the bishop of Nola (*Saint Paulin, évesque de Nole*) (1686); another dedicated to the king's gardener, Jean de la Quintinie (*A monsieur de La Quintinye, sur son livre De l'instruction des jardins fruitiers & potagers*); and *De la peinture* (1669). Other works, from Charles's first literary efforts to *Hommes illustres*, received less attention. By contrast, his very first work, a burlesque on the Trojan War written with Claude and Nicolas, received no mention at all, and his occasional pieces dedicated to the monarchy's greater glory were mentioned only in a late edition of Moréri's dictionary (1759). In other words, the posthumous lives emphasized the works written while Charles was a member of the Académie française at the expense of his early "worldly" period and his service to the throne.

Charles's *Tales of Mother Goose* represents an ironic twist of fate in terms of his status as an author. Today, it is undoubtedly the most recognizable text produced by any of the family members. Yet its impact on Charles's career and reputation at least until the middle of the eighteenth century was quite negligible. Charles did not establish clear authorship of the tales, and as we shall see in chapter 5, he tried to promote one of his sons, Pierre d'Armancour, as their presumed author. This led to some confusion about the attribution of the tales among contemporaries and among modern scholars, whose ink wells ran dry trying to establish who of the two was the real author. As the tales represented a turn to writing in a feminine genre, relying on the support of the readership of the *Mercure galant*, Charles probably did not impress many of his fellow academicians. Indeed, except for the eulogy published in the same *Mercure galant*, the tales do not figure prominently in the descriptions of Charles's life, and they began to exert a larger influence only in the latter decades of the eighteenth century.[41] The tales gained their current status only in the nineteenth century, when scholars began to devote much attention to them, at the expense of other texts Charles authored.[42]

The authors of his obituaries and dictionary entries believed that Claude's reputation rested on his creative work. They did not distinguish in this sense between his work as an architect and that as a translator and member of the Academy of Sciences; on the contrary, his status as a man of letters has been amplified thanks to his ability to draw on skills relevant to all these domains. Biographers divided Claude's work into three main clusters: the buildings he designed, his publications on architecture, and the publications stemming from his work at the Academy of Sciences. They all gave pride of place to the first and attributed to him not just the work on the Louvre but the Paris observatory and a triumphal arch planned for the road leading to the Faubourg Saint-Antoine, to the east of Paris. Germain Brice, who opposed the attribution of the Louvre façade to Claude, had no qualms about attributing the unbuilt arch to him, describing it as "one of the most beautiful monuments of this age."[43] Among the architectural writings for which Claude was praised was his translation of Vitruvius's *De architectura*; as a practicing architect and a scholar, it was said, he was destined to best all predecessors in handling the book's technical and linguistic challenges. He subsequently produced—with novice architects in mind—an abridged version, followed by a book on the order of columns in ancient architecture. Those were mentioned, as were *Mémoires pour servir à l'histoire naturelle des animaux* (Memoirs on the natural history of animals), the four volumes of his *Essais de physique* (Essays on physics), and a collection of new mechanical designs of machines. Since this last collection appeared only posthumously, Claude's early eulogies stated that it would be published by one of his brothers, "Perrault from the Académie française"; Charles indeed published it in 1700.

As for Nicolas, he published only the *Morale des Jésuites*, so naturally those who wrote about him used it as the cornerstone of their discussions, even when they were aware of other works in manuscript. Since this was an erudite and extremely polemical attack on the Jesuits, Alexandre Varet, Dom Clemencet, and Moréri all organized their presentations of Nicolas around his Jansenism. In this case, the printed work proved crucial, since Nicolas had no formal or informal connections to the Jansenist stronghold of Port-Royal, whose nuns played a crucial role in the public debate on Jansenism, and he did not contribute to the collective publications spearheaded by Arnauld, Blaise Pascal, and Pierre Nicole, the movement's leading spokesmen.[44]

As he wrote so little, the role of biographical texts in shaping his status as an author becomes especially intriguing in Nicolas's case, and here he stands for a broader phenomenon. The inherent ambivalence resulting from the contradiction between contemporary definitions of authorship, based on publication, and the literary status obtained by these men of letters, who did not publish much, reveals the early modern tension between print publication and the establishment of status in the world of letters. To cope with authors who had published little in their lifetimes, biographers sometimes turned to posthumously published works or to other categories of authorship, established ad hoc by such criteria as membership in academies. In Charles's life of the poet Vincent Voiture, he explained that "even though he never published anything in print, he acquired a great reputation, not only in France, but also in foreign countries" and that "the Roman Academy of the Umoristi sent him the letters of an academician." When Voiture's works were posthumously published, they obtained a great success. Only after mentioning these features of authorship did Charles claim that Voiture was one the greatest jewels of the Académie française.[45]

Nothing by Valentin Conrart, the first secretary of the Académie française, was published until the nineteenth century, making things quite difficult for Charles Ancillon, his biographer. Desperate to credit Conrart with the attributes of a literary author, Ancillon argued that since he had written the registers of the academy, on which Paul Pellisson's history of the Académie française was based, he deserved partial credit for that work.[46] And Ancillon dwelt on the many comments and evaluations Conrart had offered regarding the works of other authors, meaning that Conrart could in fact be considered their principal author, in contrast to the authors whose name appeared on the title page.[47]

As these cases demonstrate, those who wrote lives of authors effectively assembled their reputation and authorial status. They situated printed works in the context of the other categories discussed here, such as official positions, patronage, kinship, and moral traits. Thus when Charles discussed the life of the worldly poet Jean-François Sarasin, whose works were published only posthumously, things were even more challenging, since few credible details about his life were known. So Charles discussed his literary style, his charming character, his relation with his patron, the prince de Conti, and his family. The biography opened with the words "Jean-François Sarasin, born in Caen, son of a treasurer of France [trésorier de France] from the same city."[48] Readers expected discussions of works anchored in a broader context of kinship, origin, and family position.

Grounding the Perraults' lives in the context of kinship addressed several important issues for early modern readers. Like the other topics associated with authorship, they placed authors in the context of important or emerging Old Regime institutions. In a society that paid ever-increasing attention to lineages and kin groups, even considerations of literary creativity acknowledged the significance of kinship. In fact, the number of family histories produced and published on behalf of the aristocratic families, for example, soared in the early seventeenth century.[49] Therefore, readers who set out to learn something about one of the Perraults got more: the biographical entry of each often contained significant references to other brothers. To give a few examples, eulogies to Claude explained how Charles would posthumously publish his brother's work, the entry for Claude in Moréri's dictionary included information on Nicolas and Pierre, and even a Jansenist literary history listed the achievements of Pierre, Charles, and Claude before an in-depth discussion of Nicolas's work. This was quite a common phenomenon: the entry on the writer and philosopher Bernard le Bovier de Fontenelle detailed his connections to his maternal uncles, the renowned authors Pierre and Thomas Corneille, his literary collaborations with Thomas, and the legal fracas precipitated by Fontenelle's decision to leave some of his property to Thomas's grandchildren.[50] Since Madeleine de Scudéry published works under her brother's name, it could seem banal that the entry on Georges de Scudéry identified him as Madeleine's brother—just after listing his formal titles as governor of Notre Dame de la Garde in Provence and member of the Académie française.[51] Yet this simply demonstrated how tangled authorship and kinship could be for contemporaries.

All of Charles Perrault's biographies set him squarely in the context of his family, which was presented as the group he would be most loyal to and as a source of pride. The writer Abbé Tallemant underscored Charles's fairness and his critical acumen when he claimed that he "did not think of his illustrious brothers" when distributing royal funding for authors, a task he handled between the 1660s and the early 1680s. By complimenting him for recognizing talent and not simply serving the interests of his kin, his biographers acknowledged the importance of kinship as a constitutive principle even in the context of evaluating intellect and creativity.[52] The second paragraph of Charles's eulogy in Mercure galant listed the achievements of Pierre, Nicolas, and Claude. These very brief résumés noted the brothers' formal appointments as well as some of the works they were known for.[53] These may have served as the starting points for the much longer biographies in the Moréri dictionary and Dom Clemencet's literary history.

Some biographers went to great lengths to place authors in the context of their kin, usually in order to show the source of virtues or noble intellects. In the case of Paul Pellisson, the historian of the Académie française and a prominent literary figure in the middle decades of the seventeenth century, this was taken to an extreme. In Hommes illustres, Charles noted the juridical offices held by Pellisson's father, grandfather, and even his great-grandfather.[54] In some cases, the importance authors placed on their genealogy could backfire. Charles commented on the genealogy that Jules-César Scaliger invented—he claimed descent from Veronese princes; out of respect, his son, Joseph-Juste, did not disavow this fabrication. Charles added, "Regardless, they have acquired for themselves the status of princes among men"— thanks to their scholarly achievements.[55] In other cases, the virtues of family members complemented each other, to the greater glory of the house. In this manner, Robert Arnauld d'Andilly's valor in combat combined with the erudition and piety of Antoine Arnauld and the eloquence he and his father displayed, adding to the virtues for which the entire family was known.[56]

Information on the familial backgrounds of authors also anchored them geographically. One's native place was endowed with rich meaning in this period, and geographical mobility made the careers of numerous authors, especially as Paris was becoming the cultural capital of France. In fact, during that period the majority of the members of the Académie française had been born outside Paris: about 40 percent were born there in the seventeenth century, and the number declined in the following centuries.[57] Although Pierre, Claude, Nicolas, and Pierre Perrault grew up in Paris and spent their entire careers there, biographers sometimes mentioned their father's origins in Tours.[58]

Authors sometimes reflected on the reputation of their place of birth or looked to it to confirm their own virtues. The famous poet François de Malherbe, for example, came from Caen, a city "renowned for bel esprit, which was almost natural for its inhabitants." And even though the city produced numerous men of letters, "it would have merited the praise it receives even if it had been only the cradle of Malherbe."[59] Rouen would be honored by posterity as the birthplace of Pierre Corneille.[60] In other cases, the geographical location served to tell the story of mobility, geographical as much as artistic. Paul Pellisson came to Paris as soon as his parents agreed to the move, since "it was impossible that such a beautiful genius... would remain enclosed in a provincial city."[61] In this sense, these early modern lives had to walk a fine line, stressing the significance of a move to Paris without giving up the author's connection to his family.

Charles's management of his dead brother's literary estate belonged to a broader phenomenon: kin were expected to publish the works and manage the reputations of their deceased family members. After the death of Pierre Dupuy, guardian of the royal library, his brother Jacques took care to publish Pierre's works and to oversee the continuing series of learned assemblies that the brothers had initiated.[62] Jean de la Quintinie's work on gardening, esteemed throughout the continent and quickly translated into English, was published posthumously by the author's son.[63] Voiture's works were posthumously published by his nephew, Étienne Martin de Pinchesne.[64] In some cases, this responsibility extended to writing a narrative of the deceased relative's life, as Gilberte Périer did for her younger brother, Blaise Pascal.[65] In others, it also included taking care of those left behind: the scholar Jacques-Auguste de Thou relied on Nicolas Rigault not only for the posthumous publication of his works. He had such a great esteem for Rigault that "he asked him in his testament to take care of the education of his children, to guide them in the study of belles lettres, and to supervise them and their teachers."[66]

This concern for the legacies of family members seems natural for a society that considered dead members as essential as live ones.[67] Unsurprisingly, efforts to commemorate family members went beyond the medium of print, though the printed word amplified other forms of commemoration. Charles's eulogy of Antoine Arnauld reported, for example, that this great scholar had hoped that his heart would be carried to the monastery of Port Royal, "since his mother, six of his sisters, and five of his nieces had been nuns there, all of exemplary piety, filled with the spirit and the virtue of their family."[68] The commissioning of Claude's portrait from Charles and Charles's incorporation of the text registered in the Faculty of Medicine exemplify the concern with the legacy of family members.[69]

The death of a family member was also a time for more familiar memorials, which were mentioned in some biographical notices. Charles reported that Jacques-Auguste de Thou erected and wrote the inscription for the magnificent monument in honor of his father in the church of Saint-André-des-Arcs.[70] Such monuments sometimes became attractions for visitors to the city, and indeed Brice mentioned De Thou's monuments and copied the inscriptions honoring both father and son into his guide.[71] And just as Charles's obituary for Claude in the *Hommes illustres* brought a text from the Faculty of Medicine into a much wider readership, the medium of print gave familial tombstones greater visibility.

Little known on his own account, Pierre Perrault owed his literary reputation to his position in a family of authors. No scholar found his career worthy of discussion in its own right, and he was mentioned only in the Moréri, in the eulogy to Charles that appeared in *Mercure galant*, and in Dom Clemencet's article on Nicolas. All three presented him first as a receiver-general in the financial branch of the monarchy. The publications they attributed to him are only the printed ones: a treatise on the origins of springs published in 1674 and a translation of Tassoni's *Secchia rapita* (The kidnapped shield), a satire that took the modern position in the quarrel of the ancients and the moderns that raged in France in the seventeenth century.[72] Only the author of Charles's eulogy in *Mercure galant* added that this was one of several translations he made from Italian.[73] Had the three pieces about his brothers never appeared, Pierre would not have existed in the world of dictionaries and eulogies.

The narratives of the Perraults' lives thus formed a strong intertextual web, which crossed not only the boundaries of individual narratives but also different genres and types of publications. The Perraults appear to have enjoyed particular prominence because they constituted a family of letters; their inclusion in the royal genealogical collection was clearly based on their intellectual achievements. As we saw, Baillet explicitly referred to the Perraults as one of France's many houses that "makes letters [its] profession." Charles himself mentioned the assistance that Palamède Fabri de Valavez provided to his older brother, Nicolas-Claude Fabri de Peiresc, in the "commerce of letters and curiosities."[74] Contemporaries clearly recognized that authorship could be a family endeavor.

The work the Perraults did for Colbert points to the significance of patronage as a category for understanding early modern authorship. Biographers stressed that it was Colbert himself who selected Claude's designs for the Louvre, and they claimed that he commissioned Claude's translation of Vitruvius to help educate French architects. These intellectual and artistic achievements were assessed not only for their merits but also for how they came to be commissioned. In contrast with post-Romantic notions, the identity of the patron was part and parcel of the merit assigned to such projects.

The importance of patronage for the world of letters has been widely recognized, and as we will see in the following chapters, the Perraults relied heavily on links to the powerful to advance their careers. Patronage also played a part in their authorial figures as a routine component of the life of letters. Serving the state provided many opportunities, most notably by allowing Charles to fulfill the role of a "cultural broker." Assigning that service due weight permits us to add much nuance to two narratives used for explaining the history of early modern men of letters: the shifts from patronage to producing for the market and the takeover of literary life by the French monarchy around the middle decades of the seventeenth century.

Claude's case demonstrates the importance of the monarchy to cultural patronage. His biographers placed him squarely in Colbert's network of patronage, a configuration devoted to the glory of the monarchy. Colbert's commissions connected Claude to Louis XIV himself and to the greater glory of France; as a native son who had triumphed in a competition with foreign architects, his contribution to French architecture was considerable. Those who wondered at Charles's extreme promodern position expressed similar sentiments and suggested that he had pressed "his love of country" too far.[75] Charles stressed loyalty to the nation even when he wrote about Antoine Arnauld, who had chosen exile in the Netherlands after his expulsion from the Faculty of Theology and the monarchy's persecution of Port-Royal. According to Charles, in spite of the suffering Arnauld's politics had caused him, "his zeal for his monarch was extreme. Several times during his self-imposed exile, he swung at hornets' nests because he detested those who, ignorant of the king's heroic qualities, allowed their passions and interests to dictate their comments about him."[76]

Even before embarking on an exploration of the intricate dynamics of patronage in the following chapters, we can see that for early modern readers, patronage provided a meaningful context for understanding Charles's career, and not in a purely literary sense. Unlike seventeenth-century readers, we tend to see authors simply as the producers of written texts. Yet all those who wrote about Charles devoted special attention to his role as a cultural broker, mediating among authors, artists, and the monarchy. Even in the context of patronage, Charles's role as a man of letters was not limited to dedicating his works to the high and mighty.[77] As Colbert's confidant and his arbiter in matters relating to artistic and scholarly genius, he "sought to examine in good faith anything that contributed to the arts and sciences."[78] As we have seen, Charles also spent his nights writing the briefs that played a crucial role in the establishment of several academies: the Academy of Inscriptions and Belles Lettres, the Academy of Sciences, and the Academy of Painting and Sculpture.

Further, contemporaneous accounts devoted as much space to Charles's institutional contributions to the Académie française as to his literary career. Charles was praised for winning Louis XIV's sponsorship for the academy in 1672, after the academy's previous protector, Chancellor Pierre Séguier, had died. He won plaudits for moving the academy's assemblies to the Louvre and for ensuring that members received compensation for their labors. Even Dom Clemencet's Jansenist literary history mentioned that "the Académie française, in which he [i.e., Charles] was received in 1671, felt the effects of his influence [crédit], and is much obliged to him."[79] The "protobureaucratic" space of these institutions, underscored whenever Charles's biographers mentioned his role in composing briefs, allowed him to promote his own reputation and influence in the world of letters.

This emphasis on Charles's role as a broker placed him squarely within important relations of patronage, which added to his prestige. Here, the personal did not conflict with the bureaucratic but rather complemented it. By serving Colbert, the biographers claimed, Charles promoted the glory of Louis XIV and the French monarchy. But as Tallemant's eulogy shows, Charles was also in a position to promote his own favorites. Tallemant explained that he was obliged to praise Charles because of "the friendship he displayed toward me since my youth, the social relations that we had in common, but mostly the benefits that he procured for me so gently and so generously."[80] It was precisely Charles's services to Colbert that allowed him to display his virtues, since "Mr. Perrault sought only to please him" when he was exalting the merits of painters, sculptors, architects, astronomers, and physicists, "soliciting for them the compensation" they deserved.[81]

Further, those who chronicled Charles's life presented his relation to Colbert as the explanation for his career. They saw the loss of his position of influence after Colbert's death as a part of the normal course of events—the death of a powerful minister usually presages the removal of his followers from positions of influence. And they saw the change as a boon for his literary career, as from that moment on Charles could devote himself completely to the muses. As we shall see, these accounts erred, since Colbert had begun to relieve Charles of his duties about two years before his death. This biographical slippage only demonstrates how powerful patronage was in shaping seventeenth-century thinking on the careers of men of letters. The "fall of the favorite" was a common trope used in explaining the dynamics of service around courts and the monarchy more generally, and it certainly exercised an influence in this case.[82] Indeed, Charles himself used the same script in his life of Paul Pellisson, when he explained how Pellisson had been thrown into the Bastille after the disgrace of Nicolas Fouquet, whose affairs Pellisson had previously looked after.[83] One rose and fell as a result above all of whom he knew and served.

Patronage is a basic category for understanding the careers of the Perraults and other authors. Its effects extended beyond the inclusion of august names in books' dedications to include all the rewards that might be accrued through service to the throne and to grandees. The monarchy's prominent role in providing patronage did not exclude other patrons and did not prevent other institutions, such as the family, from shaping literary careers. Furthermore, service to the monarchy could open routes for personal patronage. Authors—even under the regime of patronage and before writing for the market became prominent—were not hapless instruments controlled by the monarchy and social elites. So while Colbert made forceful interventions in French culture by founding numerous academies and creating a formal system of state patronage, we can see that the monarchy was far from sweeping aside all other elements in the world of letters. Membership in academies became important for status considerations, yet it was one element among a host of others. The monarchy's patronage conferred status and access to resources, but contemporaries often presented it as Colbert's doing and not as some form of impersonal bureaucracy. While these academies initially adopted a form of collective authorship, readers soon learned who was responsible for many projects. And rather than working against kinship, family connections became building blocks in the emerging literary field.

While authorship often implies a highly defined professional persona, especially as crystallized in our notion of literary genius, the character traits attributed to the Perraults did not stem from a single and powerful persona or one cultural model. As we have seen, the attributes assigned to their written lives came from a heterogeneous set of categories, with no obvious relation between their character and their works. Even the "moral portraits" that appeared in many biographies do not present a clear persona. They, too, were a composite of different models. The influence of any single model or persona should not be exaggerated, as in practice they were the result of contingent compromises.[84]

Nicolas was a theologian, a domain long marked by clearly defined institutional and intellectual boundaries, and we might have expected his biographers to describe him using attributes selected from a narrow repertoire that stresses devotion as well as intellectual ability. Indeed, Nicolas's career determined many aspects of the moral character attributed to him. Varet and Moréri presented him as a penetrating theologian devoted to the Jansenist cause, or "the defense of truth," as they put it. They described Nicolas as prudent, devout, and humble. Dom Clemencet argued that Nicolas's indignation over Jesuit policies had driven him to an early grave.[85]

Yet even as they detailed the heated religious polemics he had penned, Nicolas's biographers presented him as "eloquent," "clear-thinking," and fond of mathematics—virtues drawn from rhetorical and philosophical models. Varet's account exemplified this heterogeneous compound, revealing that Nicolas had to struggle with his love for mathematics, finally giving it up in order to devote himself completely to the study of theology.[86] In fact, piety was attributed to authors with varying religious beliefs working in a wide range of genres. In his life of one of the most famous skeptical philosophers of his day, François de la Mothe le Vayer, Charles acknowledged his subject's Pyrrhonism but specified that "all opinions were the same to him, except for the ones faith does not allow us to doubt." And in the context of a dispute between Le Vayer and Claude Favre de Vaugelas, Charles even compared Le Vayer to a monk, who remains virtuous and wise in spite of his slightly relaxed discipline.[87]

Similarly, while Charles was seen as an *honnête homme*—literally, "honest man," this essentially untranslatable phrase was applied to connoisseurs of polite and courtly works—this was only one persona found in accounts of his life.[88] All the authors stated that Charles was very devout, honest, devoted to friends, lacking in jealousy, brilliant, and likable: traits that conform to the notion of honnête homme but enjoy a much broader resonance than idealized court life. Even the notion of honnête homme itself was flexible enough that men of letters could imagine Socrates to be the first of this kind and see him as a model of learned friendship based on leisure.[89]

Similarly, even the ideal of conversation was not tied exclusively to the style of the honnête homme. Biographers did refer to conversation in polite society: Fontenelle claimed that if Claude saw the systems he presented as "probable" and did not dogmatically insist on them, this made his conversation more entertaining for polite society. In fact, men of letters—and members of the elite more broadly—were expected to speak in a witty and fluent manner; in many cases, though, a reputation for conversation grew out of printed records rather than word of mouth.[90] But the topics for conversation could vary enormously and contradict the norms associated with the model of the honnête homme. Philippe Fortin de la Hoguette recalled harmony, sweetness, and discretion as the principal traits of the conversation of a scholarly circle known as the Cabinet Dupuy.[91] Yet the erudition of this circle stood in direct contrast to the norms of polite conversation, since it was generally held that witty epigrams uttered at the court should not "reek of study."[92] The fact that the same norms could be applied to almost diametrically opposed types of conversation suggests that conversation was a diffuse model and did not dictate the topics or even style of discussion.

This brief overview suggests that while moral traits were constitutive of the authorial figures of the Perraults and other seventeenth-century authors, they may be of limited utility for explaining how authors chose to work in one genre or another. Certainly, categories such as honnête homme could be marshaled to explain literary success or to rebuke a rival author, but the careers of most authors were too complex to be explained by the values associated with any single category, as Nicholas's relation to theology suggests. While changes in such values can be useful for tracing long-term developments in intellectual life, their relevance to the lives of particular authors can be limited. For authors in seventeenth-century France, categorical personae appeared in clusters; authorship was a combination of traits of a heteroclite nature, far from representing a single, unified subject.

An analysis of the posthumous reputations of the Perraults reveals some of the inadequacies of using a modern, individualized notion of authorship when considering early modern men of letters; it would be a mistake to rely on the idea of the solitary writer for the Perraults, who made up a literary family in the minds of their contemporaries. But the Perraults were *men* of letters,[93] and this chapter has left open the question of female authors, especially the question of whether the categories that applied to male authors also applied to female ones.

This is a vast question and one that cannot be given a satisfactory answer without much more research. As it happens, the materials on the Perraults do not lend themselves easily to this type of analysis. Still, on the basis of several examples, it is possible to suggest the outline of an answer in the form of two preliminary hypotheses. Briefly put, the categories applicable to male authors were applicable to female authors but with somewhat different emphases, and the media environment that shaped literary reputations did not exclude female authors. Rather, male and female reputations grew alongside each other, diverging around publications that used the gender of authors as a criterion for inclusion or exclusion.

Madeleine de Scudéry, Marie-Jeanne l'Héritier de Villandon, and Madame de La Fayette received eulogies and were mentioned in biographical dictionaries, and their lives were recounted using many of the same categories as those used for their male counterparts. Scudéry's euology in *Journal des sçavans* praised her virtues: she had "all the virtues, all the talents, and all the different merits of both sexes."[94] The eulogy also gave her an illustrious genealogy, surveyed her publications (even anonymous ones), discussed her letter of appointment to Padua's Academy of the Ricovrati, and highlighted the pensions she received from patrons such as Mazarin; the chancellor Louis Phélypeaux, comte de Ponchartrain; and even the king himself, who awarded her a pension of two thousand francs in 1683, at the request of Madame de Maintenon. The eulogy strategically omitted the name of Fouquet, with whom Scudéry had been closely associated before his disgrace. Scudéry was so famous that young princes who visited Paris were ordered not to return home before they had met her. So while Scudéry's sex was often mentioned, the categories used to narrate her life closely resembled the ones used for describing male authors.

But if it could be said that Scudéry was an unusual female author, since she developed a profile close to that of a male, professional writer, the same cannot be said for L'Héritier or La Fayette. L'Héritier specialized in the feminine genre of the fable, and La Fayette published her novels anonymously in order to protect her identity.[95] Yet both received detailed entries in Moréri, and L'Héritier's eulogy in *Journal des sçavans* included the same categories used for male authors. La Fayette's entry in Moréri described her family origins, her role as a protector of men of letters (including Pierre-Daniel Huet, Jean Renault de Ségrais, and La Fontaine), her piety in later years, and her novels, explaining that even though *Zaide* appeared under the name of Ségrais, it was solely La Fayette's work.[96] L'Héritier's eulogy and dictionary entry noted the education she received from her father, an "amateur of science"; mentioned the offices held by her male relatives; exalted her connections at court and with other famous personalities, most notably Scudéry; surveyed her publications in some detail; noted the duchess of Némours's fondness for L'Héritier; mentioned the literary gatherings held at her house; and described her "heroic" generosity and disinterestedness.[97] The similarities, both in terms of the contents and the visibility of both authors, are impressive.

Yet some important differences do emerge between male and female authors, particularly as far as offices and appointments are concerned. Since women were excluded from holding offices or membership in formal academies, their authorial figures never included these components except by association with family members. Biographers did report their membership in nonroyal academies and the literary prizes they received. For example, L'Héritier's eulogy mentioned the prize she received in the Palinot competition held in Caen in 1692 and the prizes she received in 1695 and 1696 from the Lanternistes academy in Toulouse: "When awarding her the second prize, this famous academy made her a member of its corporate body, an honor it had not yet accorded to any lady."[98] This seems to be an effect of a differentiation between the crown's courtly and bureaucratic functions. As we have just seen, the biographies of these female authors routinely mentioned connections to the king and the court. Some organized brilliant literary gatherings, but unlike Charles Perrault, for example, they never held the posts that would have permitted them to dispense state patronage.

Furthermore, there appears to have been a partial divergence in the media in which the lives of male and female authors were published. While dictionaries and learned journals discussed both male and female authors, some biographical collections were dedicated to either male of female personalities. So whereas Charles's *Hommes illustres* included no females, other publications included many.[99]

Jean de La Forge's dialogue on "the circle of learned ladies," for example, was dedicated to a female patron, the comtesse de Fiesque, and its introduction was addressed to female readers. In fact, La Forge's introduction shows how a growing female readership could become an authorial and a publishing concern. La Forge even hinted that he might publish a second edition if he learned of more contemporary learned ladies.[100] Other works, such as *Le grand dictionnaire des précieuses,* by Antoine Baudeau, sieur de Somaize, also devoted numerous entries to female members of the Parisian elite.[101] During this period, publications that were prominently devoted to female personalities became a distinct strand of biographical discourse, using many of the same categories in discussions of female authors that were used for male authors. And while women usually wrote anonymously, this appears to have been less important for their biographies than the formal exclusion of female authors from formal institutions. Female authors were not erased from the discourses that defined male authors, as a few examples suffice to show. The categories applicable to men of letters seem, therefore, largely applicable to female authors.

What did early modern readers know about the lives of the authors of their day? By approaching the Perrault brothers from that angle, this chapter has charted the place of the family of letters within the discourses that defined seventeenth-century authorship. The representations of the individual Perraults linked them to the texts they produced as well as to their relatives: clearly their contemporaries defined them as a group, drawing on the powerful concepts of the family and the house.

This chapter has also traced the ways changes in authorship related to a new media environment that reflected a growing complexity of the world of letters. Writing in 1610, well before many of the works mentioned in the foregoing pages appeared, Charles Loyseau could still confine the term "men of letters" to a narrow range of subjects based on the university model: "Our men of letters are divided into four faculties or major sciences, namely, theology, jurisprudence (including civil law and canon law), medicine, and the arts."[102] By the end of the seventeenth century, as we have seen, men of letters participated in a much broader range of institutional contexts. Behind the expansion in the printed materials about writers was the early modern "information lust," inspiring readers to demand more than another hackneyed list of the moral qualities associated with learning. It is possible that the sheer growth in the size of publishing ventures such as the Moréri led to the inclusion of more varied biographical information to avoid a monotony of similar entries.

Why were these changes taking place? Current explanations ring true at a general level, yet they do not converge in the details. It is clear that the reading public expanded and became more diverse over the course of the seventeenth century.[103] This is especially evident in the appearance of a substantial female readership for literature, a development surely linked to the appearance of biographical works devoted to female authors.[104] It is also clear that authors perceived this growth of the reading public; the "new philosophy" of the seventeenth century, in contrast with scholastic philosophy, was written for a nonuniversity audience.[105] But there are other factors that contributed at least partially to this phenomenon, from rising interest in the man of letters as a model for citizenship to the internationalization of the scholarly world.[106] Readers in Berlin, a relatively provincial town that was home to Huguenot refugees, became more dependent on journals published in Amsterdam to learn about French books printed in Paris or Rouen. Authorship was being redefined in a much more complex environment, both in terms of the number and reach of the different media and in terms of the level of detail they offered. But as d'Alembert's eulogy of Charles Perrault—which portrayed him as a would-be philosophe writing for a nation that "wanted and deserved to be enlightened"—would show, new values and further growth of the world of print would bring yet more changes to authorship by the second half of the eighteenth century.[107]

The family, just like official positions, institutional affiliations, and patrons, was for the French reading public a means to gauge the figures of men of letters and their relation to the bodies of texts they produced. Focusing on the way seventeenth-century authors saw their lives and organized their activities allows us to sketch the contours of early modern authorship as a more fully historicized phenomenon, in which authors' careers reflected family strategies just as much as individual desires.[108] In order to give substance to this assertion, we need to examine the Perraults' family strategy in detail, starting with their arrival in Paris in the early seventeenth century. That is the task of the next chapter.

CHAPTER TWO

Finance and Mobility

Pierre Ascendant (1600–1660)

Blue Beard's wife was about to lose her life at the hands of her monstrous husband, who discovered that she had been poking her nose where she shouldn't have, even infiltrating the chamber of horrors that held the remains of Blue Beard's previous wives. Fortuitously, her two brothers saved her in the nick of time and impaled Blue Beard on their swords. To this happy end Charles Perrault added details on inheritance and family fortunes:

> Blue Beard had no heirs, so his wife gained control of all his property. She used a part of it to marry her sister Anne to a young gentleman, who loved her for a long time. With another part, she bought the offices [*charges*] of captain for her two brothers. And the rest she used to marry a very honnête homme, who made her forget the awful time she had spent with Blue Beard.[1]

Just like the ending of "Cinderella," the ending of "Blue Beard" is cast in family terms. However, it adds several new nuances: it underscores the influence of a woman over the transmission of property; the mutual dependence among the siblings, whose fates were intertwined; and the importance of the venality of office as a means of securing mobility. All these aspects had a role to play in the history of the Perraults.

Nothing in the Perrault family's early history augured the literary and intellectual distinction they had achieved by the early eighteenth century. Even Pierre Sr. and Paquette Le Clerc, the parents of Jean, Pierre Jr., Nicolas, Claude, and Charles, had no direct contact with the world of letters. Yet the strategies they developed after Pierre Sr. left Tours for Paris deeply influenced their children. This chapter examines the first phases of this strategy, up to about 1660, setting it in the framework of Parisian social history. The family's integration into the city's social fabric, and particularly into the economy of offices generated by the French monarchy, proved to be of enormous significance for the Perraults' economic as well as intellectual fortunes.

The seventeenth and eighteenth centuries, so we are told, saw the gradual emancipation of literary writers from their dependence on patrons. Instead of relying on the pensions, gratifications, and employment that patrons routinely offered, authors supposedly gained autonomy—taking on the mantle of modernity—when they managed to "live by the pen" by writing for the market, free from the constraints imposed by a society of orders.[2] Living by the pen was an ideal early modern authors consistently failed to achieve, however; furthermore, many of the battles over the income drawn from writing were waged by printers and jurists rather than writers. Geoffrey Turnovsky has argued that the tension between the essentially unrealizable ideal of living by the pen and the social and economic realities that shaped literary careers was one of the structuring principles of early modern authorship.[3]

In the following chapters, I argue that while a writer's career rested on a bedrock of social and economic circumstances, this had little to do with the autonomy of writing, reflected in the ideal of living by the pen. The questions, What kind of remuneration did authors receive? and When did it become possible to live by the pen instead of depending on patronage? do more to obscure than to illuminate these connections. Whereas the publication of a book might bring an author sales revenues and gratifications that totaled between several hundred and two thousand livres, approximately equivalent to the annual income of a professor and probably less than the annual income of a notary at the Châtelet, the economic impact of a literary career could operate on a much larger scale.[4] As we shall see, to understand the economy of letters we must scrutinize family strategies and "court capitalism," that is, the market for the offices and favors that revolved around the court. As the French monarchy relied on the sale of venal offices for growing portions of its revenue, it created both a bureaucracy whose members saw their offices as their private property and a huge market for government posts. This market shaped the strategies of numerous well-to-do families. As chapters 3, 4, and 5 will show, the social and economic strategies of the Perraults were intimately connected to their literary activities. Only by bearing in mind the kinship ties among the Perraults can we fully appreciate these connections and understand how the Perraults ultimately became a family of letters.

When the Perraults arrived in Paris, deep changes were afoot. After almost a decade of intense loyalty to the Catholic League (1585–1594), the city reluctantly adapted to the control of Henri IV. An apparent calm concealed a basic shift in the relations among the monarchy, the city, and leading elites—members of Parlement, holders of judicial and financial offices, municipal notables, and nobles of different origins.

Social mobility in early modern France could be achieved through various means, from commerce through military service. However, in the first half of the seventeenth century, in the judicial milieu to which the Perraults belonged, social mobility was deeply tied to achieving noble status through office holding. In principle, the French nobility comprised two categories whose identities emerged over the early modern period: "sword nobles" and "robe nobles." The sword represented the older families that claimed descent from medieval warriors. The robe, on the other hand, signified the officeholders, predominantly those affiliated with royal courts. Only the loftiest offices provided ready entry to the nobility. And usually, the sons of the ennobled could not expect to inherit their fathers' status unless they held an identical office; requirements varied with each office. For instance, officers in sovereign courts in the provinces could expect to acquire hereditary nobility only if the family had held the office for two generations; the office of *secrétaire du roi* (royal secretary) was especially attractive, since it conferred hereditary nobility after twenty years in service.[5]

Yet ennoblement seldom followed simple formulae. As Robert Descimon has forcefully argued, it is best to view nobility not as an essence but as a social relation, reflecting conflicts of definition and interest.[6] In fact, the codification of noble status that took place in the second half of the seventeenth century masked the plurality of strategies used to attain noble status.[7] In Paris, most of the families who sought promotion through office holding had made their headway into Parisian society in the sixteenth century. The crucial moment came in the 1520s, when François I's monarchy laid out in some detail how offices would be sold. The first step taken by those who sought ennoblement was to gain the informal status of notables. This generally involved purchasing a municipal position, which could lead to a minor financial position in the king's service and ultimately a career in the judiciary. The trajectory was neither clearly defined nor completely predictable, prompting families to spread their investments across a wide range of options. While some bought lands (noble fiefs conveyed feudal rights to the new owners), others invested in royal offices, took positions in the service of the high nobility, or tried to obtain ecclesiastical benefices. If such families continued to engage in commerce, they did so increasingly discreetly; such pursuits were considered inappropriate for those aspiring to noble status.

During the late sixteenth century and the early seventeenth century, the lines demarcating groups in Parisian society became more rigid and pronounced.[8] This certainly affected barristers, the occupational category to which the Perraults belonged. So in 1602 those members of the French Parlement who were barristers went on strike for two weeks, protesting the requirement to register in their own hand the fees (*salaires*) received from parties. Though it revolved around an apparently trivial formality, the strike exposed a growing rift within the judicial community. Parliamentary barristers and presidents (presiding judges) had much in common, but at the turn of the century their status and interests were drifting apart, since the presidents were officeholders and the barristers were not. The status of the presidents was improving as the value of their offices increased. The profession of barrister ceased to be a desirable status in itself and turned into a mere stepping-stone for more prestigious occupations. By moving to Paris, Pierre Perrault Sr. became part of a social group that offered members opportunities for social improvement but ones that might necessitate leaving this group.[9]

In that world, finance became one of the most important avenues upward. The narrow definition of *financier*—anyone who deals with the king's money—is too vague to capture the social and economic realities involved in the functioning of the monarchy's financial system.[10] In reality, the financiers were a variegated group of notables, usually holders of offices in the financial administration, who profited from their credit and connections while dealing with the king's money. During most of the seventeenth century, and especially during wartime, the French monarchy was hard-pressed to raise the cash necessary for maintaining a vast army, which at its peak numbered some four hundred thousand troops. Taxes rose, and the crown implemented a number of other measures to increase revenues: creating and selling offices, farming out taxes to tax collectors, issuing state bonds through the legal fiction of rents backed up by Paris's Hôtel de Ville, and borrowing at rates that soared from 20 to 50 percent. The financiers bought and sold the offices, funded chartered companies, and leased the collection of taxes, essentially paying a lump sum for the right to collect a particular tax in one region. Through these deals, the thirst for cash created opportunities for financiers to turn quick profits at considerable risk—about 20–25 percent of them went bankrupt.[11]

My argument regarding the Perraults' careers places them in the context of what Gail Bossenga, following George Taylor, has called "court capitalism."[12] This term describes the particular situation of Old Regime France: the state generated large markets for offices (and credit more generally), but in a situation of legal uncertainty and lack of a modern distinction between public and private spheres, connections and personal influence held tremendous importance. Nobles and financiers wove networks connecting the world of finance, the court, and the army in order to gain lucrative contracts. Cold calculations of supply and demand intermingled with personal ties of patronage to produce this form of capitalism.[13] I shall show how the Perraults' literary careers related both to careers in finance and, later, to connections at the court. More than the literary market, court capitalism governed the strategies of the Perraults.

It is hard to pinpoint the exact origins of the Perrault family. Pierre Perrault Sr. was in all probability born in Tours, the son of Jaquette Denis and Jehan Perrault, a royal embroiderer. Pierre had at least one brother, who inherited both their father's name and his occupation.[14] In the late sixteenth century, Tours was a city with a glorious past and an uncertain present. A century earlier, the French court had spent much of its time in the Loire Valley, often settling in Tours for long spells. King Louis XI (1423–83) had brought the silk industry to Tours and encouraged workers from Lyon and Lombardy to settle in the city. François Rabelais was born in the area, and Leonardo da Vinci, who followed his patron François I to France, died in the region in 1519. However, when the court shifted to Paris, economic and cultural stagnation set in. Dozens of notables left the Loire and headed to Canada in the first half of the seventeenth century.[15]

Pierre Perrault emigrated to Paris at some point before 1609, and it is probably around this time that he married Paquette Le Clerc—an early indication that he had achieved some success. Jean, their first son, was born during the same period, and two more children soon followed—Pierre Jr. in April 1611 and Claude in September 1613. The next group of children to reach adulthood came a decade and more later: Nicolas was born in 1624, Charles in 1628.[16]

Initially, the family relied on Paquette's existing network in Paris and on the ties they developed in their parish. Pierre and Paquette settled in a house on the rue Saint-Jean-de-Beauvais, living there until their deaths, his in 1652 and hers in 1657. They took an active part in local religious life. At least five of their children were baptized at the parish church, Saint-Étienne-du-Mont: Pierre, Claude, Nicolas, François (Charles's twin brother, who died at six months), and Charles. Baptisms meant choosing godparents, cementing social ties within the community.[17] Charles, for example, was held over the baptismal font by his brother Pierre and his cousin Françoise Pepin.[18] The latter was the daughter of Françoise Le Clerc, Paquette's sister, and François Pepin, a *conseiller du roi* (royal councillor), a rather frequent title often used to designate officeholders. As the Pepins lived on the same street as the Perraults, this ceremony shows that the Perraults belonged to a closely knit world, defined by the parish.

Slowly, it seems, Pierre Perrault Sr. also obtained a measure of local notability by serving as a churchwarden (*marguillier*), the layperson in charge of the parish's charitable register and the church's finances.[19] In the early 1630s he accepted donations from two widows of parliamentary lawyers: 400 livres from Marie Delisle and 450 livres from Marie Torse, the latter intended for the instruction in the catechism of uneducated parishioners. The identities of Pierre's fellow churchwardens evoke the milieu he had attained: François le Saulnier, a conseiller du roi in Parlement; Jehan le Juge le Jeune, a merchant and a bourgeois of Paris; and François Orry, a draper and a bourgeois of Paris.[20] These were the sorts of men one would have expected to meet at Saint-Étienne-du-Mont, a modest Left Bank parish in the university quarter that housed students, printers, small traders, and lawyers.[21]

Pierre worked as a barrister, but there is no way to estimate his professional successes or failures. It seems plausible that his legal work sustained him and his family. The family did not go back to Tours, and the children received an expensive education that prepared them for relatively prestigious positions in law, medicine, and theology. That implied either substantial financial means or connections with generous patrons.

Only slowly did Pierre establish himself outside the parish; in the 1640s we get a glimpse of his life outside his church as he developed connections in the household of Gaston d'Orléans, Louis XIV's uncle. In October 1644 he witnessed the marriage contract of Marie Tavernier, the daughter of a *controlleur d'office* (comptroller of office) in the household of the Duc d'Orléans, and Anthoine André, a bourgeois of Paris residing in the Saint-Germain-l'Auxerrois parish. Then, in March 1648, Pierre refused to execute the will of Pierre Corneillau, who was a lieutenant of the Swiss guards assigned to the Duc d'Orléans and held the post of a *maître d'hôtel ordinaire du roi*.[22] These new connections attest to geographical and social expansion of the Perraults' networks at the moment when Pierre's children were beginning to make a name for themselves.

The family's financial security relied on its integration into Paquette's network. It is possible that Paquette's father, Jehan Le Clerc, had been a printer.[23] When his property was divided on 7 November 1626, Jehan was identified as the "honorable man, Jehan Le Clerc, lord of Pebray, close to Corbey," indicating some distinction in Parisian society, though sometimes such titles were usurped, and hence they testify to the ambitions rather than the status of their claimants.[24] Pierre and Paquette divided with Françoise and François Pepin a considerable inheritance—66,000 livres—that established them comfortably within the ranks of the Parisian bourgeoisie. The Perraults inherited two houses: one, located on the rue Saint-Jacques, close to the shop of the famous printer Sébastien Cramoisy, was estimated at 16,000 livres; the other, located outside the city walls, between the Porte Saint-Jacques and the Porte Saint-Marcel, was estimated at 4,000 livres. Beyond the two houses, the couple received rents worth 13,000, generating an annual income of 818 livres and 15 sols.[25] The Pepin's share included a seigniorial fief called Pebray, consisting of a house, a farm, and lands amounting to about 200 arpents, approximately 168 acres in modern units. Such wealth places the Perraults within the middling ranks of the urban notables.[26]

The importance of Paquette's network in the geographical, religious, and economic integration of Pierre Sr. in Paris was paramount. In general, Paris offers an exception to the generalization that the early modern patriarchal family made women strangers in their own families—and in the families of their husbands.[27] In a study of 9,226 witnesses to Parisian marriage contracts recorded in the 1660s, the brides provided 52 percent of the witnesses, while the grooms provided only 44 percent.[28] The brides' networks also included a much larger share of family members, while grooms called on both professional connections and relatives to witness the contracts.[29]

Since Paris saw a constant influx of male migrants, many grooms lacked a well-established local familial network. This was certainly true for the Perraults, and it helps explain why Paquette's relatives, the Pepins, would remain a presence in the Perraults' networks. Furthermore, since Parisian grooms tended to be older than their brides, it is likely that they would have fewer potential witnesses to draw from, since more of their elders would have died.[30] Much like other Parisian families, Paquette's family would have provided crucial social and economic support for the Perraults during the first decades of the seventeenth century. Such support ensured that even as Paquette, Pierre, and their children formed ties to their parish, they also did the preparatory work needed to move the younger generation into milieus quite different from the small world of jurists, traders, and printers that met for prayers at Saint-Étienne-du-Mont.

The Perrault family recognized the social value of education early on, and while the legal domain took pride of place, a pool of potential careers was fostered by seeing to it that the boys were educated in other fields. Initially the family focused on social reproduction in the legal milieu: if Jean, the eldest son, succeeded, that meant that the family would perhaps remain in the world of the barristers rather than seeking more prestigious and lucrative offices in the judiciary or financial administration. However, once Pierre landed a position in the financial bureaucracy, it became apparent that Charles could work to their mutual benefit. Only this shift would start the process of transforming the Perraults into a family of letters.

Charles stressed the involvement of both his parents in his early education—it was clearly a family priority. His mother taught him how to read, and after supper his father made him recite his lessons and summarize them in Latin. If this method was used with all the brothers, it probably yielded results. Charles later claimed that none of the brothers were ever whipped by their teachers.[31]

Observers saw the Perrault household as one that combined piety with an esteem for learning. Alexandre Varet, the presumed author of the introduction to Nicolas's *Morale des jésuites*, described the family atmosphere much as Charles did: "He [Nicolas] was born to a father who made a particular effort to fortify, at the opportune moment, his children against popular errors, to inspire them with the purest maxims taken from Holy Scripture, and to open their minds to the most beautiful forms of knowledge."[32] Varet was an intimate friend of the Perraults. He probably lived close to them, shared their Jansenist sensibilities, and took his law degree with Charles; most important, his sister married a cousin of theirs named Pepin, most probably a son of Françoise and François Pepin.[33]

The children's curriculum aimed, first of all, at social reproduction, but mobility was also a concern. The eldest sons, Jean and Pierre, received legal training, allowing them to follow in their father's footsteps. Jean, indeed, practiced law, though he appears to have been something of a malcontent: Charles claimed that even though he was extremely competent and eloquent, he felt he was not receiving the recognition he deserved.[34] Pierre's education in the law also provided ample training for entering the French bureaucracy or finance.[35] Claude, younger than Pierre by a couple of years, studied at the Parisian Faculty of Medicine and became a doctor, also adding to his duties teaching at the faculty. Nicolas, who was born in 1624, eleven years after Pierre, also pursued an education that diversified the family's options: he studied theology and could have opted for a position in the church.[36]

Charles, the youngest surviving son, left the college after quarreling with the teacher. As was perhaps fitting for a Perrault, he subsequently studied at home: he and a friend called Beaurain met twice daily to read the Bible, classical writings, and histories of France.[37] Charles's description of how he obtained his law degree borders on the comic while reminding us of his assid-uous studies. In July 1651 Charles traveled to Orléans with Varet and a third law student named Manjot. They arrived late, but the local doctors of juris-prudence were still happy to quiz them. Three examiners, wearing nightcaps over their lawyer's bonnets, asked them a series of perfunctory questions, to which Charles and his friends replied in kind, the whole thing performed in Latin. As Charles explained, "I think that the sound of our money, which we counted behind our backs while they interrogated us, was somewhat useful in making them overvalue our answers." Charles went on to study Justinian's *Institutiones* by himself, afterward embarking on his brief legal career.[38]

Claude's studies followed a more routine pattern. In seventeenth-century France, medical studies lasted at least seven years. When Claude completed his studies in 1639, he presented his two quodlibet theses and his cardinal thesis for the bachelor's degree. His choice of subjects was utterly typical for the period, and his theses did not anticipate his future work at the Academy of Sciences: his two quodlibet theses dealt with whether the soul aged just like the body and whether a cautery could be used when the head or other body parts shook incessantly; his cardinal thesis dealt with whether it was healthy to consume iced wine during the summer heat. Claude finished his training in 1641 by presenting a dissertation on questions such as whether a doctor could abandon a sick person. The following year he presided over the thesis of a younger student, symbolizing his new status as a doctor and regent of the Parisian Faculty of Medicine.[39]

His younger brother Nicholas also traveled a conventional route to his degree. In January 1647 Nicolas was awarded a bachelor's degree in theology after discussing a question from Psalm 4:7: "Who will show us good things?"[40] He received his doctorate in theology from the Sorbonne in 1652.[41] The costs related to medical studies barred all but the wealthy or well-connected from becoming doctors; a theology degree involved similar costs, but preparing for the examinations took even longer—a minimum of sixteen years, compared with eleven years in the other faculties.[42]

The Perrault family, then, invested its resources in formal degrees. A substan-tial part of the investment was devoted to the education of the older sons, who went into legal professions, ensuring the family's social position. Yet investment in medical and theological learning opened up new avenues of social mobility for the family—these paid off after 1660. Until then, however, Pierre's career in finance represented the most promising prospect for the family.

Pierre began working in financial administration in the mid-1630s or early 1640s. He started out as an aide in the *parties casuelles*, the administrative body responsible for handling revenues from venality. His first post was as an aide to a certain M. de Vassan, followed by a post with a certain M. Sabatier, a treasurer at the parties casuelles, who employed the young Jean-Baptiste Colbert at the same time. Claude Housset, who also worked under Sabatier, bought Sabatier's office and retained Pierre as his aide. By the time the civil war known as the Fronde broke in the late 1640s, Housset had already acquired a reputation as a financier who, beyond his formal role, benefited from lending money to the monarchy at exorbitant rates, to the detriment of the public good.[43] In 1657 Housset arranged for Pierre to buy the office of an "alternative receiver general of finances in the Paris generality" (*receveur général alternatif des finances en la généralité de Paris*) from Henri and Claude Bonneau, members of one of the most important families in French finances during the first half of the seventeenth century; the "alternative" added to the title meant that he filled this function in rotation with two other officeholders, the "old" and "triennial" holders of this office.[44]

A gauge of Pierre's overall success in the world of finance is the tax imposed on him by the *chambre de justice* of 1661. Formally, the chambre was a tribunal charged with investigating and punishing abuses in the financial administration. In practice, the monarchy used such tribunals to purge the ranks of the financiers and install new ones, effectively dismissing past debts without publicly declaring bankruptcy. The king's judicial powers, delegated to the chambre, compensated for his lack of financial resources, especially acute during the ongoing wars waged by the monarchy against the Hapsburgs.[45] Chambres de justice had been held before, in 1563, 1577, 1585, 1597, 1601, 1624, 1635, and 1648. Yet the one inaugurated in 1661 was unusual: it was protracted; it covered eight years of financial dealings, going back to the early 1650s; and it had an extremely wide reach, as hundreds of financiers were prosecuted. In a remarkable study, Daniel Dessert used the documents generated around the hearings to create a prosopography of the financiers of the day. As Dessert argued, in most cases the tax burdens of the financiers correlated well with their general wealth and importance.[46]

The proceedings of the chambre led to Pierre's disgrace, and he was forced to sell his office, as we shall see in chapter 4. The proceedings offer the means to understand Pierre's social standing, when he is placed alongside the anatomy of the financiers produced by Dessert. The sums in Pierre's file add to 117,487 livres, meaning he belonged to the lower echelon of this group.[47] This was an economically stratified lot: of the 248 individuals in Dessert's sample, a small minority—less than a third—had to cough up 79 percent of the total fines imposed; each had to pay the state over 500,000 livres. Pierre belonged to the lowest range in this group, the 71 individuals taxed at 100,000–120,000 livres.[48] The difference between Pierre and his patron, Claude Housset, is apparent when we learn that Housset was taxed to the tune of 2,000,000 livres.[49]

The financiers' trajectories and familial background also reveal Pierre's social mobility. Like the vast majority of the financiers, he had come to the financial world through office holding rather than commerce. In contrast with the majority of the financiers (71 percent of those identified), Pierre was not noble. Most of those who were (63 percent) had arrived at that status by holding the office of secrétaire du roi.[50] While Pierre had managed to obtain a lucrative office in finance, he had yet to make the leap to the nobility of the robe. More significant, whereas most of his fellow financiers were second-generation (74 percent) or third-generation officeholders (64 percent), Pierre belonged to a minority group (less than 8 percent) whose fathers were barristers.[51]

Pierre's career did much for the Perrault family's success. Until 1662, for example, Charles depended on his work for Pierre for much (if not all) of his income. He hardly practiced as a lawyer. Jean did work as a lawyer, but he does not appear to have enjoyed a resounding success; as we have seen, Charles claimed that Jean did not receive the recognition he deserved. As to Claude and Nicolas, serving on distinguished faculties would have granted them status and dignity, yet their income probably paled in comparison with Pierre's. Though it is notoriously difficult to estimate the income of seventeenth-century university teachers, who supplemented their salaries with private tutoring (which could also include housing students), one study suggests that the average Parisian professor would have earned under 1,000 livres per year.[52] Sought-after physicians probably made slightly more than 1,000 livres per year, and in an extreme case, Eusèbe Renaudot earned 7,500 livres from his patients in 1666, though it is probably far from representative of the broader community.[53]

Marriage could exert a far greater influence over family wealth than salaries, and until 1672, when Charles wed Marie Guichon, Pierre was the only son with a wife. His marriage to Catherine Lormier in November 1656 set him firmly in the middling ranks of the financiers. From Catherine's perspective, too, the marriage represented an opportunity for social advancement. If plans for the marriage proceeded once the decision had been made to purchase an office for Pierre, it would have cemented a move from the world of the sovereign courts to the world of high finance. Catherine came from a family of officers in the cour des aides, the court that rendered final decisions in disputes over internal custom duties and other taxes. Both her father and grandfather held the office of conseiller at the cour des aides, so the Lormiers must have lived in Paris since at least the middle of the sixteenth century. In fact, her father, Charles, inherited the office from her grandfather, Jean, in September 1597, and his heirs sold it in August 1649, seven years before the marriage.[54]

The Lormiers had not risen along the social ladder for some time. Charles, Catherine's father, had perhaps slipped a bit when he married into a family involved in commerce. His sons did relatively well: Charles—the most prominent—became a financial officer and came to present himself as noble; Nicolas and Antoine became barristers in the Parlement; the profession of another brother, Étienne, remains unknown. The dowry Catherine's brother Charles received in his marriage—25,000 livres—was comparable to the sums Catherine and her elder sister Madeleine brought to their marriages.[55] Catherine was a widow when she married Pierre, meaning that she was older than the average wife and possessed property she controlled herself. She and Madeleine both handled property transactions, and Madeleine especially was involved in the constitution of rents with the Baron de Bazin and with the financial officer Sébastien Hardy.[56] This meant that Catherine had access to the networks of credit that Pierre would have needed to purchase of the office of receiver general.

Pierre hardly needed to rely only on such resources. Catherine brought to her marriage 150,000 livres, and six months later, on 2 May 1657, Pierre purchased the office for 190,000 livres, just 20,000 in cash—the remaining 170,000 livres were received in installments.[57] The credit arrangements were complex: two deferred payments of 55,000 livres (on 1 January and 1 July 1658) and an annuity of 3,000 livres to be paid by Pierre, covering the remaining sum of 60,000 livres. A house on the rue Simon-le-Franc owned by Catherine served as a guarantee for future payments.[58] It should be clear that Catherine's contribution to Pierre's financial career was essential.

If the information collected by Jal in the nineteenth century can be trusted, the witnesses to the wedding of Pierre Perrault and Catherine Lormier comprised the groom's brothers, Jean, Claude, Nicolas, and Charles; Paquette, their mother, was also present at the ceremony.[59] Pierre's failure to produce a more impressive roster stands in contrast not only to the routine practice of displaying one's status through a list of stellar witnesses but particularly to the group of witnesses drummed up by Charles for his marriage in 1672 (a question treated in depth in chapter 4). Further evidence for the importance of Catherine's family, and an indication that the Perraults were shifting within Parisian geography, is the location of the wedding. According to Jal, it took place in the parish of Saint-Merry, where Catherine's husband had passed away in 1655.

It is also worth noting that Pierre was forty-five years old by the time he married for the first time, far above the average age. Among the conseillers at the cour des aides, Catherine's milieu, the median age of marriage in the seventeenth century was thirty.[60] As Charles's case will also confirm, late marriage appears to have been a strategy the Perraults used for social advancement. Since Pierre presumably anticipated that his fortunes would improve, it would have made perfect sense to delay his marriage as long as possible: the higher his status before marriage, the more advantageous his marriage would be. He put off marrying, presumably, in hopes of a larger dowry and connections with more powerful relatives.

The marriage and purchase of office consolidated Pierre's standing in a position crucial to the functioning of French finances. Receivers general were responsible for delivering taxes collected in their region to the treasury in Paris. They relied on considerable credit and were often involved in complex deals: before they had collected any tax payments, the receivers general advanced the state a fraction of their anticipated receipts out of their own pockets. Since they handled large amounts of cash destined for the monarchy's coffers, they routinely turned a profit with it before completing the delivery. As they collected direct taxes every year in office—instead, for example, of making a single killing by completing a deal for selling offices—receivers enjoyed a relatively stable revenue stream. For them, each year in office was an opportunity to use the cash at their disposal for other deals, and their regular access to cash meant that they could easily find partners or investors in their financial initiatives.[61]

Pierre carried out his duties with the normal mix of public service and private gain. He was involved in the collection of the taille in the years 1658, 1661, and 1663—and quite possibly in several other years. With Claude Coquille he formed a canny partnership, overseeing the collection in all its machinations. When things did not go quite as they had hoped, they promptly cast the blame on René Souchu, a receiver working underneath them in the election of Meaux. On another occasion, when the inquiries of the chambre de justice got too close for comfort, Pierre got word to his aide, François Maillot, to cook the accounts.[62]

Lists of Pierre's creditors from 1688 have survived, and they document the means he had at his disposal for raising money.[63] They also suggest ways his marriage built on his existing networks. These documents provide only a partial view of Pierre's financial career—for example, they do not tell us about debts he may have contracted and paid back before his disgrace—but the data they provide are detailed enough to sketch the different economic actors with whom Pierre interacted and their relative importance.

As tables 2.1 and 2.2 show, not all the actors in Pierre's economic network played an equal role. We can conceive of the information in three tiers, based on the various amounts Pierre owed. The first tier comprises the sum Catherine Lormier, his wife, brought to their marriage: 150,000 livres. That is more than twice the amount of any debt Pierre had, 40 percent of the sum total of all his debts. The next tier comprises three very large debts. The first debt in this tier was 60,000 livres owed to Claude Bonneau and his brother Henri, the result of the purchase of Pierre's office. The second debt, totaling 63,074 livres and 6 deniers, was owed to Claude Coquille, a major partner in some of Pierre's most ambitions deals.[64] Through his family connections, Coquille was well integrated into the world of high finance: he was the nephew of the financier Denis Marin, who was married to a cousin of Colbert, and he was also related to another receiver general in the generality of Paris, Pierre de la Croix.[65] Such connections ensured that Coquille received special treatment from the chambre de justice, which fined him 380,000 livres—far less than the fines meted out to other financiers in his caliber.[66] It is hard to evaluate the circumstances of the third large debt, totaling 50,000 livres. However, since it is dated to 1664, it probably related to the proceedings of the chambre de justice or to a property transaction somehow connected to those proceedings.

Table 2.1   Pierre Perrault's creditors, 1688

CREDITOR	TITLE/ PROFESSION	DATE	SUM[a]	COMMENTS
Madeleine de Bailly, dame, married to Jacques de Vassan, together with Pierre Perrault to Jean Dorieux[b]	De Vassan, seigneur de Morsan, conseiller du roi en ses conseilles et trésorier des parties casuelles, conseiller du roi en ses conseilles président en sa cour des aides	4 December 1647	9,500 (original principal, some paid back)	
Catherine Lormier	Pierre's wife	6 November 1656 (the day of their marriage)	150,000 given to the partnership between them as part of the marriage contract	
Claude Bonneau and Henry Bonneau (brothers)	Claude Bonneau, chevalier seigneur de Purnon cy devant premier maitre d'hôtel de Monsieur; Henry Bonneau, chevalier seigneur de Tracy, at the time of his death maréchal des camps et armées du roi, gouverneur de la ville et citadelle de Tournay	12 May 1657	60,000	
Jean Pepin (through his widow, Anne Raout)	Conseiller et secrétaire du roi	22 February 1657	10,000 (principal of a rent of 555 livres, 3 sols)	

CREDITOR	TITLE/ PROFESSION	DATE	SUM[a]	COMMENTS
Pierre Pepin	Conseiller du roi, élu en l'élection de Paris	21 March 1657	8,000 (principal of a rent of 444 livres, 8 sols, 2 deniers)	
Pierre de Chesneau, his sister (her husband in fact), also as inheritors of their father, Jean Baptiste de Chesneau	Jean Baptiste de Chesneau, écuyer sieur de Mareil, capitaine des grenadiers du régiment du Conty	24 May 1659	18,000 (rent of 900 livres)	
Claude Louvain, transfer to Pierre Bullin, from Claude Savot	—	8 February 1664	50,000 livres (or a part of it)	
André le Grand	Conseiller et secrétaire du roi	6 June 1664 (based on a promised from 13 August 1663)	6,039 livres (original sum)	
Claude Coquille	Conseiller du roi, secrétaire ordinaire du conseil d'état	19 June 1664 (based on promise from 3 October 1663)	63,074 livres, 6 deniers	
Moret, separated wife of Pierre Belin, wife of André Combault	Pierre Belin, bourgeois de Paris	5 June 1664	3,000 livres (principal of a rent, date could be slightly different)	
Nicolas Coquille, acquired from Jacques Josse and his wife, Marie Tubier, through Crespin	—	28 August, 1664	7,200 livres	Interest mentioned in separate entry

[a]The sums represented here are not the actual sums owed by 1688 but the reconstruction from the text of the original debt. This reconstruction is supposed to reflect the original commitments Pierre took, stripped of further interests.
[b]Since this is not a debt, I have excluded it from the calculations.

Table 2.2 Pierre Perrault's *Créanciers chirographaires* (creditors with no collateral), 1688

CREDITOR	DATE	SUM
Claude and Charles Perrault	22 March 1658	3,730 livres
Claude and Charles Perrault	22 March 1658	580 livres remaining from an original sum of 860 livres
Madeleine Lormier, passed to her children, Jean Philippe and Alfonse Charles Philippe	5 March 1661	18,000 livres
Marie Rousseau, widow of Jean de Brye (original creditor), and her minor children	3 August 1662 + 14 February 1662	750 livres, 140 livres
Philippe Daudier	24 March 1664	5,000 livres

The third tier of creditors, those owed less than 20,000 livres, probably comprises people close to Pierre who would give him credit. An important contingent is those related to Pierre through his marriage and the marriage of his father. Pierre borrowed 18,000 livres from Madeleine Lormier, his sister-in-law, and the same amount (over two transactions) from Jean and Pierre Pepin, most probably his maternal cousins.[67] By comparison, his brothers Charles and Claude together lent slightly less than 5,000 livres. Family networks thus accounted for about 50 percent of the debts in this category, with relatives outside Pierre's immediate family making far larger loans than Charles or Claude, attesting to the brothers' modest economic stature. Furthermore, the identities of the creditors demonstrate Pierre's integration in the world of office holding and finance; they include royal councillors, royal secretaries, receivers general, lawyers, Parisian bourgeois, and minor nobles.

As it was common for the names of family members to occur in records of loans, it appears that Pierre and Catherine's two children—Claude, born on 15 March 1658, and Jean, born on 14 June 1661—nowhere mentioned in this document from 1688, may have predeceased them.[68] This hypothesis *ex silentio* appears to be reinforced by the decision Charles made, in 1698, to renounce any claims as Pierre's heir, again with no mention of Pierre and Catherine's children.[69]

In comparison with the careers of his brothers, Pierre leapt most nimbly up the social ladder, and his career represented the most promising path that could lead to social advancement for the Perraults as a group. As Pierre's marriage to Catherine Lormier and his purchase of the office of receiver general show, the sums Pierre obtained made him the "high roller" of the family. Placing Pierre against the backdrop of the other financiers shows the extent to which he was a newcomer to this milieu and strengthens the claim that he should be seen as the central actor in the Perrault family's strategy.

As some Perraults moved up the social ladder, they moved away from their birthplace. By following their moves beyond their native parish and their integration into wider urban networks, we see how a kinship network expands out of a single location and how new households took form as part of this process. Viewing the family's dynamism keeps us from reifying it as a compact and homogenous unit. And the shifting social geography bespeaks changes in the status of the displaced family members, revealing the immediate context of their networks, as we shall see when we look at Nicolas's activities in his parish.

Pierre Sr. and Paquette resided in the same house on the rue Saint-Jean-de-Beauvais in Saint-Etienne-du-Mont until their deaths in the 1650s. Their sons moved away when their careers took them into a different milieu. Pierre and Charles left the parish for the more central Marais, where many royal officers and financiers lived. In general, the geographical patterns reveal both the continued importance of the parish and the effects of Pierre's entry into the world of finance.

Nicolas remained in his parents' house. Though he had become a Sorbonne theologian involved in the debate on of Jansenism—a topic that linked him to many others across Paris and farther afield—his main circle of activity remained centered on the family household. According to Charles, he was active in theological discussion and resolving moral dilemmas in the parish of Saint-Étienne-du-Mont, where he and his brothers and sister (who died by the age of thirteen) were baptized. In 1656 he defended the Jansenist leader Antoine Arnauld at the Sorbonne and lost his position. From that date, he ceased to attend the assemblies of parish clergy. He also refused to set his name to the *formulaire*, a condemnation of five articles supposedly found in the Augustinus, the fundamental Jansenist book. According to Charles, "One thousand people kept telling him that he should sign the formulaire, that a man like him ought not to allow something so trivial to keep him from being useful to the Church in his preaching, confessing or in ecclesiastical conferences."[70]

The household and the familial milieu were also instrumental in spreading Nicolas's opinion on grace, the main point of theological contention between Jansenists and the mainstream Gallican Church. As Charles recounted the story, his brothers, Pepin, and others asked Nicolas to explain the controversy surrounding divine grace, as Antoine Arnauld had been driven from the Sorbonne for his opinions on the matter. They met "at the house of my late father, where my brother the doctor [of theology] explained to us that all questions of grace, which lead to so many discussions, revolve around the question of a close power and a distant power that grace gives us to do good."[71] Pierre subsequently repeated the exchange to the *intendant* of the duc de Luynes, a notable Jansenist, who floated the idea to explain the controversy to the public, ultimately leading Pascal to write his *Lettres provinciales* (Provincial letters). Charles appears to have been determined to reflect some of the literary glory that the *Lettres* gained onto Nicolas, a subject to which I shall return in the epilogue.

The local nature of the Perraults' early networks can also be seen in their activities as patrons. In 1654 the five brothers all served as witnesses to the marriage of Bénigne Poplard to Anne Charpentier. Poplard was their father's former clerk. They were probably asked to sign because of their relatively high status, and even though they signed as witnesses for the bride this may simply have been because she had no relatives in the city. As the dowry amounted to about 1,000 livres and the groom's witnesses included a baker, the Perrault brothers must have looked like local notables on that occasion. And as the bride and groom resided on the same street, this marriage was a parish affair, creating no additional ties of solidarity across wider stretches of Parisian geography.[72]

But social and geographic changes were already under way. By the date of Anne's marriage to Bénigne, Pierre and Charles had moved to rue Saint-François.[73] While the Perraults' original residence was close to the Left

Bank's university faculties, the brothers' new neighborhood, the Right Bank's Marais, occupied a more central place, closer to fashionable quarters inhabited by financiers, nobles, and municipal notables. It was also closer to the home of Pierre's future wife, Catherine. When they married, the ceremony was registered in the parish of Saint-Merry, a relatively short distance west of Saint-Gervais, and their two children were baptized in Saint-Gervais. The importance of this geographical shift can also be seen through the location of Pierre's creditors. While the debt documents contain only the addresses for the creditors involved in the selling of the family's house in Viry, they reveal a significant pattern (see table 2.3): while we continue to see connections in Saint-Étienne-du-Mont—especially ones based on family, since the Pepins

Table 2.3   Creditors related to the sale of Viry

CREDITOR	FUNCTION	ADDRESS
Mre. Jean Rouillé	Chevalier comte de Mesle et cy-devant conseiller d'état ordinaire	Paris île notre dame quai des baleons paroisse saint louis
Mre. Claude Coquille	Conseiller du roi en ses conseilles secrétaire du conseil d'état et direction de ses finances	Paris rue du grand chantier paroisse Saint-Jean-en-grève
Mre. Claude Bonneau	Chevalier seigneur de Purnon cy devant premier maître d'hôtel de Monsieur duc d'Orleans	Rue d'Argenteuil paroisse Saint-Roch
Mre. Pierre de la Croix	Cy devant receveur général des innocents de paris	Rue Saint-Antoine paroisse Saint-Germain
André le Grand	Écuyer conseiller secrétaire du roi contrôleur général de son domaine	Rue perdue paroisse Saint- Étienne-du-Mont
Pierre Pepin	Noble homme, cy devant conseiller du roi élu en l'eléction de Paris	Rue de Bièvre paroisse Saint- Étienne-du-Mont
Dame Margueritte Naver (?) veuve de Jean Pepin + their children	Écuyer conseiller secrétaire du roi	Rue saint jean de beauvais en la susdite paroisse
Mre. Jacques de Raincy	Noble homme, conseiller du roi contrôleur des trésors et payeur des gages des Messieurs les secrétaires du roi	Same street and parish
Mre. Pierre du...	Avocat en la cour (de Parlement)	Same street and parish
Jean Vincent (?) Philippe (through Lormier, from other document)	Avocat en Parlement	Rue Simon le franc paroisse Saint-Merri
Alphonse Charles Philippe	Sieur de la Buissonnière	Rue du temple paroisse Saint-Jean-en-grève
Charles Lormier	Sieur de la Tour	Maintenant a paris logé rue Saint-Antoine paroisse Saint-Paul
Mre. Pierre Guerrin	Bourgeois de Paris	Rue et paroisse Saint-Nicolas-du-Chardonnet
Claude Bounot	Bourgeois de Paris	Rue jean Saint-Denis paroisse Saint-Germain-de-prés
Louis Baunet	Sieur de Cernan	Rue et paroisse Sain-Merri

who lived there were Pierre's maternal cousins—we cannot help noticing that at least half of the creditors lived in the more central and prestigious parishes of Saint-Roch, Saint-Jean-en-Greve, Saint-Louis, and Saint-Germain-des-Prés, alongside many financiers and nobles.[74]

Pierre's rise expressed itself in sociogeographical terms. No longer attached to the parish like his father or even like Nicolas, Pierre became socially integrated into networks that took him into central and more fashionable parts of the capital. He took Charles with him: the brothers shared a residence in the Marais, demonstrating how physical proximity related to professional relations. This dynamic would repeat itself; when Charles became Colbert's aide, he obtained an office (cabinet) in the minister's house.

I have said almost nothing about Jean's education and career as they related to other family members. His presence in the documentary evidence is fleeting and uncertain—I have mentioned that he was one of the signatories to Bénigne Poplard's marriage contract, and as we will see in chapter 6, he traveled with Claude and a group of jurists to Bordeaux in 1669. There, stricken by an unidentified illness, he was tended by Claude and local doctors, who performed bleedings. But despite these efforts, Jean died.

The distance between Jean and the activities of his brothers shows that kinship ties have to be actualized in practice. His training and chosen vocation served a conservative function in the family strategy: to follow in his father's footsteps. Under these conditions, Jean could do little to assist his brothers. Nor did he take part in the early familial writing projects, such as the paraphrase of the *Aeneid*, and he was not mentioned in the discussions of the family's country house in Viry, though the documents relating to the house's sale do mention Charles and Claude as past creditors. It seems plausible that he was following a different path, one that did not lead to much cooperation—social, economic, or literary—with his brothers. So when the image of the family of letters crystallized around the Perraults, Jean was left out; in his *Mémoires*, Charles alluded to him only as "my brother the barrister."[75]

Thanks to Pierre's career in finance, many new opportunities opened for the Perraults, and the very stakes for which they were aiming changed. The brothers entered the prestigious world of office holding after Pierre had won the position in the parties casuelles that he used to home in on the office of receiver general. Especially after the death of the Pierre Sr. and Paquette around 1657, Pierre Jr. seemed poised to assume the leading role in the family. He had acquired the most prestigious and lucrative office, taken possession of the family's country house in Viry after Paquette's death, and contracted a socially beneficial marriage with Catherine Lormier—all over the span of just two years. There is some irony in the fact that the world of office holding, traditionally blamed for siphoning off capital that could have helped modernize the French economy, proved so important for a family long identified with the "modern party" of seventeenth-century French culture. Such was the impact of court capitalism on the Parisian elite.

The legal profession lost the central importance it had had for the previous generation as investment in education opened up potential avenues for advancement in the Parisian professoriate and, more important from the economic point of view, the world of finance. This change probably led to internal fissures—Jean would have been the loser—but it also consolidated family ties. Nicolas, who as a theologian was not involved in the purely financial aspects of the family's trajectory, became a part of the model family of letters even though he maintained strong relations in his local parish, where networks built up around the Perrault household propagated his religious views.[76]

The limited role of writing and literature at this phase of the family's history is noteworthy. In 1653 Charles, Claude, and Nicolas, along with a friend called Beaurin, published a satirical, burlesque version of the *Aeneid* under the title *Les Murs de Troie ou l'origine du burlesque*. This work presented the reader with a humorous rewriting of the foundation of Troy in a style then very popular. The standard approach was to puncture famous classics by placing their heroes in rude, everyday situations. Dedicating their effort to the "bowl" of Paul Scarron,[77] the most famous author writing in this genre, the Perraults published anonymously, and no one appears to have recognized their pens in that frolic during their lifetimes. Just as well, since naming names would have, in this case, exposed the young authors to a real peril. As Marc Soriano has shown, the youthful burlesques were actually Mazarinades: works that took aim at Cardinal Mazarin. Because the poem supported the parliamentary factions against Mazarin and the monarchy, attributing it to the Perraults could have stained their reputations and placed them in a dangerous position. Instead, those playful brothers convincingly portrayed themselves as loyal servants to the monarchy.[78]

The Perraults' aspirations and mobility probably led them to identify with the officeholders surrounding the Parlement. This milieu ignited the first phases of the Fronde by fostering protests against Mazarin's financial scheming. These officeholders also proposed changes to tax regulations and the laws regulating the inheritance of offices. This did not make a mockery of the Perraults' own involvement in finance, since the Frondeurs wanted to ensure that offices remained hereditary, a topic that became more and more important for the Perraults as Pierre advanced within the financial bureaucracy.[79]

Mobility is not simply a question of moving from one level of income to the other. It entails changes in expectations, comportment, and behavior as the historical actors react to new problems—and one of the most pressing problems for financiers was credit. Credit, in its most basic meaning, represented the faith other notables were willing to place in financiers' solvency, and it led to the adoption of a lifestyle that projected an image of luxury. As La Rochefoucauld pithily phrased the issue, "In order to succeed in the world people do their utmost to appear successful."[80] To see how the Perraults dealt with this problem and why they came to see literature as increasingly important, we shall zoom in on their country house in Viry.

# CHAPTER THREE

The Perraults in the Countryside

Viry and Literary Sociability (1650–1680)

When Puss in Boots was sending gifts to the king and inventing a new persona for his owner, he partook in an aristocratic lifestyle. He promised his master a better future, put on his boots, and promptly went hunting. His wit and cunning netted him rabbits, partridges, and other animals, which he brought to the king over a period of two or three months. These gifts served as the basis of his access to the court and ultimately of the new identity he tailored for the miller's penniless son.[1]

The Perraults themselves took part in the exchanges of grouse and capon while they were acquiring an aristocratic lifestyle for themselves. Between the 1630s and the 1680s, they owned a county house in Viry, several miles to the southeast of Paris. The Perraults did not use their second home to escape from the city's madding crowd but as a key site for organizing their financial and literary careers. Poems and letters by the Perraults and their guests mentioned festive meals held at Viry, painting the Perraults in aristocratic colors. By analyzing these literary works and connecting them to the trajectories of the Perraults' careers, this chapter shows how literary sociability related to financial careers and sheds new light on Charles Perrault's first steps as a recognized literary author. By scrutinizing the connections between the careers of Charles and Pierre, I present a close-up view of a crucial phase in the process that turned the Perraults into a family of letters. The connections between a career in letters and family strategies will become even more crucial after Pierre's disgrace, as we shall see in the next chapter.

Writing and circulating poems helped lend the Perraults an aristocratic, affluent image, which was important for two reasons. First, financial careers required credit, and financiers had to adopt a lifestyle that would inspire confidence on the part of potential lenders.[2] Second, a family aspiring to recognition as a "house" and to noble status had to adopt an appropriate lifestyle and maintain an appropriate image. The home in Viry was crucial for this effort.

The Perraults' rural retreat, where social and literary gatherings were routine, recalls one of the strongest images we have of seventeenth-century France—the salon, an institution crucial for understanding the relations between men of letters and urban elites. And in fact, we shall see striking parallels between Viry and urban salons. But the country house also suggests a new way of thinking about the salon. Instead of viewing the salons as rigid institutions, having clearly defined personnel and characteristics—promoting the purity of the French language under the civilizing influence of aristocratic women—I propose to anchor literary sociability in a wider set of practices prevalent among Parisian elites. Therefore, instead of identifying a specific institution, such as the Rambouillet salon, and labeling it by the types of activities or discourses that prevailed there ("literary," "Cartesian," "Jansenist," or any other label), I ask how and why specific sites of elite sociability were represented in ways that led future scholars to label them "salons."[3] While some critiques of the salon model have introduced a valuable corrective, the complex texts used for analyzing the problem of the salons and literary sociability—from poems and novels to records of scientific observations—cannot be reduced to a monolithic explanation based on the social context. In other words, I endorse social historians' reactions against the salon model—their comments are quite applicable to the Perraults—while stressing aspects of the sources that point away from seeing them as mere reflections of social reality and underscore the multiple layers of meaning that actors introduced in them.

I propose a middle ground between two established approaches to salons. One approach, which usually takes the gatherings at the house of Madame de Rambouillet as its model, sees seventeenth-century salons as relatively well-defined institutions. Distinguished writers met in the homes of aristocratic ladies, most often in the *ruelle*, a space in the lady's chamber between the bed and the wall. The participants were a mixed group of men and women who entertained themselves with games and the reading of literary works. They promoted a new and refined aesthetics and etiquette, different from the rustic manners that prevailed at the court, and prized a pure French language.[4] This approach relies on eyewitness descriptions, most of which are passing mentions in letters and the literary productions of those who frequented salons. The support for this approach relies, therefore, on the assumption of a strong continuity between literary texts and the social context that produced them.[5] Since such a view attributes considerable importance to the salons and sees them as a clearly delineated institution, I shall call it the "maximalist approach." Maximal as it is, this line of inquiry leaves a good many questions unresolved: Were salon women politically defiant?[6] What were the attitudes toward women of male authors active in the world of the salons?[7] Were the salons a way to promote the "fusion of elites," or were they a site for the diffusion of aristocratic codes down the social ladder?[8]

As a reaction to such questions, a second approach, which I shall call the "minimalist approach," emerged. Its proponents argue that the salons, as described by the maximalists, never existed. For example, while each gathering was supposed to have a specific literary or philosophical stance, leading men of letters frequented many of them, demonstrating that a given gathering could comprise a multiplicity of stances. Furthermore, the minimalists point to a very real problem with the sources, since the available letters and literary representations eulogized the participants in very broad terms and did not ground them concretely in a particular location. These sources also subsume a range of cultural practices under the umbrella term "conversation"—we have little idea of how conversation actually worked in these assemblies.[9] The time has come to return the practices usually associated with salons to a broader elite sociability that included dining, gambling, and discussions of politics.[10] However, the texts circulated among Parisian elites cannot simply be reduced to their social context, and I shall try to resist the temptation of a too-facile reductionist reading. Even in the case of the Perraults, who certainly harbored grand social ambitions, the labor invested in the creation and circulation of texts cannot be explained by mere worldly aspirations, as the texts do not always form a coherent whole that reflects the social strategies of their authors.

The Perraults' case liberates us from the small group of canonical literary texts, opening up many more sources relating to elite sociability. Underused and unpublished sources shed significant new light on the problem. "Voyage to Viry" (1635, with later revisions) provides an idealized yet detailed description of the country house.[11] A collection of poems and letters assembled by the poet Étienne Martin de Pinchesne describes the dinners held there and opens a window onto their broader literary contexts. The poems allow us to integrate the Perraults into the wider literary and worldly circles in the Parisian countryside.[12]

However, instead of trying to describe only what really took place at Viry, I shall focus on the inconsistencies among the surviving records. I want to know what was achieved by the different modes of representing Viry, what the manuscripts were used for, and, by thinking about the Perraults' careers, what literary sociability amounted to as a social institution. After I have shown that the Perraults' rural activities had real consequences for their social mobility, I offer a critique of the salon model as a way of understanding the connections between literature and society. However, social mobility is not a skeleton key that unlocks all the representations surrounding literary sociability. On the contrary, I insist on the variety of the representations and on the way they could be reappropriated.

At least from the 1630s, the Perraults owned a country house in Viry, located to the southeast of Paris, and used it to entertain guests—from the Dutch philosopher Christiaan Huygens to poets and members of the Parisian legal courts. A declaration made by Pierre Perrault Sr. in 1641 shows that his property in Viry consisted of five plots of land. Built on the first and second plots were the main house and a smaller house called "the convent," as well as a dovecote, stables, a winepress, and a garden. On two other plots (in les Chaulmiers and in Trémézolles) grapevines were grown, and the fifth (in the rue aux Loups) provided water.[13]

By purchasing a country house, the Perraults joined many well-off inhabitants of Paris who wanted a place to spend the hottest summer months. As a guide to the capital noted, "In the summer people like to take walks, and whoever has a country house gladly spends the time there."[14] Financiers, who needed to own impressive residences in town, were even expected to own country houses, where they could drink fresh wine in the summer.[15] The privileges of *bourgeois de Paris* allowed them to bring wine they grew on their estates into the city, exempt from taxes.[16] Valentin Conrart, the secretary of the Académie française, spent his summers at a country house in Athis, close to Viry, which he bought in 1654. Conrart joined the "great summer migration" of Parisian elites for social reasons; he was fond of entertaining writers such as Madeleine de Scudéry and Perrot d'Ablancourt, who later mentioned Athis in their works and letters; Conrart had no interest in drawing profits from the land.[17] Pierre Bayle even claimed that numerous scholars required trips to the countryside, as well as social visits, dining, and gambling—the exact activities we shall see around Viry—in order to produce their works.[18] In this sense, the country house, or villa, had belonged more to urban than to rural society since the creation of the Roman villa.[19]

In many cases, the ownership of a country house was not enough, and some owners turned to the circulation of literary texts. Distinguished nobles had poets and authors spread word of their worldly splendor to audiences outside their circle. The list is lengthy, from Ronsard on Fontainbleu in the sixteenth century through Desmarets and Richelieu, Scudéry and La Fontaine on Vaux le Vicomte, to Versailles and the host of poets and artists hired to sing Louis XIV's glory.[20]

The men of letters who could sing the praises of such rural retreats themselves cherished a multifaceted ideal of *otium*, an ancient ideal of leisure that they had inherited and transformed. Otium meant a retreat from the world and its commotion, but it had several formulations that made it relevant for textual descriptions of country houses or distant castles. *Otium rusticum* recalled the bucolic myth of the countryside, and *otium litteratum* reminded authors that the muses demanded they seclude themselves to create. The saying *otium sine litteris mors est* (leisure without culture equals death) emphasized that culture is indispensable to proper leisure.[21] Otium in fact characterized the numerous intellectual and literary circles active in Paris in the first half of the seventeenth century, groups that at times sought in the life of culture a retreat from public life.[22] As the countryside became a counterpart to their urban lives, the texts extolling these forms of otium brought together country homes and urban readers.

In 1635 a counselor at the Châtelet court named Corneillau composed a poem in eight parts called "Voyage to Viry"—perhaps the same person connected to Gaston d'Orléans, the king's uncle, whom we met in the previous chapter when Pierre Sr. refused to execute his will. If this was the case, the author was clearly close to the circles that the family developed even before Pierre Jr.'s career in finance took off. A manuscript copy owned by the British Library has illustrations drawn by Claude Perrault and shows that the manuscript was revised and augmented. In the first couple of odes, which serve as an introduction, the narrator stressed the honesty of his description before moving to a description of his voyage on the Seine to Viry. Upon his arrival, the narrator described the house's environs, ending the poem with lengthy descriptions of the house, its rooms, and especially the garden, conveying the sense of a luxurious retreat in a beautiful setting.[23] The poem about Viry, rather labored if seen in purely poetic terms, performed a number of "textual services" for the Perraults. In contrast with all the grandees who had poetry written in their honor, when Corneillau composed his ode, the Perraults were a middling family, fairly recent arrivals in the capital. Though they did not possess the wealth or the pedigree of nobles or wealthy judges, representing their country estate in aristocratic terms could have improved their prospects of social mobility.

The aristocratic allure of the country house was evident to seventeenth-century readers. This setting was chosen for the dialogues in Fontenelle's *Conversations on the Plurality of Worlds*, one of the period's philosophical block-busters, which substituted cosmological discussion for the usual activities taking place in the countryside: parties, gambling, and hunting.[24] How might the Perraults be fitted into such an image? First, Corneillau inscribed them in an aristocratic geography. After bidding his servant farewell and strapping on his long sword, the poem's narrator embarks on the actual voyage:

> We let our thoughts wander
> To the planned voyage . . .
> Finally, this great machine
> Allows us to climb on its back,
> And moves from hill to hill
> On the watery road of the river.
> On its lovely banks we find
> Conflans, Choisy, and Villeneuve.[25]

One of the drawings Claude Perrault made for the poem contains a map showing the location of Viry as well as the other places mentioned. The region to the east and southeast of Paris was popular among Parisian financiers, and

FIGURE 3.1. Viry placed on a map. From "Voyage to Viry," British Library, MS, Add. 20087, fol. 7. © British Library.

the map related the Perraults' property to villages like Ivry and Charenton, where several financiers resided.[26] It also showed Athis, the residence of Valentin Conrart.

When he comes to the Perraults' house, the narrator pauses to describe the building as graceful and symmetric, an important aesthetic value that shaped contemporary descriptions.[27] Once he enters, he inspects the rooms, comparing them favorably with the most famous palaces of Europe:

> Now the whole facade
> Of this superb building appears.
> Its symmetry and grace
> Have a charming *je-ne-sais-quoi* . . .
> Two adjoining rooms, almost equals
> Put to shame the royal chambers
> Of Madrid and Saint Germain.
> They are full of paintings.[28]

The narrator added that a gallery in another room held rare works worthy of Michelangelo's studio.[29] Again, the description conforms to aristocratic expectations; the great collections of the day were in the homes of dukes and marquises. Financiers also collected, taking their lead from their noble clients.[30]

Beyond these markers of status, the narrator dwells on the house's gardens and its natural setting, and complements the descriptions of nature with descriptions of art. The natural ambience conveys beauty and grace:

> There we see the cicada who,
> Before the birth of a new day,
> Warms her spread wings
> In breezes that offer alms.
> The fine pearls with which dawn
> Washes and tints her dress
> Make her feel so proud
> That with a voice that seeks the angels
> She goes to sing her praises
> Before the door of the sun.[31]

As Krzystof Pomian remarked, nature was seen as the source of art's beauty. Art, empowered by nature, was the only way princes could preserve their glory—only their representation allowed them to last beyond the fleeting moment of victory in battle.[32] Some of the features mentioned repeatedly in the poem, such as the grotto and the fountain, straddle the boundary between nature and art.[33] The magnificent globe that the narrator encounters inside the house straddles the same boundary: it is a unique machine that shows the earth and the heavens, that is, a technical achievement that represents nature.[34]

Nature is on display in another of Claude's drawings, representing the inner garden. By the middle of the seventeenth century, the role of gardens

FIGURE 3.2. The garden in Viry. From "Voyage to Viry," British Library, MS, Add. 20087, fol. 9. © British Library.

as places for sociability and privileged retreat was already highly codified. The Tuileries gardens and the Cours de la Reine served as meeting grounds for aristocrats (and some commoners), and access to the gardens of the Palais-Royal was highly restricted.[35] Even designs for town houses from the period sometimes included gardens as part of their plan, though these would be cramped between buildings and streets rather than open to the countryside.[36] The depiction of the garden at Viry, set against the backdrop of an aristocratic retreat, probably resonated with such examples.

The natural and artificial elements all point to the dignity of the owners, the Perraults, who partook in these learned and rarefied forms of leisure. Further, the poem also reflexively refers to its own function of spreading the image of the Perraults' country house. The narrator strikes up a conversation with the reader, a witness to his voyage to Viry:

> You, who witnessed my voyage,
> The subject of my verse,
> For whom I have created a work
> That ought to travel across the entire universe . . .
> Recall your fantasy
> And revive your recollection,
> As my inspiration is exhausted
> And this work is almost finished.
> Will you not bear in mind
> A place visited by glory
> And the name of this lovely shepherd
> Who sees coming into his domain
> All the voyager admires
> In a strange land?[37]

This request to the reader underscores the poet's intention to see his poetic message spread far and wide, and these verses harp on an aristocratic theme in fashion. Hints of the pastoral vogue that swept the French aristocracy of the seventeenth century—Honoré d'Urfé's *L'Astrée* is the classic example—aroused nostalgia for a lost golden age, as did the repeated references to memory in "Voyage to Viry."[38]

This poem performed two textual services for the Perraults: first, it generated an image of pastoral aristocracy; second, it extended that image to a readership that presumably went beyond those who had visited the "superb building." If the poem was indeed revised and augmented by Corneillau, as Charles Perrault claimed, it was probably circulated in at least a couple of versions and over a significant period of time.[39] Claude's drawings show, once more, the extent to which the Perraults' social mobility was a collective effort.

Their country house served as a node of sociability for the Perraults well into the 1650s and 1660s. We know something about the more elaborate gatherings at Viry thanks to Étienne Martin de Pinchesne, a minor seventeenth-century poet mostly remembered as the nephew of the much more famous poet Voiture.

Pinchesne prepared a collection of *rondeaux*, short rhymed poems, that deal mostly with large feasts he attended between 1660 and 1662.[40] As Jean-Luc Gautier has established, these took place in the early 1660s in at least three separate locations—the house of Robert Nanteuil in Paris, the Perraults' country house in Viry, and the Melson sisters' house at Antony, not far from Viry.[41] But these meetings are inserted into the framework of a longer poetic friendship: Pinchesne and Costar, a fellow poet who lived in Le Mans, corresponded regularly between 1655 and 1660. Costar would ship capons and grouse to Paris for dinners organized by Pinchesne. In return, Pinchesne would send lighthearted poems describing the dinners. Even after Costar's death in May 1660, his secretaries, Girault and Pauquet, continued to provide Pinchesne with birds. In return, Pinchesne promised them poems by Perrault.[42]

Culinary pleasures dominate Pinchesne's rondeaux; even elevated topics such as art and literature play a subordinate role for the group of friends. This was an ideal with deep roots: Seneca, a much celebrated model in the seventeenth century, claimed that public spectacles, private homes, and dinner parties are where friendship is made.[43] To take one example: Nanteuil, a painter and royal engraver, was also known for his ability to versify;[44] here is the subject of one of these ditties, which challenged him as a host:

> You know which is big Nanteuil,
> Whom God created to please the eye,
> Who can produce multifarious marvels,
> Charming our ears tomorrow
> With the most sensible words, and above all
> Piquing our sense of taste with two good dishes.
> His thoughts on physiognomy,
> The art of painting, or anatomy
> Are worth much more when they are presented
> Between well-seasoned courses.
> Just so are the ones which, as he reasons,

His wife seasons with good salt.
Her face, if we dwell on it,
Is a pleasure to our eyes no less than his,
With such grace, and full of charming traits;
She never grumbles at good people.
I do not believe that it possesses for fools
Such sweetness, charms, or enticement.[45]

Even this short excerpt shows how food and dining can provide a context for discussing the nature of literary sociability, the role of polite conversation, and the place of women in the whole. Nanteuil's wife seems to have filled an ambiguous role. On the one hand, she performed a fine service by seasoning the dishes for the merry company; on the other, the appeal of her face is denied to fools, making her into a judge of intellectual qualities.

The mix of food and poetry stood at the foundation of these amicable exchanges. In a letter dated 20 July 1661, Pinchesne asked for copies of two works by Charles, his odes on the peace and on the king's marriage. Pinchesne intended to send some of the copies to Charlotte Melson, as part of an effort to compare Charles's work with poems by Jean Chapelain. He also passed two copies to Pauquet and Girault, Costar's secretaries, who still lived in Le Mans.[46] Pinchesne shared with Pierre Perrault some of the birds he received in return for the poems and sent the others to Charles. And he placed another request: a copy of Charles's recent work on the "talking mirror" (undoubtedly a *galant* piece entitled "Le miroir; ou, La metamorphose d'Orante") and a poem thanking Pauquet. More poetic thanks followed. Grouse then made the world of poetry go round in two different ways: they served as an occasion for circulating work by Charles Perrault that was only beginning to find its way into print in the early 1660s; they also provided the reason for writing more poetry.[47]

Rather than visiting just one house and forming what we would call a salon or informal academy, Charles and his friends frequented several different places in Paris and its environs. The collection of rondeaux permits us to reconstruct three separate meetings with identifiable participants.[48] The first took place at Nanteuil's house in Paris in September 1662; present were Nanteuil, his wife and daughter, Pinchesne, and both Pierre and Charles. A few days after this meeting, the small company spent a day at Viry. This time, the poems attest to the presence of Pierre and Charles, Nanteuil, Pinchesne, and two others named Bellin and Paillot.[49] About two weeks later, this same group paid a visit to the two Melson sisters at their country house in Antony. Country houses were indispensable for this urban form of existence.

This series of visits draws attention to several phenomena: first, whereas a small nucleus of men was present at all three events, the women remained stationary. Also, all the locations were viewed as fit for poetic description. This form of sociability probably depended on the ability to move among several locations in Paris and its environs. Since the exchange of invitations and hospitality provided the basis for the different visits and the friendly challenges among the hosts, moving among houses was crucial for writing this type of poetry. No single site of these exchanges was more crucial than the others for their writing. This strikes a sharp contrast with our usual image of the salons, which involves a veritable pilgrimage of literary authors to the ruelle of a distinguished woman.

The poems by Pinchesne and Perrault aspired to a model of distinguished hospitality, always highlighting the importance of food. In their descriptions of the Perraults' house, they mention the same features as the author of "Voyage to Viry," mainly the grotto, and cast the property as a seigniorial possession; a reference to Viry as a "feudal" possession clearly presents Pierre Perrault as a master of the domain: "Perrault will look upon it kindly, in his little *Seignory*."[50] A rondeau Nanteuil dedicated to Charlotte Melson made these points evident:

Rondeau, Recited as a Compliment to Coralte, by M. de Nanteuil

Among my friends, Pinchesne is the hook,
And just as he would catch a fish,
He lures them, and knows how to take them quickly,
When with a single word he makes it clear
    That they should love me like a good fellow.

At the Perraults', in their drinking grotto,
Where the drinks are so cold we shiver,
He brought Belin, Paillot and made them
    My friends.

But it pleases God that the agreeable Melson,
The beloved among nine sisters,
Without despising my wish to be heard,
Tells me here, with a charming and tender air,
"Be Nanteuil, and be quite simply
    My friend."[51]

While it is certain that contemporaries saw women as possessing a critical capacity, enabling them to serve as arbiters of literary taste, a closer look at the Perraults' social circle adds nuance to this image.[52] Although those who dined at the Melson house viewed Charlotte as someone who could evaluate Charles's poetry, it was other actors who did the actual evaluating. In the summer of 1660, Pinchesne asked Charlotte to rank two odes on the recent peace treaty with Spain: one by Charles and one by Jean Chapelain. An evaluation, titled *Jugement de Coralte*, was read at a meeting held at the Melson house; it found Perrault the better poet. However, Pinchesne revealed in a letter written to Charles less than two weeks later that while Charlotte had indeed favored Perrault, the *Jugement* was by Pinchesne.[53]

Later that summer, Charles evaluated a work by a young poet sent him by Nicolas Vitart, the intendant of the duc de Luynes.[54] It was Jean Racine's "La Nymphe de la Seine." A letter by Racine shows that the circumstances of this evaluation were much like those of the other poetic gatherings just described. After Vitart showed the poem to Chapelain, who offered many criticisms, he went to see Perrault, though Racine protested. Still, Perrault's opinion of the piece was positive, and when his friendly suggestions were passed along to Racine, almost all of them were heeded.[55]

Viry served as a central axis that brought together poets and subject matter, a node for the circulation of letters and manuscripts. This circulation proved important both for the creative process, even for a talent like the young Racine, and for the establishment of Charles as a literary author. Here Charles's "Portrait d'Iris" can serve as example. Charles composed this poem at Viry, according to an "idea that was in the air."[56] When Philippe Quinault, a writer known at the time for plays in the gallant style, paid a visit to Viry, Charles read the poem to him. As Quinault liked the poem, Charles provided him with a copy. However, the playwright used the poem for his own purposes: he presented it to a young lady, neglecting to correct her impression that he had composed it for her. For a time the poem circulated in Paris under Quinault's name. When the truth was discovered, Quinault was embarrassed, but he managed to salvage his reputation by offering a forthright confession and explaining that he had been courting the young lady.[57] Charles's early works probably circulated extensively through such means, as many are preserved in Valentin Conrart's collection of manuscripts. Conrart, the secretary of the Académie française, copied many of the literary works circulating in fashionable circles at the time, and he preserved copies of Charles's "Ode sur le mariage du Roi," "Chambre ardente de l'amour," "Portrait d'Iris," "Portrait de la voix d'Iris," "Le miroir," and "Parnasse pousseé au bout."[58]

So far, my exploration of the Perraults' country house has revealed that the representations circulating around Viry presented an aristocratic image. This was part of a general strategy aimed at supporting Pierre's financial career, and it fits Alain Viala's claim that bourgeois families used noble imagery in the salons to distinguish themselves.[59] Furthermore, these poetic gatherings possessed all the attributes of what later scholars called salons, including a woman schooled in letters exercising her aesthetic judgment over a group of authors. But several puzzles remain. How did the lyrical images of these joyful dinners function? Why did the Perraults participate in this activity? And finally, how does this connect to what other sources say about the Perraults' social life in Viry? I shall start with the last question first.

The letters Christiaan Huygens wrote about his time at Viry strongly suggest that his presence there helped to spread the reputation of the Perraults.[60] They also show how that sociability at Viry belonged to a varied gamut of sociable activities that connected Paris with its countryside. A comparison of Huygens's relatively unembellished letters with the poetic descriptions that we have already seen demonstrates how seventeenth-century literary authors selected narrow and clear-cut representations from a broader repertoire of sociability.

Huygens became a regular guest at the country house as part of his Parisian social life. Just like other notables, he looked forward to leaving the city during the summer.[61] When Huygens's sister, Suzanna, wrote after their mother had died, she expressed the wish that her brother were back in the Netherlands, only to acknowledge that walking and wandering in the French countryside might be good for him, as Viry was the "sweetest place in the world."[62] He probably had not met any of the Perraults during a visit to Paris in late 1660 and early 1661, but at that time he did meet Robert Nanteuil, who may have provided the link to the Perraults.[63] By 1663, members of literary circles in Paris were addressing correspondence with Huygens to Viry. Valentin Conrart wrote to Huygens there in October, inviting the scientist to his own country place, since they were in the same area.[64] The presence of so celebrated a figure would certainly have increased the Perraults' profile in the world of letters.

Huygens also fit well into the varied social life the Perraults led in Viry and in Paris, and he quickly became a good friend of the family. As he wrote to his brother Lodewijk on 28 July 1673, "Monsieur Perrault will be back from Viry tomorrow, and I will convey to him your compliment. I am a close friend of this house [maison], and there's hardly a day I don't see them. Almost every day, after dinner, there's gambling, food, and good company at their place, or at [the house of some] other member of the group. I have to gamble too, and since I don't pay close attention, it costs me several pistoles [type of coin] from time to time."[65] Huygens was evidently quite fond of the Perraults and their friends. In 1671 he compared recent trips to Viry and to Beaulieu, another country house. He had found the company at Beaulieu "good, but a little savage, and the company at Viry is better, in my opinion." The ladies he met at Viry included Mademoiselle de Nielle[66] and a young niece of the Perraults. In his opinion, the people at Viry "know how to live."[67]

The relations between the Perraults and Huygens seem to have been very close and supported the networks of sociability for both parties. When Marie Guichon, Charles's wife, passed away in 1678, Philips Doublet, Suzanna Huygens's husband (and cousin), wrote to his brother-in-law, asking him to convey his condolences to Charles and the "other members of this generous family."[68] Huygens invited the Perraults to dine with him in Paris, and other family members exchanged letters and even presents. Claude wrote to Lodewijk Huygens, one of Christiaan's two younger brothers, and Pierre's wife, Catherine, wrote to Christiaan himself. Suzanna even sent Catherine a sizable piece of cloth, measuring fifty-two *aunes*.[69] And when Lodewijk sent a letter congratulating Charles on his marriage, it was read in the company of several *beaux-esprits*; the letter was highly esteemed, as if Lodewijk had been a "second Voiture."[70] As we shall see in the next chapter, these personal relations also intersected with the work that Charles and Claude undertook under Colbert.

Huygens and Claude Perrault also used their time in Viry to perform scientific measurements. In 1692 Huygens recalled in a letter to the astronomer Philippe de la Hire that while at Viry he and Claude had used a telescope to carry out measurements of atmospheric refraction.[71] In 1669 he also conducted measurements of the speed of sound at Viry, surely something that was easier to do in the calm of the countryside than in the crowded streets of Paris.[72] Both observations were related to important problems that preoccupied Huygens for quite a while: the improvement of telescopes and the propagation of light and sound in a medium.[73]

The unique place that the Perraults occupied in Huygens's Parisian world, and the intermingling of his scientific publications with his worldly sociability, can be seen in the distribution of his masterpiece on pendulum clocks. When *Horologium Oscillatorium* appeared in 1673, he sent three copies to the Perraults (Pierre, Claude, and Charles), and in his list of recipients, Huygens placed their names immediately after those of Louis XIV and Colbert, indicating their importance.[74] The Perraults and Huygens were joined here as clients of Colbert, but their relations went much deeper than owning a debt to the same patron.

Huygens's letters break free of the poetic and literary conventions of the poetry circulating around Viry. The point is not that the letters are more "objective" than the poems. Rather, poetry "objectively" established for the Perraults an image of aristocratic sociability.

The manuscript evidence for life at Viry comprises materials from the second half of the 1650s and the beginning of the 1660s, a transitional period in the careers of Pierre and Charles Perrault. These transitions were related. Charles's entry to the world of letters was facilitated by Pierre's career and in time came to support it.

As we have seen, Pierre began his career in the world of royal finance. At an early stage (either during the 1640s or a bit earlier), he served as an aide to François Sabatier, a treasurer in the parties casuelles, and then to Sabatier's successor, Claude Housset. In 1657, following Housset's advice, Pierre bought the office of receiver general in the Paris generality. He remained in this position until 1664—the period of the literary activity around Viry documented in Pinchesne's collection of poems.

Like his father and elder brother, Jean, Charles began his career by training as a barrister. He passed the oral examination at Orléans's Faculty of Law in 1651, as we have seen in the previous chapter.[75] As young barristers were required to follow the work of more experienced ones before they could plead cases themselves, Charles attended trials and studied Justinian's *Institutiones*, probably the most important classical text for jurists. By 1654 he had successfully pleaded two cases at the Châtelet, attracting the attention of Dreux d'Aubray, the civil lieutenant. But Pierre's position as a receiver changed all that, and Charles's brothers soon convinced him to leave the legal profession, which had not provided Jean with a fulfilling career. As Pierre's aide—he later said that his sole duties were receiving money and delivering it to the treasury—Charles had plenty of free time.

This move caused a chain reaction, nudging Charles toward the world of literature. While he and his brothers had already published their paraphrase of *The Aeneid*, he was not recognized as a worldly author, and he had not penetrated fashionable literary circles. A short while after buying his office, Pierre purchased the library of Germain Habert, abbé de Cérisy and member of the Académie française.[76] The presence of so many good books inspired Charles, as he put it, to resume his studies. He also began to write poetry, and in 1656 a short work appeared in a collection published by the printer Sercy.

Over the second half of the 1650s, Pierre assumed a more prominent role in the family. He married Catherine Lormier, a widow from a family of officeholders at the Cour des Aides, on 6 November 1656, showing he could continue the lineage. When his mother, Paquette Le Clerc, passed away a few months later, Pierre inherited the house at Viry. According to Charles, he began building a central building (*corps de logis*) there. Charles took charge of new construction, and in his *Mémoires* he mentioned the construction of the rock garden in the grotto. Once these works had been completed, the stage was set for the dinners that brought together the Perraults, the Melsons, and Pinchesne.

The sociability in Viry relied on the Perraults' existing social networks, but it also transformed them. Housset, Pierre Perrault's patron, had established connections with Costar and Pinchesne before the Perraults. In one of the letters related to the grouse dinners, Pinchesne requested that Costar send some birds to Housset and his wife. Pinchesne described "Monsieur Du Housset," the "intendant des finances," as a reputable person, known for his good qualities, who entertained his friends with fine food. He expatiated on the good qualities of Madame Du Housset, who was an "illustrious woman" with literary interests: "You may know [her] reputation as a good friend of Mademoiselle de Scudéry and Monsieur [Gilles] Ménage, your good friend, which should allow you to judge whether she is a rare and precious person." He had occasionally brought her books, both on his behalf and at Ménage's request.[77]

It therefore seems likely that Housset provided a first link to Pinchesne and the grouse he furnished from Le Mans. Certainly, the Perraults were not well known to some of the members of this network before they started entertaining at Viry. In 1660 Pauquet, Costar's secretary, did not know whether Pierre was the uncle or the father of Charles Perrault, and Pinchesne had to explain that they were brothers.[78] But by the early 1660s, the Perraults had already played host, in this fashionable atmosphere, to Pinchesne and his small group of dinners, to the poet Quinault, and to Huygens. The exchange of favors the dinners entailed allowed them to visit the Melsons and to circulate Charles's poetry.

As Pierre's financial career allowed Charles to become a literary author, Charles's writings supported Pierre's status as a financier and the family's ascent up the social ladder. Viry proved crucial for both, as the manner in which the Perraults' sociability integrated Charles into the world of fashionable literature also generated an aristocratic air, easing Pierre's integration into the financial milieus revolving around the court and high nobility. This first phase of "literarization" established Charles as a recognized author, but it did not encompass the family as a whole. As it turned out, while activities at Viry may have influenced the careers of Charles and Pierre, they did not become a permanent facet of the family's reputation. Later versions of the texts produced around Viry even obscure the country house's importance for the Perraults' social strategy.

The representations of salon activities did not always overlap with the circles that later scholars saw as salons. A closer look at some later representations of the Perraults, the Melsons, and their relations reveals the fragility of the salon model by pointing up the heterogeneous nature of worldly sociability. And yet the work invested in these representations of literary life shows that they cannot be reduced to their social context. The cultural form of worldly sociability could be used and adapted in a variety of ways.

A standard source for the study of salons is *Grand dictionnaire des précieuses* by Antoine Beaudeau, sieur de Somaize. Published in 1661, it profiles many of the most celebrated practitioners of the "precious" style of writing and speaking so prized by members of the Parisian elite in the middle decades of the seventeenth century, which stressed the creation of supposedly noble and refined neologisms. The *Grand dictionnaire* lists 251 women who frequented or hosted salons, the most extensive and detailed evidence of its kind, and it indicates who was associated with the vogue for preciousness.[79]

Somaize's comments on the Perraults and the Melsons made them sound very much like anyone else who ever frequented a salon. Charles appeared as "Polidor, a young man of wit and merit, who composed galanteries in prose and in verse." Somaize mentioned two works by Perrault, a dialogue "held in esteem in all the ruelles" (most probably the *Dialogue de l'amour et de l'amitié*) and the "Portrait d'Iris," which, explained Somaize, "Quinault attributed to himself for a long time." The mention of the *ruelles* as the place in which Charles's work gained legitimacy and literary fame makes it easy to see Charles as a salon author, an impression that Somaize reinforced. In a section devoted to precious expressions, he presents a turn of phrase attributed to Charles: instead of saying "she likes company," one could say "she inclines toward communication."[80] Charles (Somaize called him "the second of this name," probably having Pierre in mind as the "first") was said to visit "Tubérine, a precious woman who entertains men of letters who write only when inspired by some sort of galanterie."[81]

Somaize's descriptions of the Melsons fully assimilated them to the model of the creative lady of the precious sort. "Ménoppée and her sister" were two precious young ladies, rather good-looking and witty. They provided Quinault with the inspiration for an allegory, and they were themselves able crafters of verse and prose. Somaize claimed that Ménoppée had previously been known as Iris, establishing a link between her and the two portraits Charles had composed.[82]

If we heeded only Somaize, we would be inclined to label the events at Viry a salon, in spite of the divergences we have already noted from the salon model. But if we turned to Gédéon Tallemant des Réaux, the poet who provided most of the evidence for the Rambouillet salon in the *Historiettes*, his collection of satirical anecdotes and biographies, we would have much greater difficulty in portraying Viry as a salon—not least because the *Historiettes* make almost no mention of Charles or Pierre Perrault.[83] The Melsons do feature but not as we would imagine salon women to appear; there is no resemblance to Somaize's portrait of the sisters. While Tallement described Charlotte as a "rather amusing person," the anecdotes he provided about her have little to do with any type of literary activity. One regarded the Melsons' fasting habits during Lent; the other concerned Charlotte's repeated attempts to obtain face powder. And Tallement mocked Charlotte's father, who despite serving as interpreter for the queen, knew no foreign languages. Apparently, when the Swiss ambassadors paid a visit to the queen and began to speak among themselves, the queen called upon her interpreter to do his duty. He replied only, "They are praising your beauty, Madame, and if not, they should be."[84]

Charlotte Melson also appeared in collections that anthologized the activities of learned ladies. La Forge's *Le cercle des femmes sçavantes* reported, "One of the most learned men of our age assured me that she was beautiful, spiritual, and learned. Judge for yourself if she is not worthy for inclusion in the *Circle of Learned Ladies.*"[85] Titon du Tillet mentioned her membership in Padua's Ricovrati Academy and described her as a person of "distinguished merit." Citing Vertron's *La nouvelle Pandore*, he mentioned a poem Charlotte had dedicated to Louis XIV, and he quoted four lines from a poem Vertron had composed in her honor.[86]

As often happened to early modern texts, the poetry that had originally circulated around Viry entered a new context that altered its meaning, recycled and rewritten by Pinchesne himself.[87] From a celebration of dining in distinguished settings, the poems became works of galanterie.[88] This transformation entailed a change of medium: from a manuscript collection, the poems became a part of a printed work, comparable to other published poetry collections. He selected and edited, surrounding choice Viry poetry with other works. The poems in the collection all belong to similar genres, but they lack the unity of place and theme found in the manuscript collection: the works from Viry dissolved their specificity into a general atmosphere of worldly sociability. Other poems in the collection bore titles such as "For a Young Lieutenant, Whose Children Are All Girls," "For the Same Person, While His Wife Was Pregnant," and "On the Three Beauties at the Ball."

While the manuscripts were dedicated to Charles Perrault, the collected poems appeared with a rather glib dedication to the Duc de Montausier, who at the time was responsible for the education of the dauphin. Pinchesne's introduction to the reader repeatedly characterized his audience as a small group of honnêtes hommes, harping on a familiar theme of gallant literature. The poet also created a poetic genealogy for himself, alleging a connection through his uncle Voiture to the Hôtel de Rambouillet, where one could acquire a more polite and refined style.[89]

The legacies of literary sociability varied considerably. The same group of people—the Perraults and the Melsons—could be described in very different terms, making the very thought of rigidly defined salons a problem. Even scholars like Alain Viala, who tried to sketch the contours of formal as well as informal academies, notice that in some cases the most basic distinctions would not hold, as contemporaries started calling salons "academies" once they discussed basic notions of language.[90] This is not merely the effect of our distance from seventeenth-century Paris. After all, three hundred years ago German tourists risked mistaking brothels for houses in which one could politely converse with French ladies.[91] We have seen how many operations Pinchesne had to perform in order to make the poems written around Viry into a framework that is much closer to an image of salon sociability. The heterogeneous nature of the texts, which do not form a single and coherent whole, shows that even if we accept the minimalist critique of the salon model, we ought to acknowledge the different discourses revolving around worldly sociability and the variety of contexts in which they could be embedded.

Written records of gatherings at the Perraults' country house have contributed to our understanding of two related issues: the image of the Perraults and the significance of how we think of seventeenth-century salons. The in-depth examination of the texts clarifies the circumstances of Charles Perrault's entry into the world of letters by placing it in the context of his entire family. He was not moved to take his first literary steps out of frustration with his legal practice or infatuation with the library recently bought by his brother Pierre, notwithstanding the image Charles himself tried to convey in his *Mémoires*. During a crucial phase of his career in finance, Pierre took a series of steps that enhanced the family's literary sociability, suggesting that a growing literary reputation could shape the Perraults' status in elite circles. Viry was not an egalitarian haven, as certain images of the salons would suggest, but part and parcel of the struggle for rank and power in a hierarchal society.[92]

The relations between literary sociability and the texts it generated were manifold and did not simply reproduce social strategies. The vision of Parisian literary society presented in this chapter shows that these relations were more ambiguous and fluid than is usually admitted—reducing these ambiguities required a creative effort on the part of writers such as Pinchesne and the Perraults. This chapter shows that rather than equating literary sociability with the salon, we should look at the circulation of men, women, and texts around different sites in Paris and its environs. I argue not that contemporaries somehow felt lost in this fluidity but that the meaning of these events became clear only after an investment of textual and social labor, just like the effort necessary to establish the image of the Hôtel de Rambouillet.[93] Authors had to transform social gatherings, fitting them into literary conventions. They could "stabilize" or "atomize" the meaning of these events in various forms, neglecting to mention scientific measurements of the speed of sound and underscoring the flavors of grouse and capons. Authors did not select events, characters, locales, and productions at random—they had specific goals, ambitions, and aesthetic preferences. While we usually try to assemble a coherent image out of the pieces, the seventeenth-century authors I have examined could use the same texts to create different images altogether, meaning that we have to be especially cautious in trying to reconstruct them.

When viewed through the perspective offered by the Perraults, even canonical works reveal how elite sociability provided the wide gamut of components for future representations. Two examples will suffice here to show how the Perraults' country house was hardly exceptional. Molière's *Les Précieuses ridicules* (1660) presents the brief and amusing story of two provincial women, Madelon and Cathos, who try to imitate the preciosity of the local elite, expressing itself in a refined manners and speech.[94] Once they reject two bourgeois men who court them, the men send a servant, who pretends to be the marquis de Mascaraille and courts the young ladies. As the marquis knows how to push the right buttons, by presenting a mastery of the codes of preciousness and polite society, the young ladies are smitten—only until the truth about the marquis's real identity is revealed. Courtship provides a clear script for sociability here: Madelon complains that they should not be married after a simple visit of their future husband. Instead, she details the course of events that includes the activities we associate with the salons, a course that should have been easily recognizable to the spectators. First, the lover has to see his future wife in a public ceremony or be led to her by a friend or relative. While hiding his passions, he should pay her several visits, in which the assembled company discusses a question of galanterie. After the obligatory declaration of his feelings, the woman chases away the man, who has to find ways to appease her and to overcome the obstacles put in place by relatives and rivals.[95] Further, the presence of men of letters is seen in the *Précieuses ridicules* as a means for establishing the reputation of the ladies. Madelon explains to Mascaraille that they are still not known in Paris but that the situation should change: a friend has promised to bring to their house the authors who participated in a collection of poetry. Even the academic model seems rather blurred in this context: Mascaraille promises to the précieuses that he will make them famous, stating, "I will establish at your house an academy of beaux-esprits, and I promise that you will know every single piece of verse produced in Paris before everybody else.... You will see in the beautiful ruelles of Paris two hundred songs of mine, the same number of sonnets, four hundred epigrams, and more than a thousand madrigals—not counting the enigmas and the portraits."[96]

Similarly, Antoine Furetière's *Roman bourgeois* (1666) satirized the culture of the Parisian urban elite. The plot followed young Nicodème's attempt to obtain the hand of the lovely Javotte, thereby also recounting Javotte's initiation into the cultural life of the Parisian bourgeoisie, composed of social events and literary discussion. Nicodème pretended that he could get excellent rabbits from the countryside, as a ruse for obtaining invitations to dinners. Nicodème also started playing *boule* with the father and allowed him to win some money. His most successful ploy was betting a capon on the last round of play, which they would then eat together. This was his only means of getting to see Javotte at her house, but unfortunately, she kept her manners and did not join the conversation. Only later, and especially after reading *L'Astrée*, would Javotte learn how to display her wit in these gatherings.[97] Here, too, men of letters played a role in the gatherings, but it could be an unwelcome one: Charroselles, a character based on the real-life author Charles Sorel (1602–74) (the name is an anagram of Sorel's name), was a figure of mockery. The members of a literary gathering knew that he was trying to read his work there simply because the printers were not interested in publishing it and he thought their gathering could lend his work the legitimacy it lacked. The other participants even foiled Charroselles's cunning plan to steal a story read there.[98] Clearly, Furetière could use this character to settle real-life accounts because he could pick and choose elements of elite sociability familiar to his readers and combine them as it suited him.

The Perraults, too, played this game to underscore one particular side of these practices. The sociability around Viry generated an aristocratic reputation for the family, one that could serve Pierre's financial career and further the goal of acquiring nobility through office holding. But owning rural property and generating cultural capital through it were not enough. Thanks in part to the changing political conditions of the 1660s, this phase of the family strategy ended in failure, as we will see in the next chapter.

Failure in Finance and the Rise of Charles Perrault (1660–1680)

"Diamonds and gold coins [pistoles] have great sway over minds / However, sweet words are even stronger and more valuable."[1] So began the moral of Charles Perrault's "The Fairies," also known as "Diamonds and Toads," which recounted how two stepsisters were transformed by a fairy—the kind one started to produce diamonds out of her mouth, the unkind one, toads. In the early 1660s, the Perrault family was itself forced into a tough choice between diamonds and "sweet words."

The Perraults used Viry to project the image expected of a family with social ambitions who was involved in finance. Mixing with poets and writers on a handsome estate led Charles—in several ways subservient to his older brother Pierre—to embark on a career in letters. Then things changed. The strategy the Perraults had followed in the second half of the 1650s, when Pierre took the lead in the family, reversed itself through a quick succession of events in the early 1660s, which saw Charles become an important aide to Colbert and Pierre lose his financial office. The relations between finance and literature flipped. Charles's literary career became the main engine for the Perraults' economic and social mobility. This chapter charts this new regime of social mobility through the life of letters, dwelling on Charles and his impact on Claude's career.

The literary sociability around Viry fostered Charles's poetic creations in a fashionable style, and it connected him with more established literary authors such as Philippe Quinault and Jean Chapelain. In this period, Charles also expanded his repertoire to include political encomia, and in early 1660 he composed the *Ode sur la Paix* mentioned in the previous chapter. This rather clichéd poem celebrated the recently signed Peace of the Pyrenees between the French monarchy and Hapsburg Spain, which was sealed in June 1660 by the marriage of the young Louis XIV to the Spanish *infanta*, Maria Theresa. Such odes were routinely used to attract the eyes of potential patrons, and the ode caught the attention of Colbert, an event of extreme importance for Charles's future.

In 1660 Colbert was still a financial officer working as intendant de la maison for Cardinal Mazarin, who had survived the challenge of the Fronde.[2] Colbert seems to have received an "advance copy" of *Ode sur la Paix*, since he sent a copy to Mazarin on March 2, well before the publication privilege for the poem was granted, on March 14.[3] Colbert probably anticipated that Mazarin would view the poem as useful for royal propaganda, and he explained in a letter, "I am sending to Your Eminence an ode written on the peace, which you will appreciate."[4] Indeed, Mazarin did appreciate it, as he wrote back to Colbert on March 13, saying, "It contains very good ideas, and I would like to know who wrote it." Colbert replied that the author "is called Perrault, a barrister in the Parlement, who has talent and writes verse very well."[5]

This new attention from Mazarin did not bring Charles any immediate benefits, and when the cardinal died a year later, the young Louis XIV announced to his ministers that he intended to rule without a "first minister," presiding himself over the monarchy's administration. Six months later, Nicolas Fouquet, the superintendent of finance and previously considered the man most likely to succeed Mazarin, was arrested in Nantes, removing a threat to Louis XIV's ability to reign alone. The king replaced the position of the superintendent of finance with a four-member council, which included Colbert.[6] By late 1662, Colbert was taking an active role in the monarchy's broader affairs and cultural projects. He corresponded with Jean Chapelain on the most effective ways for glorifying the monarchy through poetry, medals, statues, buildings, and panegyrical histories. And so, thanks to a recommendation from Chapelain, Charles Perrault was named secretary of a committee created to draft official inscriptions for buildings and medals and to encourage literary works intended to glorify the king; the group came to be known as the Petite académie.[7]

Charles's literary works won him his appointment. When Chapelain mentioned him as a candidate for the Petite académie, Colbert asked if Charles was the brother of the receiver general—in other words, Pierre. He also asked whether Charles was the author of two odes, one on the peace and the other on the king's marriage.[8] Colbert trusted Chapelain, but he wanted to see an example of Charles's prose. A piece on the recent conquest of Dunkirk met with his approval. Finally, on 3 February 1663, Chapelain and Charles went to Colbert's house, where they met the Abbé Jacques Cassagne and Amable de Bourzeis, the other members of the Petite académie. Colbert explained to them the goals for the new institution and asked them to keep his instructions for the academy a secret.[9] Chapelain's role in procuring this position shows once more how the internal dynamics of the family depended on relations with outside brokers, who helped the Perraults weave their networks.

Charles's role as secretary of the Petite académie brought him to the forefront of the cultural politics of the monarchy and even to a rare direct contact with the king. For the better part of 1663, the group did not receive specific commissions from Colbert, but it kept busy writing and revising works that glorified the monarchy. For instance, when Louis XIV recovered from a bout of measles, the members of the academy reviewed works related to his recovery, such as Henri de Valois's *Elegia. Ob restitutam Regi valetudinem* (Elegy on the king's recovery). Charles composed a sonnet on the same topic, and when, in September, French forces took the town of Marsal in the Mosel region of what is now Germany, that became the topic of another sonnet.[10] In May 1663 Colbert presented the Petite académie to the king. Louis assured the group that he held each of them in the highest esteem; had he not entrusted to them the thing he valued most: his glory?[11]

In January 1664 Colbert received an official appointment as superintendent of the Royal Buildings, having informally carried out these duties during the two years prior. Since this department handled royal patronage of the arts and manufacturing, as well as the palaces implied by its name, Colbert could deploy a man like Charles in many capacities. So Charles, too, received a formal appointment as his aide; official accounts spoke of "Sieur Perrault, one of our aides, in charge of visiting all the works commanded by His Majesty's buildings and to overseeing the punctual and diligent execution of all of our orders in fulfilling the king's wishes."[12] In the span of less than two years, Charles's literary endeavors had landed him a position as Colbert's right-hand man, supervising royal building projects. The vagueness of his duties implies that Charles functioned as Colbert's personal emissary in matters of architecture and art. Consider, for example, the far more specific brief of a certain "Pierre Francine, engineer [in charge] of waterworks and decorative fountains."[13]

In literary matters, Charles served initially as an intermediary, delivering messages between Colbert and Chapelain, and Chapelain intended that Charles take his place in handling Colbert's relations with foreign authors.

In a letter from 1671, Chapelain, who was seventy-five years old, stated, "My age and poor health permit me little hope that I shall live much longer or be able to help my dear friends with their needs. This has convinced me to think about how this might be done differently, through others who are loyal to me. In that which regards M. Colbert, [it shall be done] through M. Perrault, my friend and one of his [i.e., Colbert's] foremost aides, so when I'm gone, they will not be left without someone to take my place."[14]

The services Charles provided for Colbert also led to his appointment to the Académie française. Shocked to hear that Charles was not already a member, Colbert explained that his need for regular reports on the academy meant Charles should seek the first seat that became available.[15] He succeeded in 1671. His friend Huygens attended the induction ceremony and reported to his brother Lodewijk, "I quite enjoyed being among all those old poets and authors—Corneille, Desmarets, Quinault, Cottin, et cetera—who spoke among themselves only of verse and of novels. It seemed to me like I was on my own Parnassus."[16]

Even though this was the institution that consecrated Charles as a writer, the way he presented his academic activity in his *Mémoires* makes him seem far more an aide to Colbert than a Parnassian. He underscored his quite bureaucratic contributions to the organization and its public stature, offering few comments on literary creativity. He wrote at length about opening up the activities of the academy to the public, about the creation of new protocols for electing the academicians and for compensating them, and about Louis XIV's taking the academy under his personal protection after the death of its former protector, the chancellor Pierre Séguier.[17]

The day-to-day work Charles performed under Colbert consisted of supervising artistic and cultural projects. Quite a "protobureaucrat," he performed professional services for a state organism that became more specialized and impersonal over the course of the seventeenth century. His duties included making payments for architectural projects and serving as Colbert's representative in consultation with architects such as Le Nôtre and Mansart.[18] He visited Saint-Germain on behalf of Colbert, presumably to supervise works there, since he reported that "experts" were preparing reports.[19] And he handled a range of more loosely defined problems for the minister, from taking care of the supply of marble for the Italian sculptor Bernini to ordering the syndics of the Parisian printers to evacuate a college hall.[20]

At the time, kinship networks and bureaucratic networks were closely enmeshed. A fine example is the relationship, both personal and professional, between Huygens and the Perraults. Charles served as an emissary between Colbert and Huygens, requesting advice on proposed solutions to scientific problems, such as the design of a clock by Matteo Campani.[21] And Huygens's connections in the Low Countries could be useful for Charles's official business. For example, in July 1666, Huygens asked Philips Doublet, his cousin and brother-in-law, to send to Charles a Dutch set of engravings of French ports.[22] In June 1677 Huygens even involved his father, Constantijn—a renowned scholar, poet, and diplomat—in a campaign to release the Chevalier de la Guette, a French officer taken as a prisoner of war; "Monsieur Perrault" and the Duc de Roanez had apparently already sent Constantijn Huygens letters on the Chevalier's behalf.[23] Huygens even arranged for a visit of one of the Perraults to the Low Countries, a visit that apparently did not take place.[24]

In exchange, Huygens relied on his association with the Perraults to satisfy his duties as a member of the Academy of Sciences and to obtain related benefits. When he spent time in the Netherlands, it was Claude who kept him updated on developments at the academy and presented Huygens's work to his French colleagues.[25] And when Huygens was ill in July 1670, his father implored Lodewijk to see whether "your Monsieur Perrault or someone else" might prevail upon Louis XIV to provide for the related expenses.[26] Claude routinely served as a conduit between Huygens and French scholars, passing along to Jean Gallois, for instance, a copy of Spinoza's posthumous works obtained by Huygens, and lending his own copy of Huygens's work on telescopes to Jean de Hautefeuille.[27]

Huygens also relied on his connections with the Perraults to obtain texts or objects for himself and his relatives. The Perraults sent copies of Charles's poem *De la peinture* (*On painting*), of Pierre's translation of Tassoni's epic *La secchia rapita*, and of Claude's translation of Vitruvius, as well plans of the Louvre and Versailles, to Huygens and his loved ones.[28] Borrowings and lendings took place between various members of the Perrault and Huygens households. Catherine Lormier borrowed from Christiaan Huygens a rare print that Lodewijk had sent his brother.[29]

The Perraults also allied themselves with Christiaan when he ran into trouble with fellow academicians. In 1671 the mathematician Pierre de Carcavy and his son bitterly reproached Christiaan over the sale of a carriage. The deal had not been concluded before Huygens left Paris, so he kept the curtains and cushions locked in his room. In his absence, Carcavy and his son exchanged the carriage for another one, broke into Huygens's locked room, and took the cushions and curtains. The dispute went all the way up to Colbert, who understood that an open rupture between Huygens and Carcavy could hurt the academy and charged Charles with negotiating a compromise. Even after the affair was formally settled, the relations with Carcavy remained cold; "several times, the brother doctor [Claude] and Carcavy exchanged insults in the assembly."[30] The work done under Colbert was very much a family affair.

*

Just as Charles Perrault won Colbert's trust, Pierre Perrault nearly destroyed the family's standing. As we have seen, these were the years of the chambre de justice, used by Colbert to get rid of a great number of receivers general, forcing them to sell their offices and replacing them with his clients.[31] But there were formal pretexts. In his *Mémoires*, Charles explained that in 1664 the king decided to forgive the debts on the taille for the decade between 1654 and 1664, an act that would have amounted to "admirable generosity, had it not been made at the expense of the receivers general."[32] Charles conveniently blamed the deposed Fouquet for the sufferings of the receivers general, claiming he had not set aside the indemnity receivers general could usually count on, leaving them to be pursued by their own creditors.

Colbert's rise did not open new opportunities for Pierre, something contemporaries anticipated on the basis of the previous acquaintance between Pierre and the ascending minister. As the source of his revenue dried up, Pierre's creditors clamored, threatening to have him thrown in jail if he did not pay immediately. Out of desperation, Pierre used current tax revenues to pay off a portion of his debts. Word of this reached Colbert, who covered the difference from his own pocket but asked Charles for an explanation. Charles could only inform his superior that his brother had acted in this manner because he had not been reimbursed for the tax remissions. Determined to act the part of the righteous and impartial minister, Colbert forced Pierre to sell his office at a loss. As Charles wrote, "It was all done with extraordinary harshness, and shocked all the financiers."[33]

Charles attempted to reason with Colbert. Pierre, he explained, had been placed in an especially difficult position, compared with that of his colleagues, since he did not enjoy their close ties to Denis Marin, the intendant of finances and relative of Colbert, who had helped his favorites. Colbert had heard enough, and he told Charles that he had to choose between two alternatives, never broaching the topic again or leaving Colbert's service. Prudence dictated the former course, but Charles later claimed that Colbert himself had raised the subject several times, alleging that Pierre had tried to use their friendship to trick him. Nothing Charles said swayed Colbert from his imaginings, and when Pierre petitioned the monarchy to tender the sums it owed him so he could pay his debts, Colbert refused.[34]

The broad contours of the re-creation offered above, based on Charles's *Mémoires*, are confirmed by archival and printed documents. Pierre was not named in any financial dealings after 1663, though it seems that in 1672 (later than the date mentioned by Charles) he sold his office for about 120,000 livres, much less than what he had paid, and the income probably went toward reducing his debts.[35] After 1664 Pierre never had a meaningful economic role in the family; he and his brothers changed their strategy accordingly.

The combination of Pierre's disgrace and Charles's rise demonstrate the importance of tactical steps, as well as strategic ones. During the period of rapid transition in the early 1660s, the Perraults acted under the pressure of legal persecution and had to react to changing circumstances that suddenly propelled Charles, the youngest son, to a prominent position. At this time, mediators from outside the family—most prominently Chapelain—began to play important roles. Without them, it is easy to imagine the Perrault brothers losing all aspiration to further social advancement.

While the family strategy changed in the early 1660s, it is also worth considering a number of continuities. If we ask why the Perraults did not turn to something completely different, such as commerce with the Low Countries or ecclesiastical careers, we run up against a long-term investment in letters, which paid off in the 1660s. Pierre's disgrace collapsed the bridges that connected the Perraults to the world of finance; the family's future would be made by Charles, Claude, and to a lesser extent, Nicolas.

From the early 1660s, the Perraults pinned their social and economic hopes to the life of letters, formerly an ancillary pursuit that now became their way to serve the monarchy. Tracing the detailed impact of literary life on the family's economy will clarify the stakes.

This phase of the Perrault family strategy would have been impossible had the French state not begun hiring professional writers, something very different from the previous system of literary patronage. During the first half of the seventeenth century, writers depended on patrons of various sorts: members of the royal family who supported writers, although Henri IV and Louis XIII were not especially generous; aristocratic patrons, such as Henri de Montmorency and the Duc de Vendôme; prominent ministers, such as Richelieu, Mazarin, and Fouquet; and lesser ministers and financiers such as Montauron, who served as a patron to Pierre Corneille, François Tristan L'Hermite, and André Mareschal.[36] The writers performed a wide range of services for their patrons: they discussed literary matters with them, they guided them on matters of taste, and on occasion they tutored their patrons' children or worked as their secretaries. The dedications authors wrote served as propaganda for their patrons. The Duc de Longueville, for instance, gave Chapelain a pension for celebrating his ancestor Dunion in an epic poem on Jeanne d'Arc, *La Pucelle*. In addition to pensions, writers could expect other kinds of benefits for their services: a dedication might earn a gift (called a gratification) of as much as 2,000 livres; those who served as secretaries received salaries; some won appointments in the royal or ecclesiastical bureaucracy; writers sometimes lived with their patrons, receiving free room and board. In rare cases,

most notably Théophile de Viau's, a powerful patron like Henri de Montmorency could offer protection from persecution by the authorities. A perquisite
that was of considerable value was introduction to aristocratic circles, where
authors could hope to present their works and find other patrons. Colbert's
rise to power opened up new opportunities for writers. The years following
Richelieu's death in 1642 had seen a crisis in literary patronage, as authors
negotiated an unfamiliar terrain where financiers had assumed considerable
importance. When Fouquet was swept from office in 1661, Colbert stepped
into the patronage vacuum, mindful of the danger of appearing to be a patron
rivaling the king.[37] His solution was to remain in the background and to create a more impersonal system of patronage, remunerating men of letters for
their services to the monarchy.[38]

The services offered by writers were a state affair; they would praise Louis
XIV rather than his minister. In return, Colbert instituted a formal system of
gratifications funded by the Royal Buildings. The sums involved were high
by the standards of the period: from an initial sum of 77,500 livres to a peak
of 100,500 livres in 1671, distributed to authors both French and foreign, as
well as to members of royal academies. The system did not always operate
smoothly, as it depended on a number of variables, such as Chapelain's personal connections, that lacked much predictability. As a quarrel Chapelain had
with Gilles Ménage indicated, the implicit set of expectations underpinning
the royal gratification sometimes remained quite opaque, hardly a guarantee
of efficiency.[39] Yet overall, this system of gratifications created a new center
of gravity in the literary field, to which the Perraults were drawn.

Charles's position in the Petite académie and as an aide to Colbert gave him
the sort of influence that permitted him to assist his brother Claude. While
these gains did not entirely offset the loss of income suffered through Pierre's
disgrace, Charles earned sums that put most gratifications to shame. He
was triple-dipping in the monarchy's coffers, drawing income as a man of letters (i.e., gratifications), as Colbert's aide, and as comptroller or comptroller-
general of the Royal Buildings. Initially, between 1664 and 1666, Charles
earned 1,500 livres in gratification per year; he subsequently received 2,000
livres. The top earners, such as Chapelain and Denis Godefroy (whose historical work was extremely important for Colbert in these years), earned 3,000
and 3,600 livres, respectively, in 1667, while Pierre Corneille earned 2,000;
Conrart, the secretary of the Académie française, earned 1,500; and Molière
earned 1,000.[40] If these sums corresponded to Colbert's notions of the writers' importance, Charles stood near the top of a tiny elite.

There was also the income from serving as Colbert's aide and supervising
the Royal Buildings. Starting in 1668, Charles earned 1,500 livres annually for

that work. From 1675 to 1680 his salary was 2,000 livres. From 1672 to 1683, he also earned an additional 4,125 livres per year as "three fourths of the *gages*" for a triennial comptroller general of the Royal Buildings.[41] Overall, between 1664 and 1683, Charles earned 98,875 livres—34,500 as a man of letters, 19,000 as Colbert's aide, and 45,375 as controller general of the Royal Buildings.[42] As it has been estimated that writers had to earn between 3,000 and 4,000 livres annually during this period if they were to make an impression in society, Charles's average of just under 5,000 suggests he made quite an impression.[43]

Claude's earnings over this period were also considerable. In 1666 and 1667, he received 1,500 livres annually as a member of the Academy of Sciences; from 1668 until 1688 he earned 2,000 livres annually. In addition, Claude received remuneration for his architectural work. In 1667 he received 2,000 livres for "plans and designs"; in 1671 he received 4,000 for work on buildings done in 1669 and 1670; and in 1677 he received 4,000 for work on the Louvre, a triumphal arch (presumably in the faubourg Saint-Antoine), and other places. In 1674, Claude received an additional 4,000 livres in payment for work he did at the Academy of Sciences, on top of the 2,000 livres he earned that year as a gratification. His total earnings over the twenty-three years surveyed amounted to 57,000 livres, an annual average of close to 2,500 livres. This sum is probably higher than what he could have expected to earn as a practicing physician or professor of medicine.

This new financial landscape, in which Colbert and the economy of letters figured so prominently, may explain why Pierre chose to turn to an intellectual career, taking on projects that were related to his brothers' interests, such as writing a treatise on the origins of springs and literary criticism.[44] With his connections in Colbert's orbit, such projects could have won him gratifications or an appointment in an academic institution.

Pierre's hydrology project, in which he connected the volume of rainwater in a given place to the output of springs, is the most illuminating in this sense, since it helped in connecting him to the Academy of Sciences. For example, on 4 August 1668 the academy heard the Abbé Jean Gallois read a paper sent by a "M. Perrault, receiver," on the quantities of rainfall and melted snow in Paris between 12 October 1667 and 9 July 1668. The auditors expressed interest in the observations and asked Gallois to thank Perrault and to encourage him to pursue this project further.[45] Even though Pierre did not directly draw on these measurements, he ended up writing an entire book on the origins of springs. He dedicated the work to Huygens in terms that underscored their long friendship. The Dutchman treated it as a serious project, voicing a series of objections to Pierre's argument while the work was in manuscript, prompting Pierre to add a letter of reply to the objections from his dedicatee.[46]

★

Charles's marriage to Marie Guichon, daughter to a family from the Parisian judicial and financial milieu, opens an extraordinary window for understanding the transformation of his social networks, as well as his wealth, following the changes in his literary career and his entry into Colbert's service. According to Charles, the news that he would receive a dowry of 70,000 livres did not please Colbert. Could it be, wondered the minister, that this was a match based on sentiment? He promised to find his protégé the daughter of a financier, someone who would bring with her a larger dowry. Charles replied that though he had seen his future wife only once since she had left the convent where she had lived since the age of four, he had known her parents for more than ten years, and he was certain that they would get along well. Another sort of father-in-law, one who would pester him about his career, demanding that he ask Colbert for larger responsibilities, would be dreadful. This seemed to placate Colbert, who recommended that Charles proceed with his plan and promised to look after him.[47]

The Perraults, the Guichons, and their witnesses signed the marriage contract on 26 April 1672. This document included both the contract, with its stipulations about the dowry and property arrangements, and a list of all Charles's nonreal (or "mobile") property.[48] Marriage contracts served important practical and ideological functions in French society. They formalized the property transactions transpiring around a marriage and symbolized the arrival of the couple as full members of society through the creation of a new family, the basic unit of Old Regime social order.[49] In his 1682 work La Science parfaite des notaires, Claude de Ferrière claimed, "The marriage contract is probably the most important of all those men make."[50] The signing of the contract served as an opportunity to mobilize the signatories' networks of kin, friends, and protectors; it gives a far more accurate picture of the persons most closely associated with the signatories than most other means, including correspondence networks. In this case, we can even differentiate among witnesses of different kinds, dodging the assumption implicit in quantitative analyses that all contacts are alike.[51]

Charles's network of witnesses was highly unusual for several reasons and should be seen as evidence of rapid social mobility. As table 4.1 shows, this group was drawn from the loftiest reaches of society, including Colbert's wife, Marie Charron, and his daughters, Jeanne-Marie and Henriette-Louise, as well as powerful dukes such as the Duc de Chevreuse and Anne, Duc de Noailles. Of the eighteen witnesses who signed for Charles, more than half were noble.[52] The sheer number of his witnesses places Charles in the upper percentile of the Parisian population.[53] Even in relatively prestigious professions related to justice and finance, the average number of witnesses to a first marriage was 12.8.[54] The internal composition of this group is even more

Table 4.1 Witnesses for Charles in his marriage contract, 1672

NAME	TITLE	RELATION TO CHARLES
Pierre Perrault	Noble homme, conseiller du roi, cy devant receveur général des finances de la généralité de Paris	Brother
Catherine Lormier	Pierre's wife	Brother's wife
Claude Perrault	Docteur régent en la faculté de médecine de Paris	Brother
Marie Charron	Colbert's wife	Friend
Jacques de Johanne	Chevalier, seigneur de Sonnecy conseiller de roi en ses conseils, maréchal de ses campagnes, grand maître des eaux et forêts au département de l'Isle de France, gouverneur de Chambord	Friend
Charles-Honoré d'Albert	Duc de Chevreuse, Baron de Charet, seigneur de Marigny et autres lieux, capitaine lieutenant de chevaux légers de la garde du roi	Friend
Jeanne-Marrie Colbert	Duc de Chevreuse's wife	Friend
Henriette-Louise Colbert	Wife of très haut et puissant seigneur Mre. Paul de Beauvilliere, chevalier comte de Saint-Aignan reçu en survivance en la charge de premier Gentilhomme de la chambre du roi	Friend
Anne	Duc de Noailles, pair de France, chevalier des ordres du roi, Premier Capitaine des Gardes du Corps de Sa majesté, Gouverneur et Capitaine général des Comtes de Roussillon Conflans et Sardaigne et Gouverneur de Perpignan et autres lieux	Friend
Anne-Julles de Noailles	Comte d'Agen, aussi premier Capitaine de gardes du Corps de Sa majesté	Friend
Henri Pussort	Chevalier, Baron des hommes saint martin Cernay et autres lieux, conseiller ordinaire du roi en tous ses conseils et du Conseil Royal	Friend
Monsieur le Marquis de Pienne	Marquis	Friend
Nicolas Lambert	Chevalier, seigneur de Thorigny villegrand et autres lieux conseiller du roi en susdits conseils et président en sa Chambre de Comptes	Friend
Henri de Pallart	Chevalier, seigneur de Bouron Jacquevilles et autres lieux	Friend
Marie Loucert	His wife	Friend
Nicolas Desmaretz	Conseiller de sa majesté en susdits conseils et en sa cour de Parlement	Friend
Jean Pepin	Écuyer, conseiller secrétaire du roi maison couronne de France et de ses finances	Friend
Pierre Pepin	Noble homme, conseiller du roi et élu en l'eléction de Paris	Friend

striking, as the ratio between family and friends is highly unusual. In general, the groom's witnesses typically included almost 57 percent family members and 42 percent friends.[55] Fewer than a third of Charles's witnesses were family members.

His friends can be roughly divided into two groups, based on their relation to Colbert. Colbert's wife, daughters, and their husbands represent about a third of the witnesses. Even Henri Pussort, Colbert's uncle, and Nicolas Desmaretz, Colbert's nephew, who served as director of finances and comptroller general of finances in the early eighteenth century, signed the contract.[56] The second group ranged from the powerful Anne and Anne-Julles de Noailles to humbler royal councillors and secretaries.

The ratios between these groups provide the most convincing evidence, in my mind, for Charles's social mobility. The network is heavily weighted toward recent patrons and acquaintances; family and members of Charles's original milieu—the middling ranks of Parlement lawyers and barristers—are in relatively short supply. With the exception of the Pepins, none of Pierre's business collaborators in finance and not a single member of the literary circle formed around Viry were deemed worthy to serve as witnesses. Charles had gravitated almost completely into Colbert's orbit.

Marie's network of witnesses conforms much more to her natal milieu of judicial and financial officers. Like her groom's, Marie's list of witnesses is considerable—twenty-five signatories. Their internal composition, however, is closer to the normal ratio, with fourteen family members and eleven friends (the usual ratio for brides was 63 to 35 percent).[57] Nearly all came from the judicial and financial groups that aspired to noble status. The signatories included no prominent nobles, but seven claimed to be "sieur" or "seigneur" of a domain identified by name, and three more claimed the honorific title "écuyer" or "noble homme." The most common honorific was conseiller du Roi, and the treasurer general of the Royal Buildings signed. Noteworthy is the signature of Claude le Pelletier, provost of Paris's merchants, the position closest to what we would call today "mayor." Le Pelletier would go on to have a brilliant career, replacing Colbert as controller general of finances. Great-grandson of the sixteenth-century humanist Pierre Pithou, he was well established in the judicial elite of the capital.[58] In conclusion, the Guichons were deeply rooted in the world of judicial and financial offices; in sharp contrast with Charles, they exhibited weak connections to the court or to senior ministerial functionaries.

The only witness on the bride's side connected to the court was Claude Housset, a name that prompts some questions about the joint history of the Perraults and the Guichons. In 1672 Housset was the chancellor of the Duc d'Orléans, the king's only brother. But we have encountered him in the past as the dedicatee of a manuscript by Claude and as Pierre's patron in the early stages of his financial career; by the marriage, he had certainly known the Perraults for decades.[59]

The Perraults and the Guichons were neighbors prior to the marriage: the latter owned a house in the rue Saint-François (as part of the dowry, the young couple would benefit from the rent on this house). This was the street on which Pierre had lived with Charles in the late 1650s, and Charles and Marie were wed at the parish of Saint-Gervais, to which the street belonged.[60] As we have seen, Charles reported that he told Colbert that although he did not know his future wife, he "had known the mother and the father for over ten years, as we lived in close familiarity at the time."[61] Another potential basis for a previous acquaintance was the du Metz family, who were Marie's cousins. Gédéon du Metz signed the contract as an intendant and comptroller general of the king's furniture, which would place him close to Colbert. The latter had informed Charles, in their conversation about his marriage, of a marriage he had arranged for a certain "M. du Mets [sic]."[62] While the Guichons aimed for ecclesiastical positions—all three of Marie's brothers at some point held church positions (see appendix)—they shared with the Perraults broad Jansenist sympathies.[63]

Similar social groups, different trajectories: the Guichons seem to have been more firmly entrenched in their milieu, while the Perraults seem to have been more upwardly mobile, in spite of the failure of the most promising brother. As in Pierre's case, the couple's age difference attests to the groom's ambition: Charles was forty-four, while Marie was only nineteen. Years later, Charles explained in the moral to "Sleeping Beauty" that waiting for a rich, kind, well-behaved husband was best, though few women could wait for a hundred years.[64] Charles preached what he and his brother practiced.

The networks of the two families were shaped by divergent family strategies. They came from similar milieus, but the Perraults, and Charles in particular, now mixed with persons connected to Colbert and to courtly milieus. This distinctly new network did not include many family members or friends who could have known the groom for a long time; the list of witnesses mainly advertised the connections he had made while in Colbert's service. Charles sought avenues for social mobility and profited from the opportunities his literary career afforded him.

Dowries have traditionally been seen as a good indicator of the wealth and status of the bride. Marie's was valued at 70,000 livres: 30,500 in cash; 18,000 in the form of a house on the rue de Cléry, which brought an annual rent of 700 livres; and the house on the rue Saint-François, worth 21,500, which brought an annual rent of 800 livres.[65] This sum was considerably lower than the contribution made by Catherine Lormier to her marriage with Pierre, which was valued at 150,000 livres. Charles had not, or rather could not, set his social sights as high as Pierre had.[66]

The marriages of several other Parisian authors and men of letters— Molière, Racine, Conrart, Scarron, Quinault, and Donneau de Visé—show a pattern in which the pursuit of the life of letters went hand in hand with social mobility (see table 4.2).[67]

The life of letters did not provide them with a clearly defined social identity. Jean-Baptiste Poquelin came the closest when he used his theatrical moniker,

Table 4.2   Marriage and social milieu of Parisian authors

AUTHOR (YEAR OF MARRIAGE)	AGE AT MARRIAGE	TITLES CLAIMED	WIFE	MILIEU/TITLE OF FATHER
Molière (1662)	40	Only stage name of Molière	Armande Béjard	Parisian notability; father "sieur de Belleville"
Jean Racine (1677)	39	Monsieur Mre Jean Baptiste Racine, conseiller du roi, trésorier de France en la généralité de Moulins; father identified as conseiller du roi, contrôleur du grenier à sel de la Ferté Milon	Catherine de Romanet	Financial officeholders; father conseiller du roi, trésorier de France en la généralité d'Amiens
Philippe Quinault (1660)	25	Avocat en la cour de Parlement; father identified as marchand bourgeois de Paris	Louise Goujon	Merchants; Louise identified as widow of sieur Jacques Bonnet, marchand bourgeois de Paris
Valentin Conrart (1634)	31	Noble homme Mre Valentin Conrart, conseiller secrétaire du roi, maison & couronne de France et de ses finances	Magdeleine Muisson	Parisian notability; father identified as "noble homme Jacques Muisson vivant sieur du Thoillon"
Paul Scarron (1652)	42	Écuyer	Françoise d'Aubigné	—
Donneau de Visé (1671)	33	Écuyer, garde meubles ordinaire du roi et des princes estrangers et ambassadeur extraordinaire	Anne Picou	Painter with court connections; father identified as "peintre et valet de chambre ordinaire du roi et garde des Tableaux du Cabinet de Sa Majesté"

ᵃAccording to Jal, the contract hid the fact that Quinault's father was a baker, with the word "boulanger" corrected to "bourgeois." See Jal, *Dictionnaire critique*, 1027–28.

"Molière," in his marriage contract. The others identified themselves according to recognized titles and professions. Yet it seems the life of letters inflected the social trajectory one would expect of them, according to their familial and professional background. The marriage contracts reveal a certain tendency to delay the age of marriage, and there are hints of social ambition. Racine, for instance, climbed higher in the financial milieu than his father, and Quinault certainly improved his position in relation to his father, a baker. Perhaps the life of letters played a part in Sacrron's decision to marry the beautiful yet broke Françoise d'Aubigné, yet another provocative and unexpected gesture from one who made a career out of shocking his audience with nasty remarks and venomous parodies.[68] The life of letters played a role in social strategies even without a codified identity for men of letters, and these authors did not form a homogeneous group. The dowry Charles received from the Guichon family, far larger than those of most of the authors mentioned above, shows that the pursuit of letters could inflect social trajectories in different ways; a small boost for a Quinault was a significant one for Charles, thanks to his deeper implication in Colbert's system.

While Charles's career could never have been as lucrative as Pierre's time as a financier, it opened up a different avenue for obtaining wealth: art. A new network had opened to him as a high-ranking official in the Royal Buildings.

Charles's nonreal property—the furniture, paintings, jewelry, and tapestries listed in his marriage contract—was held in three locations: a house on the rue Neuve-des-bons-enfants, Colbert's house, and a room in Versailles. The total declared value of these objects was 18,232 livres (see table 4.3). His tapestries, paintings, and statues accounted for 5,289 livres; books bring the total to 6,289, or 34 percent of Charles's personal property.

Table 4.3 Charles Perrault's personal property, April 1672

TYPES OF POSSESSIONS	VALUE (ALL IN LIVRES)	PERCENTAGE OF TOTAL PROPERTY
Tapestries	2,699	15
Cash, silverware, and jewelry	4,504	25
Furniture (including used by servants)	3,714	20
Paintings, drawings, and prints	1,904	10
Statues	686	4
Clothing and linen	2,450	13
Coach and related items	1,275	7
Books	1,000	5
Total	18,232	

As we saw in chapter 2, it is difficult to assess the value of the property of seventeenth-century office holders; personal property poses a special challenge. Relative to the wealth that resided in houses, lands, or offices, the value of furniture, art collections, jewelry, and so on was small. Notaries seldom paid much attention to paintings, which had little value, and were far more attentive to the frames than the canvases. Specialists were called to assess the value of art only on rare occasions, when dealing with large collections.[69] This means that the data needed to make broad comparisons are either problematic or not available, obliging me to proceed cautiously.

Let me begin, for the sake of a benchmark, with a fairly well inventoried estate: the property of Valentin Conrart, the secretary of the Académie française, inventoried in his 1675 testament.[70] As one would expect, the vast majority of the value of Conrart's property was in real estate: out of slightly more than 100,000 livres of property, two houses in Paris and a country house accounted for about 60,000 livres, while rents accounted for close to 50,000 livres. Conrart's library was much finer than Charles's: it was valued at 8,000 livres, while Charles's was worth a mere 1,000. In addition, Conrart had furniture worth about 20,000 livres. A substantial portion of this property was received as an inheritance in 1648; the three houses were not bought with the income of a king's secretary. Charles's nonreal property was worth about two-thirds of what Conrart's was, but it was exactly the kind of property he could gain in Colbert's service: a large number of paintings and statues, as well as tapestries and silverware.[71]

These luxury items can tell us a great deal about Charles's status and connections. Tapestries were found in more than 70 percent of seventeenth- and eighteenth-century Parisian households. As important as their decorative function was the insulation they provided.[72] Many of the tapestries Charles owned were of high quality, from celebrated workshops in the Flemish town of Oudenarde (450 livres), the Auvergne (1,500 livres), and Flanders (250 livres). He also owned relatively inexpensive Bergamo tapestries—a style pioneered in Lyon in 1622 and subsequently produced in other French cities, such as Lille, Rouen, and Roubaix. Tapestries from the Auvergne and Flanders were much more expensive, as the inventory of Charles's property shows; only the affluent could afford such precious objects. The Auvergne tapestry that Charles owned must have been extremely luxurious: expensive tapestries from the recently established manufactures at Beauvais and Gobelins were valued at 400 to 800 livres. How did he come to possess such fine objects? We can only speculate, but Colbert had fostered the industry in France, visited the workshops, and influenced commissions.[73] Perhaps he or his aide received them as gifts from aspiring manufacturers—or directly from the royal factories.

It seems even more likely that Charles's role in the Royal Buildings provided access to paintings and statues. When we consider the value of the paintings and who made them, we must conclude that Charles's collection was the product of opportunity rather than a particular aesthetic taste. At a time when many of the paintings and prints found in Parisian homes cost under 1 livre, the art on Charles's walls was exceedingly valuable—in part because of the gilded frames he fancied. The collection also reflected the activities at the Royal Buildings: several artists who depended on commissions from the monarchy are named in the inventory. Among them, as table 4.4 shows, are

Table 4.4   Artists in Charles Perrault's collections, April 1672

NAME	NUMBER OF WORKS	TOTAL VALUE (VALUES IN LIVRES OF EACH WORK)	COMMENTS[a]
Coipel	3	170 (100, 30, 40)	Noël Coypel, one of the first directors of the French Academy of Painting in Rome
Blanchard	2	72 (60, 12)	Jacques Blanchard, famous 17th cent. French painter
Mauperché	1	60	Henri Mauperché
Nocret	2	90 (40, 50)	One of the first professors at the Academy of Painting
Le Brun	3	680 (60, 120, 500)	Charles Le Brun, first painter to the king
Sieur Bailly	3 miniatures grouped as 2 items	120 (100, 20)	Probably Jacques Bailly, painted the 1662 carousel as well as miniatures
Patel	1	20	Probably Pierre Patel
Loir	1	25	Nicolas-Pierre Loir
Varrin	1	20	?
La Fosse	1	12	Charles de La Fosse
Michelangelo	1	50	
Boulogne (father)	1	40	
Boulogne's daughter	1	30	
Mlle. Girardon	1	25	
Champagne le jeune	1	50	Jean-Baptiste Champagne
Coipel's wife (Mlle Herrault?)	1	30	
Bourzon	1	20	Borzone Francesco Maria
Caracci	1	80	
Baptiste	2	30	Baptiste, sculptor in wood
Unidentifiable name	1	20	
Girardon	1	20	Sculptor working under Colbert (see chap. 6)
Jaillot	1	120	Pierre-Simon Jaillot, academician

[a]For more details, see Barchillon, "Charles Perrault."

Charles Le Brun and Noël Coypel. The paintings by Le Brun, including a portrait of Charles, were collectively valued at 680 livres, or roughly 36 percent of the overall value of Charles's collection of paintings. The two men had collaborated on other projects—Le Brun illustrated the manuscript collection of Charles's early works, he was deeply involved in the management of artistic elements in the king's building projects, and he directed the manufactures at the Gobelins, one of Colbert's prize projects.[74]

There are other instances of Charles's working with artists whose works he owned. For example, in September 1668 he gave Girardon an itinerary for a working trip to southern France and Italy, instructing him to view, among other monuments, the amphitheater and Maison Carrée (square house) of Nîmes, the works of Caracci in Bologna, and the works of Michelangelo in Florence.[75] Since on several occasions Charles acted as a witness at the weddings of painters and furniture makers who outfitted the Royal Buildings, he evidently established close connections with them.[76]

Charles did not conform to the taste that prevailed among the collectors of the day, who ranked the Low Countries and artists such as Rubens, Rembrandt, and Van Dyck, and Italy, with Titian, Tintoretto, and Giorgione, supreme.[77] The paintings reveal, then, not just a taste for art but the functioning of a web of connections spun around the Royal Buildings. This network allowed Charles to act as collaborator and patron of both aspiring and established artists; as his property shows, he also drew material benefits from these connections.

Leaving behind his legal training and his work under Pierre, Charles's literary career led him into Colbert's service and transformed the structure of his capital, social and material. His social network included the family of a minister, grandees like Duc de Noailles, and artists working for the Royal Buildings. His wealth, in comparison with that of a man of letters such as Conrart, reflected these newfound connections: he developed an art collection and held an office at the Royal Buildings. Such offices were treated as real estate property, a topic that merits a more in-depth look.

In seventeenth-century France, real estate was far more than land and buildings. As the sale of offices developed under the Valois and the Bourbons, they began to be considered *propres*, property that could be transmitted only within the lineage, a trust for succeeding generations.[78] In other words, hereditary offices were classed with conventional real estate for legal purposes. And real estate accounted, in George Taylor's estimate for the eighteenth century, for 80 percent of all private wealth in France.[79] In light of the documentary lacunae in the Perraults' notarial records, it is impossible to provide an exhaustive estimate of this special category of wealth. Still, it is possible to discuss the potential value of Charles's office and the long-term impact of his marriage.

We do not know what Charles paid for his office, if anything. In a letter to his brother Lodewijk written shortly after Charles assumed the duties of controller of the Royal Buildings, Christiaan Huygens wrote that he believed that his friend had paid nothing.[80] Charles complained that when he left the position in 1683, he was receiving only 22,000 livres for it; though the office (perhaps worth as much as 75,000 livres) was in fact sold for about 66,000 livres, there was the matter of gratifications for Charles Le Brun and André le Nôtre—each received 20,000 livres.[81] This division suggests that the office was seen more as a gift from Colbert to his trusted cultural advisers than as Charles's exclusive property.[82]

Charles was involved in several transactions that show the importance of real estate for his wealth. He received rental payments for a house on the rue Saint-François, probably the one that came into his control as part of Marie's dowry. The house generated an annual income of 700 or 800 livres until at least the late 1690s.[83] Charles also owned at least two houses on the Left Bank, near the rue des Postes and the fossés-de-l'Estrapade; the records suffer from inconsistent use of addresses, so the number of his properties cannot be ascertained with complete confidence.[84] Investment in real estate would have been a natural avenue for one so well placed in the Royal Buildings. Might he have drawn on professional connections in 1677, when he was involved in the sale of the Hôtel de Turenne, along with Vincent Hotman, and earned perhaps close to 17,500 livres? We will probably never know.[85]

We do know that connections in the Royal Buildings proved invaluable for building two houses in the town of Versailles. In 1671 Louis XIV decreed that some of the unoccupied land be granted to people who wished to build houses, leading to the expansion and development of the town surrounding his palace. As a matter of course, Colbert was in charge of this program, and in 1675 Charles expressed interest in building two houses. At least one of the houses was being leased in 1714, when Charles's son sold it.[86]

On the basis of these figures, it seems safe to assume that Charles held real estate worth over 50,000 livres and probably drew annual rental income of at least 2,000. This very conservative estimate is based on fragmentary evidence. It is probable that the actual figures were higher, as there is evidence that Charles had even more real estate.[87] If we take the ratio between real estate and personal property to be around four to one, as established by Taylor, and use Charles's 1672 declaration regarding his personal property as the basis for our calculation, we arrive at a rough estimate of about 90,000 livres for the total value of his property.

★

The marriage of Charles and Marie Perrault was happy but brief. In 1672 Huygens described Marie as a "good-looking young brunette," and he seems to have been quite fond of her. Only six year later, he wrote to his brother, "The young Madame Perrault died a few days ago from smallpox, three months after giving birth. My loss is heavy."[88] She was twenty-five at her death. The couple had four children, three sons and one daughter: Charles-Samuel, born in May 1675; Charles, born in October 1676; Pierre, born in March 1678; and Marie-Madeleine Perrault, whose date of birth is unknown.[89] Among the godparents were friends and relatives of both families: Catherine Lormier served as Charles-Samuel's godmother, while Claude Perrault and Laurence de Nyert held Charles II over the baptismal font.[90] Laurence had been a witness to Charles and Marie's wedding and was probably from a family closely allied to the Guichons, as three other members of her family also served as witnesses.[91]

The Perraults and the Guichons linked arms against the backdrop of a significant shift in the family strategy. In the years following Marie's death, as Charles's great protector, Colbert, sensed his own end coming, his in-laws became ever more important to Charles. In advance of his death in 1683, Colbert was determined to shift his children and other relatives to positions of influence. His fourth son, Colbert de Blainville, took over Charles's responsibilities in the king's building projects.[92] Charles lost his income as an aide in 1681 and his gratification as a man of letters in 1682. This left him with only one formal appointment, as a member of the Académie française, and more time to pursue his literary interests but without an obvious patron.

The Guichons grew to fill an important role in this vacuum in spite of Marie's death. In 1685 Charles became the guarantor of Marie's inheritance. Her father had died, and the money was destined to go to her underage children. Marie's original share would have been 47,838 livres, 4 sols, out of a total legacy of 263,853 livres, 2 deniers, but since a portion of her allocation had gone to her dowry, Charles received on behalf of the children's 24,250 livres.[93] At least one member of his wife's family was present at Claude's funeral in 1688, and the Guichons were prominently featured in the obituary for Charles published in the *Mercure galant* in 1703.[94]

The relations between Charles and the Guichons fit the new economic niche Charles found for himself. As a full-time author, he could use his increased literary production to generate new income. He wrote pieces that drew on his experiences in the Troyes region, where the Guichon country estate was located. He composed a poem titled "La Chasse" (The hunt), dedicated to Monsieur de Rosières, that is, Pierre Guichon.[95] By connecting hunting, one of the activities most associated with the noble lifestyle, to his in-laws, Charles's poem performed for the Guichons a similar service the poems on Viry had performed for the Perraults more than thirty years earlier.

Charles also published a poem on the fire that damaged the church in Troyes, dedicating it to the local bishop.[96]

Only in this late phase of the family strategy did the constellation of Charles's socioeconomic position and his publication correspond to the image of a man of letters who relied on his publications to make a living. He published in a relatively broad range of genres, dedicated works to potential patrons, and underscored his affiliation with the Académie française. As his contemporaries put it, his dismissal from royal service allowed him to return to dedicate himself to the muses.[97] In this new constellation, Charles was one of the major protagonists of the "quarrel of the ancients and the moderns." His *Siècle de Louis le Grand*, read at the Académie française in 1687, sparked yet another phase of the debate, as we shall see in the next chapter. The four volumes of his encyclopedic dialogues on the topic fully established his reputation as a modern author. On the other side of the debate was Nicolas Boileau-Despréaux, a proponent of the ancients and foe of all Perraults who castigated even Claude's skills as a doctor, describing him as an "enemy of health."[98]

Charles published religious works that allowed him to develop new patronage connections. In this category are the lengthy poems *Saint Paulin, évesque de Nole* (1686) and *Adam, ou la Création de l'homme, sa chute et sa réparation* (1697), as well as the shorter "Le Triomphe de sainte Geneviève" (1691). While I do not intend to cast doubt on the sincerity of Charles's religious commitments, which he also expressed in private, these works did play a part in fortifying his position in the quarrel of the ancients and the moderns and in establishing contacts with potential patrons and protectors.[99] The earliest of these works, *Saint Paulin*, appeared with a long dedicatory letter to Bishop Bossuet, who by that time was probably the most prominent bishop in the French clergy and an eminent orator and author. Twelve years later Charles translated into French a literary portrait of Bossuet, which appeared in the *Mercure galant* and was also published separately, dedicated to Cosimo III, the grand duke of Tuscany.[100] Charles used his work in this genre to buttress some of his aesthetic positions In *Saint Paulin*, Charles's dedication to Bossuet included a detailed defense of his selection of a protagonist who lived in late antiquity; by choosing a historical character about whom little was known, the author gave his imagination room to play while still drawing on a story based in reality.[101]

During the later period of his career, Charles was involved in several translation projects. In addition to the translation of Bossuet's literary portrait, there was a Latin translation of his short work on Sainte Geneviève, the patron saint of Paris, and his poem *La Peinture* was translated into Latin by Jean-François Lacroix (that unpublished work may have been written at an earlier period).[102] Charles himself translated the hymn to St. Nicolas from a collection by Jean-Baptiste Santeul, a canon at the abbey of St. Victor and a renowned worldly figure, close to the Condé princes; the manuscript of this translation was donated to the church of Paris by "M. l'abbé Guichon, the brother-in-law of M. Perrault."[103] Charles also translated fables by Du Ryer and by the sixteenth-century Italian author Gabriello Faerno.[104]

The publication of *Hommes illustres* shows the extent to which Charles's literary activity was dependent on circumstance and literary commissions. The idea and the funding for the book came from Michel Bégon, the intendant of Rochefort. Bégon envisioned a lavishly illustrated compendium of the lives of the seventeenth century's most illustrious personalities. He engaged Charles to provide the text to accompany the sumptuous engravings. In early 1696, when the project was going through the process of formal approval for printing, troubles arose. The inclusion of eulogies of Arnauld and Pascal, the two most prominent Jansenist authors, incited the Jesuits to complain to Louis XIV. Charles quickly promised to remove the offending entries. The only person who insisted on publishing them was the printer, Dézallier, who knew that a controversy around the publication could lead to quick profits. He printed copies that included the two offensive eulogies and distributed them clandestinely.[105]

In this phase of his career, Charles favored forms of writing oriented toward Parisian elites. He composed two short plays, which returned to galant themes such as courtship and sociability.[106] The fairy tales on which his current reputation is based affected his status as an author not very much in the late seventeenth century, as we saw in chapter 1. I discuss the different media used to spread the tales in the next chapter and in the epilogue.

The form to which Charles regularly returned during this period—one that resonated with his membership in the Académie française—was short poetic works, dedicated to important literary and political personalities. Between 1683 and 1703, Charles dedicated poems to Louis XIV ("Siècle de Louis le Grand"), to Fontenelle (On genius), to Président Rose, to La Quintinie (on the king's gardens), to the dauphin, to the Bourbon heir of the Spanish monarchy, and to the king of Sweden. While these works usually did not include elaborate dedicatory letters, they linked Charles to prominent figures.[107] All presented the author as "Charles Perrault de l'Académie Française," linking his authorship to the institutional position he still preserved at the end of his career.

Charles's marriage stabilized a crucial shift. After decades of reliance on—and rich rewards from—Colbert, in the early 1680s his connections to the Guichons became more significant. His wife's inheritance was considerable, and Charles drew on the Guichons' links to the Troyes region in his poetry, sometimes dedicating works to his new relatives. Before 1683, Charles's printed work was closely connected to his work for Colbert. Later he proudly published as a member of the Académie française, addressing a wider array of topics that permitted him to dedicate his work to a broad range of potential patrons and protectors.

Bearing in mind the material on the Perrault brothers' early careers in chapter 2, I propose a division of the family strategy into four phases, each presenting a different connection to the world of letters. After they moved to Paris, the brief first phase of their strategy focused on social reproduction in the legal domain, as represented by the career of Jean. Then, in phase two, Pierre's financial career provided the impetus for Charles's literary career, and Viry functioned as a center of worldly sociability. The Perraults' networks grew, extending well beyond the parish of Saint-Étienne-du-Mont, where the family home was. Phase three was dominated by Charles's work under Colbert. That position probably led to Claude's appointment to the Academy of Sciences, meaning that a substantial part of the family's income came from literary, artistic, and scientific services to the crown. Once Pierre had lost his office, careers in letters provided the family's social and economic capital. Pierre's scholarly and literary efforts all took place after the Chambre de justice, and followed the literary and scientific paths carved by Charles and Claude. And we have just seen phase four, Charles's post-Colbert career.

This close look at one family illustrates the limits of viewing early modern authors in terms of a move "from patronage to the market," underscoring the importance of family strategies in literary careers. This analysis also has implications for two broader issues. First, the role the family can play as a unit of social and economic organization obliges us to reconsider arguments that connect intellectual positions to blocked social mobility, which are predicated on individual notions of mobility. Such arguments have been most prominently used by Robert Darnton, but they have also been deployed to explore the attitudes of university graduates more broadly.[108]

The Perraults' case highlights the importance of court capitalism, the market in offices and favors created by the state. For Jean, Pierre, Claude, Nicolas, and Charles, offices outweighed any relation to commercial activities, including selling their works in the literary market. As we will see in the next chapter, while the court provided a model for aspiring authors and financiers, the Perraults and the Guichons belonged to the world of the city, where they resided, married, carried on with their professional careers, entertained their friends, and educated their children. The importance of the court, for them, was its function of integrating the monarchy and urban families. The market created and run by the state developed alongside the life of letters, and these social worlds shaped each other in a complex set of relations between Versailles, Paris, and the elites that staffed the monarchy's apparatus.

❦ Chapter Five

The Perraults and Versailles

Mediating Grandeur (1660–1700)

When Sleeping Beauty pricked her finger and was about to fall asleep for a hundred years, the fairy who intervened on her behalf had to act quickly. She hurried back to the kingdom of her protégée in a chariot of fire, and the king—who had been busy preparing the bed and the rooms in which his daughter was to sleep for more than a lifetime—welcomed her himself. The fairy started touching all the staff, horses, and other animals in the castle with her wand, putting them to sleep until their princess woke up. Then she turned and raised a forest around the castle, which blocked all access and hid it almost completely.[1] In her rush to succor the princess, the fairy highlighted two principles that characterize royal grandeur: first, a princess is nothing without her retinue, who make her into what she is, and second, controlling access to the royal body goes hand in hand with the sight of the castle and the image of power it projects.

Charles knew this only too well from his personal experience, as this real-life story shows. On 13 May 1672, Christiaan Huygens sent a letter to his brother Lodewijk recounting a fabulous visit to Versailles he had undertaken the previous Monday. Four carriages had conveyed the party, which included his female cousins, the Carons, and their mother. Madame Caron, who had been too ill to leave her bed for the previous three days, had met the company at Versailles—while Versailles was a usually accessible palace, clearly this was a very special occasion. Many other people from Paris came to the palace on that festive day, which apparently included a full display of the fountains and access to places from which visitors were normally excluded.[2] The poet Jean de La Fontaine indicated that the fountains were turned on only for very important visitors.[3] Huygens, for instance, in spite of his celebrity and his place in the Academy of Sciences, needed to avail himself of connections to enjoy the marvels of Versailles in all their grandeur. His visit rested on his Parisian contacts, and most particularly, on his acquaintance with Charles Perrault, who at the time held the position of comptroller general of the Royal Buildings. In fact, Huygens traveled to Versailles with Charles and his young wife, Marie, and it was probably Charles's position as an aide to Jean-Baptiste Colbert in the Royal Buildings that opened all the doors for the party.[4]

Charles had supervised construction projects for Colbert since his appointment as the minister's aide in 1664, and he drew repeatedly on his access to the palace for his writing projects. He dedicated works, from the collection of his early works to "Little Red Riding Hood," to courtly personalities.[5] As we have seen, the friendship between the Perraults and Huygens, which made the visit possible, grew in Paris and its circles of elite sociability and had nothing to do with formal service at Versailles or struggles for power among courtiers, episodes we know so well thanks to Saint-Simon's magnificent descriptions.

This chapter takes its cue from Huygens's story and examines how the Perraults appropriated monarchical symbols and resources, though their family strategy focused principally on Paris rather than the court. Even in the age of Louis XIV, Versailles was much more than the site for courtly machinations. By viewing Versailles from the outside, this chapter explores how the connections between La Cour et la Ville were shaped by mediators like the Perraults. Versailles served as link between the glory of Louis XIV and the personal status of men of letters. The Perraults used this link persistently and for a range of purposes. For them, Versailles became a family institution.

Versailles, like other institutions, encompassed different types of interlocking networks. Studies have focused on the formal propaganda machine or courtly cabals operating in Versailles, and they tend to place the huge material, cultural, and intellectual investment in the construction of the king's residence at the center of their narratives.[6] Contrary to such approaches, I begin with the assumption that understanding the royal program for glorifying the monarch requires an awareness of the full range of the functions and meanings Versailles could assume even outside the courtly milieu.[7]

Versailles was not simply an expensive instrument of power wielded by the monarch. It was a panoply of glorious images and resources that could be appropriated in local contexts. More important, as a family of letters, the Perraults produced different versions of Versailles to suit different communities.

For them, there was no single Versailles, with a coherent meaning valid in every context. This variegated process of appropriation suggests that the model of cultural absolutism must be reconnected to current conceptions of absolutism in practice.

Norbert Elias's classic studies placed Versailles at the focal point of the monarchy's cultural politics and underscored two of its functions: domesticating the nobility and providing cultural inspiration for wider circles. According to this interpretation, Versailles transmitted absolutist taste in painting, architecture, music, and courtly behavior to diverse audiences of Parisian, provincial, and European elites.[8]

In the last decades, historians have revised our view of the political structures of Versailles in their relation to royal power and cultural production.[9] The court, we now see, allowed courtiers to hold important positions in the monarchy's power structures.[10] The display of rank, for example, emerged as an important tool in the political struggle over status at the heart of France's political system.[11] But no new understanding of Versailles's role in the monarchy's cultural politics has appeared. Many still assume that Versailles's meaning arose from a system of royal propaganda, a subject studied by Peter Burke and Gérard Sabatier.[12] As Jeroen Duindam claimed, "The last decade's harvest of cultural studies dealing with the court still shows the 'goldene Käfig' [gilded cage] as a notable presence. Many historians of the cultural aspects and products of the court were persuaded to present their findings in Elias' socio-political framework."[13] It is this gap between the sociopolitical and cultural approaches that I hope to redress by placing the production of culture around Versailles in the context of a family network, something very different from the gilded cage model. My inspiration includes works by historians of literature, art, and architecture that detail how the cultural and political programs of the monarchy relied on models available around 1660 and how actors outside the court propagated the image of absolutism.[14]

While the Perraults mediated Versailles, it can be also said that Versailles mediated the Perraults, serving as an important node in the family's network. The world of finance was no longer open to Pierre, so he and his brothers turned to the pursuit of intellectual careers, facilitated by Charles's new position under Colbert. Their relation to Colbert meant that the Perraults were not embedded in courtly circles. If anything, Charles's position in the minister's circle depended on his personal service as a man of letters and on his protobureaucratic position in the Royal Buildings, not on the games of court favoritism.

For the Perraults, Versailles was many things: a place that bolstered their status in aristocratic and literary circles, a depository for texts, even a source for exotic animals dissected at the Academy of Sciences. They may also have used Versailles as a way to obtain works of art and as a venue for displaying architectural talent. Perhaps Louis XIV even dictated directly to Claude instructions for the operation of the fountains at Versailles.[15] As we have seen in the previous chapter, Charles used his position to purchase property in the town of Versailles. Here I focus on how the brothers presented Versailles to various audiences and how they harvested the benefits of mediation.

Charles Perrault's role as cultural adviser to Colbert allowed him to function as a physical and symbolic gatekeeper to Versailles. Mediating between the royal palace and its builders and publics generated the image of Versailles as a remarkable modern achievement glorifying the Sun King.

The palace was put to artistic and cultural use even before the court settled there in 1682. During construction, the king spent most of his time at the old palace in Saint-Germain-en-Laye, his birthplace, and in spite of the presumed hostility between Louis and the city of Paris following the Fronde, he routinely visited the city until 1670, almost twenty years after the end of that conflict.[16] Contemporaries noted that Versailles was constantly under construction even after 1682; to many of the visitors and residents of the palace, it could appear a strikingly unfinished project.[17] As Frédéric Tiberghien argued, the lack of a master plan led to continuous adaptations and alterations; it was always an "incomplete castle."[18] In contrast, the literary construction of Versailles provided a glorified image that could cover the dust and noise of the construction works.

Charles participated in both architectural and cultural efforts as the secretary of the Petite académie and the literary work for Colbert that led to his appointment as comptroller general of the Royal Buildings. As this title suggests, Charles's responsibility went far beyond cultural affairs; he supervised work at Versailles as well as at other royal properties and shared the responsibility for the people working in the palace. For example, he certified that two comptrollers of weights and measures had done their work at Versailles in December 1672, and he supervised the supply of materials for construction work three years earlier.[19]

Charles also relied on his capacity to mediate Versailles in a symbolic sense. Royal buildings in general provided a topic for works that were intended to glorify the monarchy. Charles composed a description of the labyrinth in the garden at Versailles, as well as prose explanations of fables meant to accompany the engravings by Le Clerc that illustrated the book.[20] These works were akin to other writing projects that conveyed monarchical festivities and events to a broader readership, such as the description of the chivalric display held at the Louvre in 1662 with the king and grandees participating.[21]

His formal capacity also benefited Charles's sociability. The visit he organized for Huygens, his relatives, and other members of Parisian elite society
would have strengthened the Perraults' status in aristocratic circles. No doubt
the outing was important: "M. Perrault" (probably Claude) took the time to
re-create the visit in writing for Huygens's brother, who could not accompany
them in person.[22]

The mediator's role has a logic of its own, one that Charles conveyed by
depicting in his writings mediators who show and explain the wonders of a
royal palace. Charles chose Versailles as the setting for his major work, *Parallèle des anciens et des modernes*, and included a tour of the palace for his readers.[23] The work takes the form of a conversation among three characters: an
abbé (abbot), supporting the position of the moderns and serving as a thinly
veiled proxy for the author; a president, hailing from the provinces and representing the position of the ancients; and a chevalier, representing a more
innocent and less biased approach to the quarrel, though he naturally falls
under the combined spells of the abbé's argument and Versailles's charms.
As the dialogue begins, the abbé is taking the other two characters on a tour
of Versailles, telling the president, "Since you are a stranger here, and haven't
visited in twenty years, I will perform the role of a concierge and tell you the
name and function of every room we will see."[24] The abbé then proceeds to
show them the courts housing the offices of the secretaries of state, officers
who need to be close to the king, apartments belonging to the royal family,
and rooms such as the Salon de la Guerre and the Salon de la Paix.[25]

Drawing on his own experience, Charles could place the characters convincingly, and whenever he includes a detail such as "turn to the right" the
reader is given a deeper sense of the building's contours.[26] In other words,
Charles transformed his knowledge into a reality effect, at the same time
stressing the role of the mediator. Further evidence for Charles's experience
as a mediator of the palace is to be found, surprisingly, in a work on a fifth-
century saint—Saint Paulinus, the bishop of Nola, published in 1686, two
years before the first volume of the *Parallels* appeared.[27] For this long poem,
Charles adapted a story told by Gregory the Great, recounting how Saint Paulinus sold himself into slavery in North Africa in order to redeem a widow's
son who had fallen into the hands of the Vandals. The Vandal king ultimately
discovered Saint Paulinus's true identity after receiving wise advice from the
bishop in disguise and decided to set him free along with other captives from
his town. Here Charles inserted an entire episode in which an aide to the
king shows the beauties of the king's palace to the bishop, just as the abbé in
Parallèle and Charles himself did. Together they admire the architecture, the
sculptures and paintings on display, which give rise to intense emotions.[28] No

such episode occurs in Gregory's account; Charles certainly drew on his own experience in Versailles.

In *Parallèle des anciens et des modernes*, Charles cast Versailles in ways that allowed him to use the prestige associated with the palace for his own literary and intellectual purposes, as a contender in the quarrel of the ancients and the moderns.[29] Ostensibly this was a good site—he called it a battlefield—for examining the claims of both sides. For the abbé, the beautiful works found at Versailles proved that under Louis XIV's august reign, the modern age could equal or even surpass that of the ancients. For the president, such glories could exist only thanks to ancient models.[30] Yet Versailles did not amount to a level playing field; in Charles's presentation, the palace supported the modern position.

There were many ways to put the palace to tendentious work, some extremely direct and some subtle. Before the tour, the abbé expressed his surprise at how champions of the ancient world could devote so much effort to the reconstruction of antique palaces without bothering to see Versailles. Once the three men had finished taking in the palace and its grounds, the president was obligated to confess to the very fault the abbé had mentioned, offering the excuse that he tended to be too busy during his visits from the province.[31] The president also placed himself this way in a position of cultural inferiority, as a provincial, as opposed to the abbé and the chevalier, who were assumed to be familiar with new developments in Paris.[32] Charles drove home this point at the beginning of the second volume, a discussion of eloquence. There the president admitted that the grand works at Versailles represented a culmination of the "arts depending on the hand." This was only a partial admission of defeat, as the president insisted that the modern era had produced nothing to match the perfection of the ancients in the "purely spiritual" arts, such as eloquence and poetry.[33]

The walk through Versailles supported another modern claim, namely, that direct experience was preferable to mediated experiences such as reading, in part because it obviated an interpretive tradition. In their discussion of Roman architecture, the abbé complained that no example of an ancient princely mansion had survived from the classical era in good condition. When he read recent descriptions of Rome's ancient buildings, he could not understand them. Even when one did see examples of ancient buildings, they had often been altered over time—had not Pope Urban VIII relocated two famous columns in Rome? The chevalier closed the circle—and rendered this parallel explicit to the reader—with the claim that anyone who relied on a commentary to make sense of an ancient text might as well judge the beauties of Versailles by reading a description instead of directly observing those beauties.[34]

This argument resonated with the abbé's comment about the Homeric epics: any educated person could read them, and there was no need to rely on previous authorities to understand them.[35] One might well ask, if direct experience is preferable to reading books, how can one write a book on the subject? A contradiction indeed, but perhaps Charles's own familiarity with Versailles, his use of detail to create a reality effect, mitigated the paradox.

Scientific and technological innovations provided potent ammunition for the partisans of modernity. Charles connected several such innovations to Versailles in a manner that allowed him to draw on his experience and to appropriate for himself some of the palace's glory. He had the abbé explain how the construction of the Grand Canal that ran through the garden had involved both ancient and modern methods. Initially, claimed the abbé, the workers carried out all measurements using ancient methods, concluding that the difference in height between the beginning and end of the canal would be ten feet (*pieds*). When members of the Academy of Sciences measured the same slope, they found that the difference would be only two feet. The construction of the canal proved them right. As with the tour, Charles peppered the abbé's explanation with concrete details that lent greater realism to the description. For instance, the abbé explained to the chevalier that the divergent measurements were attributable to the use of a thick cord in one case and in the other a thin thread.[36] In his closing, Charles lauded the fireworks displays essential to festivals at Versailles. Unknown in the ancient world, fireworks were used to magnificent effect by Colbert and Charles's colleagues.[37]

After he had seen the treasures of Versailles, the president could only argue that the ancients had inspired the whole thing. However, the abbé had an answer to this argument, and the chevalier proved ready to simplify it, as he usually did. In a nutshell, the abbé argued that even the different types of columns associated with Greek architecture were the expression of "simple common sense," something to be modified by people of different periods or cultures according to their circumstances; even the Iroquois, he said, had columns that they hewed from tree trunks. The chevalier likened architectural ornaments to fashion: beauty can be found in clothes of many different forms and shapes, but when they are in vogue—that is, worn by courtiers—the beauty and qualities of the people seem to pass into their clothes.[38] This made Versailles a concrete manifestation of aesthetic sensibilities brought to perfection in the age of Louis XIV, something quite different from classical models. Emphasizing the importance of Versailles, Charles made it harder for his opponents to contradict him: to do so could mean offending the king. In a parallel fashion, the dialogue also bolstered the status of Versailles by presenting it as the apogee of mankind's creative endeavors.

Charles received the key to Versailles from Colbert, only to transmute his role into that of a different sort of gatekeeper. Access to the royal grounds and palace became the means to augment the prestige of the Perraults' aristocratic sociability and Charles's own position in literary debates, even years after Colbert's death. Versailles received admiring visitors and became, in print, the symbol of the superiority of the moderns over the ancients.

For a long time, studies of the impact of print in early modern Europe stressed the importance of either print technology or scribal publication; scholars set the two means of producing books in opposition.[39] The publications surrounding Versailles, however, present a more complex picture. They reveal not irreconcilable contrasts between different modes of publishing but a remarkable mutualism: print and manuscript worked together to establish Versailles's reputation as well as Charles's status as a major author. The gallant texts Charles produced were quite different from explicitly political writing, yet they, too, became enmeshed in the exchanges between author and crown. In fact, Versailles served as a depository for Charles's works in a couple of crucial instances. Here I focus on the publication of a collection of his earlier writings in 1673–75 while also showing how complementary manuscript and print circulation around the court supported the publication of his renowned fairy tales in the 1690s.

By presenting his collection in print and manuscript and by drawing on his connection to Versailles, Charles established himself as a recognized author and member of the Académie française. Principally composed of works in the gallant style, the 1675 collection also includes pieces written in the service of the king: poems, dialogues, and letters dealing with subjects such as love and friendship, the royal marriage, and women praised for their beauty and charm. Charles published this collection twice. The first version appeared in manuscript form, dedicated to Alexandre Bontemps, the intendant of Versailles and one of Louis XIV's favorite valets.[40] This is a lavish work illustrated by Charles Le Brun and Sébastien Le Clerc, two famous artists who worked closely with Charles on royal projects; as we will see, Le Clerc was responsible for many of the engravings in *Natural History of Animals* and probably collaborated closely with Claude as well. Though a professional scribe probably executed the copy, the signature at the end of the introduction is in Charles's hand, and the title given to the collection stressed that it was destined "for the Versailles library."

The ability to dedicate a manuscript and place it at the Versailles library signaled to readers close connections between the author and the court. The library consisted of a single room at the palace, located on the first floor, close to the Cabinet of Medals. Access may have been difficult for those lacking the proper connections, since the Abbé Gallois did not include it in his survey of Parisian libraries, published in 1680; apparently the library did not formally belong to the more public Royal Library, located at the center of Paris.[41]

The contents of the printed edition from 1675 largely match those of the manuscript, but the dedication and other paratextual elements suggest a wider aristocratic audience. Most surprising is the way Charles's work and Versailles are presented to the public. Charles did not bring the work to print himself, which was not unusual in itself, and left this task to the court poet, Louis Le Laboureur.[42] However, Le Laboureur's dedication to the Prince de Conti presented the publication as an act of theft from the king's treasures: "I present Your Highness with a book that I stole from His Majesty. Monsieur Perrault, who is its author, destined it for the library of Versailles. These works occupied a lofty place there in manuscript; now, without any permission besides that which I give myself, I bring them to print, generously making them available to all."[43] The explanations for the "theft," which followed, added luster to Perrault and Versailles. Le Laboureur stressed an analogy between the manuscript hidden away at Versailles and the natural creation of gold and diamonds, materials meant to be used but hidden away for some time before that. In another analogy, Le Laboureur compared the glory of the monarch to Charles's skill as an author. The glory of the king was so well served by such well-crafted works, he claimed, that there was little choice but to make them available to the public.[44]

Many of the pieces had previously been published, and some of the dedicatory letters that had accompanied them were printed in this edition, with the full name of the dedicatees. This also served Charles's reputation. For example, the Abbé d'Aubignac, to whom *Dialogue de l'amour et de l'amitié* was originally addressed, was acknowledged by his full name only in the 1675 collection. Thus the collection presented to the public not only Charles's identity as the author of these works but also his ability to dedicate them to significant figures in the world of letters.

The 1675 collection complemented this image and fit Charles's new public position in the Académie française, to which he was appointed in 1671 at Colbert's behest. Proof of his literary skills and connections, the collection concealed the poverty of Charles's output during his years as Colbert's aide. The only other original works he published between his appointment to the Académie française in 1671 and Colbert's death in 1683 were a discussion of the opera *Alceste* and a royal panegyric written on the occasion of the birth of a royal grandson.[45]

Manuscript and print versions also brought Charles's famous fairy tales to their audiences. As table 5.1 shows, Charles's first three tales, which were

Table 5.1   Publication of Charles Perrault's fairy tales

TALE	PUBLICATION IN PRINT AS A SINGLE WORK	COURT MANUSCRIPT	*MERCURE GALANT*	COLLECTION IN PRINT
Griselidis	1691			1694
Les Souhaits ridicules			1693	1694
Peau d'âne				1694
La Belle au bois dormant		1695	1696	1697
Le Petit Chaperon rouge		1695		1697
La Barbe Bleue		1695		1697
Le Maître Chat ou le Chat botté		1695		1697
Les Fées		1695		1697
Cendrillon				1697
Riquet à la houppe				1697
Le Petit Poucet				1697

written in verse, appeared in a print collection in 1694, and "Les Souhaits" also appeared a year earlier in the *Mercure galant*, the literary publication that served polite society.[46] Charles followed this first round of publication by preparing in 1695 an ornate manuscript containing five new tales. The dedicatee was Mademoiselle Elisabeth Charlotte d'Orléans, Louis XIV's niece and a high-ranking person at the court. This was not a working copy but a manuscript created for presentation, with impeccable script and carefully executed color drawings. The printed version, which appeared two years after the manuscript under the title *Histoires ou contes du temps passé, avec des moralités* (Stories or tales from days of old, with morals), retained the dedication written for the manuscript and hence the underlined relation to the court. The book's appearance was supported by a publicity campaign in the *Mercure galant* and by the literary author Madmoiselle L'Héritier, a close friend of the Perraults. Another print medium, the journal, was used to draw attention to a work that had begun in manuscript form, retaining crucial elements from the manuscript even in its final printed form.[47]

The fairy tale manuscript was signed "P. P." by Charles's youngest son, Pierre d'Armancour, born in 1678. The teenager was presented as the author of the tales in the publicity campaign surrounding their publication. The question of the true authorship of the tales has vexed historians and critics since the late seventeenth century, as the contradiction between the signature and Charles's heavy involvement in the project was immediately evident.[48] Indeed, no other works bear Pierre's name—or initials—and he has left no

mark in any other literary contexts; in other cases, a father's help in composing his son's work was certainly a possibility that loomed large in the minds
of contemporaries.[49] However, attributing these stories to Pierre would have
served to raise his profile at court, where military careers like the one he
chose were being made and broken; indeed, he fit into the relatively new phenomenon of robe families that turned to military careers as avenues of mobility for their younger sons.[50] Certainly, attributing the light-hearted stories to a
youngster would also have fit their aesthetic. Unfortunately, as we shall see in
the epilogue, Pierre died in 1700, three years before his father. Viewed from
the perspective of family strategy, the question of who wrote the fairy tales
changes its meaning. Rather than establishing who wrote what, we come to
appreciate that presenting the tales to Mademoiselle would have helped a
young man anxious to make his way at court and in the army.

This series of publications reveals a complex relation between the modes of
publication and the social actors involved. First, in contrast to those approaches
that seek to document either the revolution print brought to European intellectual life or the persistence of the manuscript tradition, we see here scribal
and print publication reinforcing each other. To put it somewhat differently,
while manuscript publication could connect Charles to the highest spheres of
power at Versailles, print offered him a much broader readership. The palace
of Versailles could be translated into the world of print by presenting it as a
library, all the while preserving its relation to Louis XIV, himself a beneficiary
of this representation. Works that belonged, in manuscript form, to royal collections could offer in their printed form vicarious access to the royal domain.
Likewise, publication in two forms emphasized that Versailles possessed all
manner of rare treasures, and it established Charles as an author of considerable talent, widely connected at court and the world of letters.

Appropriating Versailles as a depository for texts brought together court
poets, princesses, printers, literary authors, journalists, and readers across
different media, in a community of practice revolving around reading, writing, and publishing—hardly the first image that comes to mind when courtly
sociability is mentioned. Perhaps a new vocabulary is needed for discussing
the impact of print on early modern intellectual life. As Filippo de Vivo suggested in the case of Venice, "What matters is not to evaluate the strength of
orality vs. manuscript vs. print, but to see the ways in which each functioned
by connecting to the others."[51] The Perraults' case shows not only the limits
of the contrast between print culture and scribal culture but also the problems inherent in the lexicon relating to the survival of manuscript versus the
continuities between the two technologies, still common in studies of print.
Such studies leave little room for the interrelated ways in which the Perraults

combined different modes of publication or for the political implications of linking Versailles to literary enterprises.

Claude Perrault became an unexpected beneficiary of Versailles, as the royal menagerie became a source of exotic animals used in the dissections carried out by the Academy of Sciences. Building on an imperial tradition of collecting, which treasured exotic beasts sent from the ends of the earth, the menagerie was one of the earliest features built at Versailles, and from the mid-1660s it could claim a range of remarkable inhabitants.[52] The story of Claude Perrault and the exotic cadavers he received from the palace demonstrates how Versailles contributed to the royal image even when it served only as a part of the material infrastructure of an intellectual project.

The foundation of the Academy of Sciences in December 1666 has long been understood as embodying Colbert's essentially utilitarian desire to promote experimental learning after the collapse of private patronage. In fact this was one of the great periods for the foundation of academies in fields ranging from literature and language to science, architecture, and the study of ancient coins and epigraphy. Colbert's involvement may also be seen as politically motivated: it allowed him to prove himself a great champion of Louis XIV without taking the risk of following in the footsteps of the deposed Nicolas Fouquet, whose personal patronage of writers and artists was seen as an attempt to outshine the Sun King.[53]

It soon became clear that the world of letters and print culture was important for the Academy of Sciences. In 1666 the academy acquired a home on the rue Vivienne in Paris, in a building that also housed the Royal Library.[54] Colbert promoted a plan to produce a set of engravings based on animals, plants, and ancient medals from the royal collection; it became known as the *cabinet du roi* (the king's cabinet). This plan was not fully realized; instead the Academy of Sciences published studies of animals and plants illustrated with the engravings made for the cabinet du roi project.[55] Since Louis XIV was not particularly interested in science, and since the academicians could not provide the monarchy with useful technology, they had to shape their research agenda to glorify the monarch.[56]

While Claude was a founding member of the Academy of Sciences, his professional status remained uncertain during its early years. Through Charles he was connected to Colbert, the founder of the academy, who had brought about his appointment. It is hard to think of any other reason why he might have gained entry. Unlike many other members—above all Christiaan Huygens but also less famous academicians like the mathematician and philosopher Jean-Baptiste du Hamel and the astronomer Adrien Auzout—Claude

could not claim to have distinguished himself in natural philosophy, mathematics, or natural history. He was a physician, and he had to establish his
position in the new institution.[57]

Claude was a very active member of the academy, but the only project that
allowed him to use his skills and led to a highly visible and prestigious publication was *Mémoires pour servir à l'histoire naturelle des animaux*, to which I refer
as the *Memoirs of the Natural History of Animals*. As the manuscript registers in
the academy's archive show, his colleagues had been critical of some of the
early ventures he took on, such as a study of the circulation of sap in plants.
Other studies, such as a report on lime, did not arouse immediate interest
and were published only close to his death in 1688.[58] Claude's experiments on
blood transfusion in the late 1660s also ended in failure.[59]

The natural history of animals project provided the fledgling academy
with an opportunity to prove its worth by producing descriptions of fauna
that no other Western scientists could lay their hands on.[60] Each publication
included anatomical descriptions of several animals, with particular attention
to the morphology of the different organs; lavish and meticulous engravings
by Sébastien Le Clerc and Abraham Bosse provided great detail. The publications followed one another in quick succession: 1667, the first full year of the
academy's existence, offered anatomical descriptions of a lion and a "great
fish"; 1669 saw the additions of a chameleon, a beaver, a camel, a bear, and a
gazelle, and the first edition of the *Memoirs of the Natural History of Animals*
appeared in 1671. When an updated version of *Memoirs* was published in 1676,
it included descriptions of more exotic animals, including the "sea fox" and
the "great turtle of the Indies."[61] The academicians underscored their connection to the monarch when they published an engraving showing an imaginary
visit of the king, who is shown observing their scientific labors.[62]

Charles's connections to Colbert seem to have landed his brother a leading role in the project. With Colbert's direct support, Claude took charge of
the dissections of the featured specimens and of the written descriptions as
well.[63] As the draft corrections in Claude's handwriting suggest, he probably
oversaw the printed edition.[64] In several cases, moreover, Claude himself did
the preliminary drawings, which served as a basis for the engravings too. After
he had written the anatomical description, he read it to other academicians,
who approved it for publication. In keeping with medical tradition, Claude did
not dissect the animals with his own hands. The 1676 edition of the *Mémoires*
noted that Jean Pecquet, Louis Gayant, and Joseph-Guichard du Verney were
responsible for the dissections.[65]

A very clear example of these roles is the observation and dissection of a
chameleon performed at the Academy of Sciences in 1668.[66] The academicians

received a live specimen after a Capuchin monk who had just returned from Egypt presented it as a gift to Louis XIV.[67] According to the registers, the king convened an extraordinary session of the academy on 20 September for the examination of this exotic species. The academicians promptly carried out a series of experiments to verify comments about chameleons found in ancient sources. For example, in contrast to the statement of Pliny the Elder, the chameleon did not burst into a fit of rage when placed on a wild fig branch.[68] Claude took part in these observations, and prepared an "exact drawing" of the animal. In an additional session held on 13 October, after the death and dissection of the animal, Claude was charged with handling the engravings. On 10 November he read his description to the assembly. This description was printed shortly after the dissection had been completed.[69]

Without Versailles, there could have been no *Natural History of Animals*. Even though some animals arrived at the academy from the menagerie at the castle at Vincennes, such as the tigress dissected in an extraordinary session on 13 October 1669, the majority of the published animals came from Versailles, in conformity with a shift in royal taste: the animals at Versailles were peacefully displayed, in contrast with the animal combat hitherto common at Vincennes.[70] According to Gustave Loisel, between 1669 and 1690 at least one animal from the Versailles menagerie or its suppliers was dissected each year.[71]

All these animals shared a basic trait: they were exotic. The publication of their dissections constituted a show of political strength, proving the king's power to bring to France marvels from every corner of the world, as was fitting for an early modern ruler.[72] Colbert even had an employee in charge of bringing animals from the Orient aboard French vessels.[73] The academicians also dissected indigenous animals, and the traces of these activities are preserved in the descriptions of the exotic animals: the anatomy of the tigress is compared with that of a dog, and references to cats, cows, and other animals turn up regularly in the descriptions.[74] In 1683, the academicians dissected four lizards, particularly suitable for comparison with the chameleons.[75] However, common animals provided background knowledge not worth publishing in detail.

Versailles was seldom mentioned in the published descriptions. When it was, the context could even be somewhat negative: the academicians examined most of the animals they described only after their death, and sometimes body parts remained at the menagerie. Thus when describing the cassowary, a large flightless bird, the academicians mentioned that they could not examine the bird's crest, which had been left behind as an ornament.[76] In other words, Versailles provided materials crucial to the functioning of the Academy of

Sciences, but in exchange it got little credit. Scientific publications displayed the relation of the academicians to the king, but Claude was not mentioned before the 1676 edition, since previous publications were anonymous. The importance of the menagerie itself as the source of specimens was only occasionally hinted at. For this community, Versailles was not an architectural wonder or even a source of patronage but a source of exotic animals, often received in less-than-ideal condition.

What might look like a failure for Versailles's image was a success for Louis XIV and Claude. The monarch benefited as the vaunted protector and sponsor of the academy and its publications. Even though Claude's personal role in the project was effaced in the earlier publications, his scientific interests and his personal reputation grew rapidly thanks to the project. The natural history of animals served as a stepping-stone to many of his future projects, from studies of animal mechanics to research on sound. When nominated to the Academy of Sciences, he was just "Mr. Pereau, apothecary [sic]"; by 1669 an observer at the dissection of a horse spoke of "Peraut, a very knowing Dr of Physick."[77] This rise in stature did not mean giving up his urban connections, nor did it mean that his work became somehow "courtly." As a man of letters, in fact, his most visible work was on architecture. But as the comments quoted above show, it was the access to the resources at Versailles that secured his early status at the Academy of Sciences

Versailles's contribution to the royal image rested not only on a well-organized propaganda campaign but also on complex processes of appropriation, which molded a different meaning for the castle in each context: a palace the Perraults could mediate, a depository for texts, or a source of exotic animals. Significantly, these appropriations resulted from local and contingent contexts in which the Perraults could leverage their relation to Versailles, as did other authors such as Jean de La Fontaine, Molière, and Madeleine de Scudéry.[78] Others, particularly architects and master builders, certainly did the same: Jules Hardouin-Mansart used his reputation as Versailles's first architect to win private commissions and to speculate in the real estate market; Jacques IV Gabriel, one of the architects who worked under Hardouin-Mansart, gained the esteem of the Grande Mademoiselle, who chose him to build her castle at Choisy, and he ultimately left to his heirs the considerable sum of 355,722 livres.[79] While these examples show how architects used their connections with Versailles for personal gain, the Perraults' case shows how their particular agendas shaped the public image of the monarch as they spread the king's image widely in unusual venues for official propaganda. A focus on the propaganda machine cannot by itself explain the fabrication of Louis XIV.

Patronage has only a limited value in explaining the relations between writers and their protectors. It provided crucial support for early modern authors, exerting a significant influence over literary forms in the seventeenth century, as we could see in the previous chapters. Versailles itself was a particularly significant nexus for the relations between family, politics, and patronage.[80] But the unique place men of letters occupied in society meant that their actions and interests cannot be fully explained by their status or their affiliation with a recognized corporate body. As Christian Jouhaud has argued, the lack of a corporate affiliation made it easy for men of letters to fill a range of social spaces, such as coteries surrounding nobles, academies, or circles of literary sociability. Writing for the monarch or a powerful noble could mean convincing readers, entertaining patrons, or functioning as a mediator in any one of a range of contexts.[81]

While the Perraults' appropriations of Versailles were based on their capacity to act in the world of letters and to operate in a fragmented social space, these appropriations elude the simple alternative between service and autonomy. A contribution to Louis XIV's image was more than the work of a client; reducing the relation to that transaction distorts it. Few of the Perraults' writings were dedicated directly to Louis XIV.[82] Colbert—whose interests were not identical to the monarch's—certainly loomed far larger in their everyday perspectives.[83] The cultural and intellectual projects studied in this chapter, with the exception of Charles's works that expressly glorified the monarch and the editions of *Natural History of Animals*, probably benefited the Perraults more than they did Louis XIV. For example, arranging visits to Versailles for Huygens and his cousins contributed to Louis XIV's glory only by proxy and not as a part of any royal program. In fact, the visit to Versailles did not prevent Huygens from sadly commenting on the state of the Netherlands in its war with France. Even in social gatherings with the Perraults, he anxiously listened to news about the Franco-Dutch war discussed in the company.[84] He was not won over to Louis XIV's side in a narrow political sense. Seeing such actions as expressing either "service" or "autonomy" ignores the "amphibious" qualities men of letters enjoyed in a society based on multiple overlapping corporate identities.

The family was among the most important networks available to writers in seventeenth-century Paris, and familial considerations had an impact on the cultural politics of the monarchy. Studies by Guy Rowlands and Sara Chapman, for example, have considered the ways "social collaboration" applied to cultural politics and to political absolutism.[85] So far, supporters of the social collaboration approach have not disputed that absolutism could and did exist as a political theory and ideology, and for the most part they have sought to demonstrate how the French monarchy functioned differently in practice.[86] The Perraults allow us to take this argument one step further. Their experience suggests that even idealized images, seemingly free from the constraints of governing-in-practice, were the product of a process of collaboration with the men of letters responsible for them. While the Perraults give added weight to studies that underscore ways in which the monarchy appropriated existing cultural models or practices, this book also shows that the Perraults were not simply tools to be used in this process. They benefited from their appropriations in ways that the monarchy could not anticipate or possibly even control. Versailles was a source of culture because of the ways strategically placed mediators could collaborate and appropriate the monarchy's initiatives. The next chapter will take us into the details of the work of Claude Perrault, one of the mediators working in the heart of just such a nexus of power and knowledge: the Academy of Sciences.

CHAPTER SIX

Claude Perrault and the Mechanics of Animals

Family and Scientific Institutions (1660–1690)

Curiosity almost killed the cat in Charles's version of Blue Beard. Unlike the heroine of that story, Claude Perrault could not rely on his brother to save his life. In 1688, he died a scientific martyr, having contracted an incurable infection following the dissection of a camel in the Academy of Sciences. However, his family did make a difference in the course of his scientific career. This is most evident in the skills and practices that went into his work. Indeed, Claude's ideas were often commonplace in the second half of the seventeenth century.[1] What distinguished him in the eyes of his contemporaries was a remarkable combination of talents and proclivities. When the writer and philosopher Fontenelle described Claude's translation of Vitruvius's *Ten Books on Architecture*, his praise for the translator's skill was unstinting:

> His success outstripped all those who had undertaken this labor before him, as they were either savants who were not architects, or architects who were not savants. He was a great architect and a great savant. He had a remarkable knowledge of all the architectural objects Vitruvius discusses, as well as paintings, sculptures, music, clocks, and especially medicine and mechanics, the first his own profession, the latter his dominant inclination. He had an extraordinary genius for machines, which he complemented with a great hand for drawing and making

models. . . . We can conclude that it would be very difficult to find another man who had assembled such different skills [*talens*].[2]

This chapter reconstructs the skills, networks, and knowledge that went into Claude's *Of the Mechanics of Animals* (1680), his attempt to explain the movement and functions of the animal kingdom through mechanical principles. It argues that this scientific project was the result of an interaction between the skills and networks that Claude developed as part of his family strategy and the institutional structures of the recently established Academy of Sciences. The family, I shall argue, had a structuring effect on these interactions, and to flesh out this point, I shall briefly review the complex relations between kinship and institutions in the cases of architect and mathematician François Blondel and of the Cassini family of astronomers.

Claude's work illuminates the interplay and affinities between incorporated skills and networks on the one hand and the resources and constraints offered by the academy on the other. Viewed this way, the academy emerges as more than an institution that defined the goals of its members and provided them with resources for achieving them. Rather, I argue that the academy allowed scholars to implement skills developed elsewhere—Claude's ability as a draftsman would be a prominent example.

This suggestion can seem somewhat paradoxical, since it claims that in order to understand the Academy of Sciences as an institution it is not enough to study its "institutional character," as expressed in a philosophical outlook, research programs, or a set of resources.[3] If we are to understand the relation between the academy and the scientific works produced by its members, we ought to see the former as a space that facilitated interactions among different networks of patrons and practitioners. This bypasses a problem common in studies of the Academy of Sciences, namely, the apparent contradiction between the courtly (and supposedly old) and the formal or rational (and supposedly new) components of French seventeenth-century science.[4]

In *Of the Mechanics of Animals*, Claude offered an account that relied on mechanical philosophy and an extensive knowledge of dissections.[5] This represented the culmination of several research agendas Claude had developed over the years, from work on noise to machines he invented. In addition to philosophical and ideological commitments, Claude's work was driven by a set of practical skills that explain significant features of his book, from its structure to its regular reliance on the machine analogy. The skills Claude acquired in the household and at the Faculty of Medicine came to fruition in interaction with the resources offered by the academy.[6]

Previous studies of Claude and of the anatomical projects of the academy more generally have privileged ideas and concepts. For example, Antoine Picon has emphasized the continuities that linked *Of the Mechanics of Animals* to Claude's earlier work on noise and on the senses. The link, according to Picon, is a coherent mechanical interpretation of the body, formulated in reaction to Descartes.[7] Claire Salomon-Bayet has argued, in a similar manner, that central to the thinking of Claude and several other academicians was the experimental method.[8] Anita Guerrini has placed such ideas in the context of the seventeenth-century dissection and showed that Claude's anti-Cartesian ideas stressing the uniqueness of each animal relied on traditional Galenic notions; a "profound conservatism" underlay the "determined modernism" of Claude and the Academy of Sciences.[9] Yet Claude did not hold ideas that distinguished him from his milieu. After all, that these ideas were so common means they provide only a poor explanation for the specific character of Claude's work; other scholars and philosophers, working with the same ideas, produced different results. To understand how Claude worked and what made him unique in the eyes of his contemporaries, we shall need to examine in detail his skills and projects and see how they were structured by his family strategy.

Of the Mechanics of Animals, published in 1680 as the third volume of Claude Perrault's *Essays on Physics*, represented almost fifteen years of work in natural history and natural philosophy. As the title suggests, Claude applied his understanding of the workings of machines to the movements of animals. Two of the work's striking features were the extent of its reliance on mechanical principles and its use of images. This section describes them, while the remainder of the chapter will put them into context, starting with the projects that preceded them and ending with the acquisition of the skills that made them possible.

By the second half of the seventeenth century, the notion of "mechanism" had become quite common in anatomical and biological thinking, and it could take on several related meanings and connotations. It could be used for highlighting the structure and function of organs; for placing an emphasis on the relations between the anatomical whole and its component parts, which can be understood separately; for determining through analogy the location and nature of mechanical processes underwriting the functioning of organs; and for contrasting material and stable mechanism with the soul or with Aristotelian notions of change.[10] For Claude, the mechanical analogy defined the limits of natural knowledge and provided a way to visualize the composition and function of each part of the body. It was possible to study each organ as a machine and understand both its structure and its function. This was a purely epistemological supposition, as far as he was concerned. He stated that animals were not pure machines, since they possessed a soul. The existence of the soul need not pose an insurmountable barrier to mechanical explanation, as he clarified. While the different parts in a musical organ produce different sounds, an organist is still necessary to animate the instrument. Similarly, the soul uses the body's organs, but their machinelike nature ensures that explanations of their function need not involve the higher principles that animate them. Knowledge of this sort—the mechanical functioning of the body as opposed to its causes—is, said Claude, the "only thing we are allowed to know in nature."[11]

Machines also provided the structure for Claude's text. Claude claimed that it was much easier to understand the workings of nature when "we consider the machines that move animated bodies" and that "the admirable functions of animals are produced by instruments, which we can observe, and whose action we know through *expériences*, based for the most part on mechanics."[12] That is, mechanical philosophy reduced the complexities of the animal world into the three basic functions of the organs: sensing, moving, and digesting. These functions provided Claude's book its three sections, which discussed at first the general use of the organs before focusing on how the organs are activated. For example, the discussion of animal movement opened by suggesting that its goal was to look for things or to flee, according to the information received from the senses. This was followed by a discussion of fibers, muscles, and the roles of animal spirits in movement, as well as different forms of movement, including walking, flying, crawling, and rolling.[13]

The role machines played in structuring the book may also be seen in the explanations Claude omitted. He foregrounded the digestive system, presenting it as the complement to the senses and movements of animals, but he struggled with the workings of other inner organs, not easily comparable to machines. He also relegated reproduction to a marginal place at the end of the work; he stated that, in contrast with the preservation of a single specimen—intelligible since we can understand how nutrition sustains it—the preservation of the species was "utterly unknown."[14] Claude also relegated to the section on digestion such phenomena as the generation of poison or ink; evidently these did not fit well into his mechanical framework.[15] No doubt Claude was aware of works that treated digestion in a nonmechanical manner. For example, a colleague at the Academy of Sciences, Marin Cureau de La Chambre, had published an account of digestion that drew heavily on Aristotle.[16] As a popularization of Pierre Gassendi's work shows, it was possible to fit into a corpuscular framework a discussion on the critical role of nerves and tendons in movement, retaining some Aristotelian elements while rejecting others.[17] The availability of other options for conceiving of these processes, as well as the limitations imposed by the machine as a model, only reinforces the importance of the machine analogy for Claude.

One of the remarkable features of the work is the engravings designed to make manifest the relations between the workings of machines and the workings of animal bodies. The increase in the use of illustrations in natural philosophy books was part and parcel of the scientific revolution. While university texts based on Aristotle relied on a deductive and semantic approach, they usually dispensed with visual aids. The "new philosophy" ushered in a different approach. Descartes's work, for example, used images as a "bridge between logical deduction and rhetorical persuasion," and visual appeal contributed "much of the suggestive force of this Cartesian alternative to Aristotle."[18]

Claude claimed to have outdone his contemporaries thanks to his unique illustrations. By no means did he assert that he had exhausted so vast a topic as anatomy; since his focus was the structure of bodily organs, he did not include "figures one can see in every anatomical book." Instead, so he claimed, he included illustrations that were both innovative and "absolutely necessary" for understanding the text.[19] In other words, Claude claimed for the illustrations in *Mechanics of Animals* the same "bridging function" that Christoph Lüthy identified in Descartes's work, while at the same time arguing for their distinctive features.

While we can only imagine how contemporaries would have reacted to the illustrations, even a brief comparison with those in Descartes's *L'Homme* reveals telling differences.[20] While both works claimed to show the mechanical principles underlying anatomy, only Claude's included several crucial illustrations of machines, key to grasping the mechanical interpretation of motion. For example, illustrations demonstrated how muscles connect to the bones in ways similar to the ropes attaching to a boat's mast, how the workings of the heart resemble a piston, and how the mechanisms necessary for the breathing in birds resemble a bellows (see figs. 6.1, 6.2, 6.7).[21] In *L'Homme*, on the other hand, no illustration clearly demonstrates the machine analogy. The illustration most closely alluding to this analogy shows how the work of memory is illustrated by piercing a stretched piece of fabric (see fig. 6.3). Even this unique appearance makes much less of the analogy between the specific structure of machines, such as bellows or pistons, and the functioning of organs. And the level of detail in Descartes suffers by comparison with *Mechanics of Animals* (see, e.g., fig. 6.4). Descartes is not the only example for works whose illustrations did not incorporate machines, in spite of their

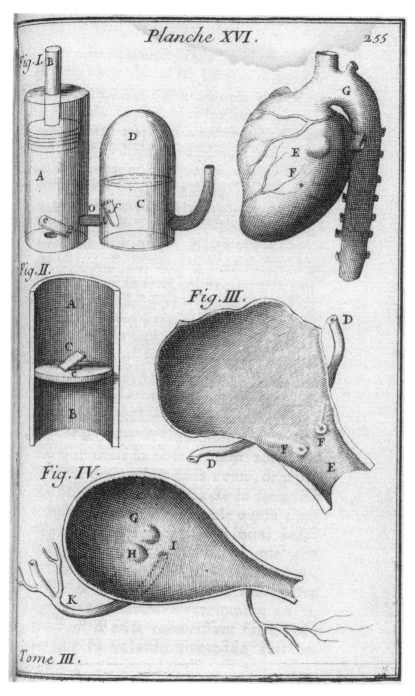

FIGURE 6.1.   The heart functioning as a piston, from Claude Perrault's *Of the Mechanics of Animals*. FC6, P4263, 680e, Houghton Library, Harvard University.

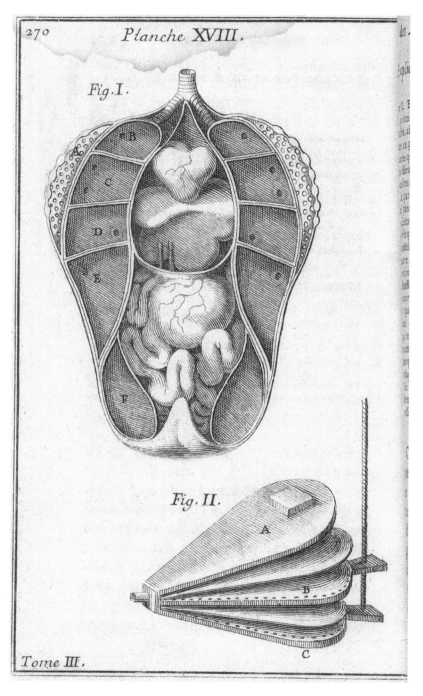

270
Planche XVIII.
Fig. I.
A
B
C
D
E
F
Fig. II.
A
B
C
Tome III.

FIGURE 6.2. Bellows as mechanical analogy to birds' breathing, from Claude Perrault's *Of the Mechanics of Animals*. FC6, P4263, 680e, Houghton Library, Harvard University.

FIGURE 6.3. The mechanical explanation of memory, from Descartes's *L'Homme*. FC6, D4537, B677h, Houghton Library, Harvard University.

reliance on certain mechanical principles. Du Verney's work on hearing, close to Claude's work on noise in terms of the focus on structure and function (though differing in the considerable space it devoted to disease), used illustrations that did not draw on the mechanical analogies.[22] These examples show that Claude was not exaggerating: his illustrations were innovative. These engravings served, then, both as a support for Claude's arguments and as a means for distinguishing his work from other anatomical work. Together with the extensive influence of the machine analogy on the structure and topics covered in the work, they were defining characteristics of Claude's work.

Claude Perrault's work on animal mechanics was not a single, self-contained intellectual project but the result of a complex and dynamic system of projects.[23] His book's structure and contents suggest that Claude created it in a

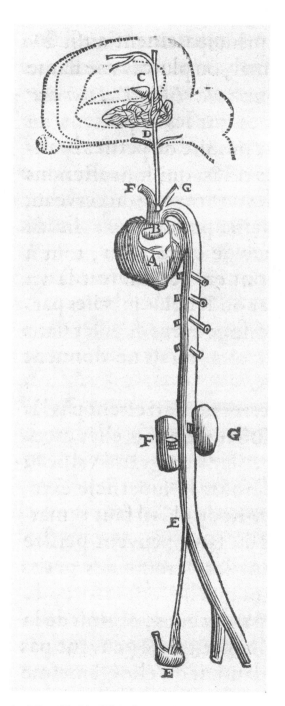

FIGURE 6.4. The circulation of the blood, from Descartes's *L'Homme*. FC6, D4537, B677h, Houghton Library, Harvard University.

dialogue with several related projects over a long period. As Gerd Gigerenzer has argued, the tools and methods that scientists use can provide tested concepts and metaphors for further work, and this section documents this effect of Claude's career trajectory on his work on animal mechanics.[24]

Claude worked within the basic structure of the Paris Academy of Sciences, which comprised two sections, one dealing with the mathematical sciences (which also included topics we would identify as engineering), the other with "physique" (physical sciences) or nonmathematical sciences concerned with the discovery of causes, such as botany, chemistry, and anatomy.[25] Academicians were appointed to one or the other section, but they were expected to attend the meetings of both.

The academicians could pursue personal projects, but their collective endeavor was supposed to be useful for the monarchy. Some of those in the physical sciences pursued work on France's mineral waters, considered a health remedy. Detailed chemical analyses were carried out, but no meaningful conclusions were drawn. The academy may also have assessed the quality of ores from the mines Colbert tried to develop in the late 1660s and early 1670s.[26] In addition, this section produced accounts of nature's two kingdoms: *Natural History of Animals* and *Natural History of Plants*, strongly privileging the former.[27] We have already taken a look at the former project in the previous chapter; the latter project relied on plants collected at Paris's Jardin des Plantes and samples sent from the wide reaches of the kingdom—indeed, the whole world. The academy published a massive collection of descriptions of plants in 1676, in parallel with the expanded edition of *Memoirs of the Natural History of Animals*, and in the same luxurious format.[28] While Claude Bourdelin carried out the relevant laboratory analysis with great diligence until his death in 1699, he did not produce significant results.[29]

During the same years, the mathematical section also developed several major projects. While individual academicians such as Huygens and Mariotte worked on the theoretical aspects of mechanics, collaborators evaluated newly invented machines and initiated a collection of machines in the Royal Library. Academicians also provided advice on the capital's and the court's water supply. Colbert asked the academy to publish a general treatise on machines for engineers; that project did not come to fruition. Considerable efforts were devoted to astronomy, and the astronomer Giovanni Domenico Cassini attempted to devise a method for determining longitude by observing the eclipses of Jupiter's moons. Other projects related to navigation and mapmaking included work on seaworthy clocks that could keep accurate time even on board swaying and pitching ships, and maps of the Paris region and France. These tasks necessitated several scientific expeditions to far-flung destinations, such as the Cape Verde islands and Cayenne, and data were solicited from French Jesuits in China.[30]

Claude had little to do with these projects, as he could have calculated neither eclipses nor longitudes better than the academy's astronomers. His interest in animals and machines obliged him to occupy a territory that defied the academy's basic structure, part physical sciences, part mathematics. To understand *Of the Mechanics of Animals*, we need to examine the relations among Claude's various projects.

The written sections Claude prepared for *Of the Mechanics of Animals* drew on the many dissections carried out over the course of the academy's natural history of animals project, which, as we have seen, Claude effectively managed from 1667 until his death in 1688. Instead of relying on bookish knowledge, that work enabled him to describe the structure of a lion's paw with its retractable claws, a porcupine's quills (the structure suggested to Claude that the lances could be launched at animals that harried it), and the chameleon's tongue—a fascinating organ, modified to seize food rather than produce sound.[31]

Claude explicitly recognized his debt to others involved in the project, as he acknowledged that some of the new discoveries relied on the unique dissecting skills of Joseph-Guichard du Verney, who had been working on this at the Academy of Sciences for several years before the publication of the work.[32] Yet while Claude relied on this previous stop in his "investigative pathway" (to borrow Frederic Holmes's term), he went beyond it in his new study. *Memoirs of the Natural History of Animals* offers descriptions without generalizations, without hazarding a hypothesis regarding cause and effect; *Of the Mechanics of Animals* does far more.

The network established around the natural history of animals project also contributed to the creation of the images that adorned *Of the Mechanics of Animals*. Twenty of the engravings in the *Mechanics* were by Sébastien Le Clerc, who had been a principal collaborator for the former publication.[33] Le Clerc, who was born in Metz, moved to Paris around 1665, at the age of twenty-eight, and struck up an acquaintance with the famous painter Charles Le Brun. Through that connection Le Clerc met Colbert, who promptly hired him. Soon he became the most important engraver working for the young Academy of Sciences, and he closely collaborated with Claude on *Memoirs of the Natural History of Animals*.[34] He also produced forty-seven engravings for Claude's translation of Vitruvius in 1673 and eleven more for the abridged edition in 1674.[35] Claude kept working with Le Clerc on additions to the *Memoirs*: on 10 March 1683, Claude brought to the academy engravings by Le Clerc and presented a program for publishing a new volume of the project.

This volume was supposed to include corrections to the old engravings, as well as new ones.[36] Claude could draw, then, on Le Clerc's unique expertise for the *Mechanics of Animals* after a long period of substantial collaboration with one of the most accomplished engravers of seventeenth-century France.

The second project in the network that supported the *Mechanics of Animals* was Claude's intensive work on machines. Machines were commonly used to explain the workings of the universe in general and of living bodies in particular, though the term "mechanical philosophy" could be understood in different ways.[37] The development of a mechanical philosophy culminating in Newton's doctrine of "the motions of material bodies," which led to a complete "mechanization of the world picture," has provided one of the most compelling entry points for interpreting the scientific revolution.[38]

The Academy of Sciences has been described, however, as lacking a commitment to a particular philosophical program beyond a general adherence to a Baconian program of experimentation; a significant number of its early members opposed Descartes's philosophy, for example, and espoused a view based more on Pierre Gassendi's atomistic philosophy. By and large, mechanical philosophy predominated, stressing motion and matter rather than metaphysical causes; it was therefore easy for Claude to use mechanical explanation without subscribing to Cartesian ontology.[39] Colbert's utilitarian interests in industrial, agricultural, and military technology may have underlain the minister's charge "to study theoretical and applied mechanics."[40]

Claude's work as an architect, however, led him to penetrate beyond mere metaphors. He designed a variety of machines, from a frictionless lifting device to pendulum clocks and a bridge. Some of his ideas never went beyond the drawing board. For example, on 4 December 1675 Claude read a description of a "machine for putting out fires" to the academy, and on 18 January 1679 he read a description of a device that would extract the "essence of carbon" (*esprit de charbons*).[41] His fellow academicians did not treat such matters as simply hypothetical: when on 4 December 1683 Claude read the description of a device meant to "augment the effects of firearms" by accelerating the speed of the projectile, the register noted, "One can experiment with it."[42]

For at least a decade before he wrote *On the Mechanics of Animals*, Claude had been making machines; he occasionally displayed models or finished machines to the assembled academy. In June 1679 he brought a model of a machine meant to produce relatively strong and slender ropes suitable for use on ships; two years earlier he had exhibited a machine he had invented for testing projectiles. The featured speaker on the latter occasion was fellow academician François Blondel, who had addressed the topic of "throwing bombs"; it seems that Claude's machine confirmed the theories developed by Blondel and Evangelista Torricelli.[43] Claude's passion was known to his friends, and even in 1686, when both were elderly, Huygens expressed his desired to show Claude a "planetary machine" that Claude had only heard about.[44]

The inspiration for many of these machines came from Claude's work as an architect, since several have architectural uses or implications. During his time at the Academy of Sciences, he worked on the eastern façade of the Louvre and designed both a triumphal arch near the faubourg Saint-Antoine and the academy's own observatory in the faubourg Saint-Jacques, on the outskirts of Paris. And Claude's most prestigious literary project, the translation of Vitruvius, benefited greatly from his deep familiarity with machines and mechanics. In fact, though Huygens was not entirely satisfied with the translation, he appears to have turned to it as a source for making a vacuum pump with two cylinders.[45] Claude's work on machines shaped his thinking about animals, resulting in a portrayal of anatomy far more detailed and sustained than Descartes's machine analogy in *L'Homme* or the mechanization of the world picture in the seventeenth century.

By 1680, many had come to see machines as crucial to new scientific work. The foundation of the Parisian Academy of Sciences, the Royal Society of London, and the Cimento academy in Florence signaled a generational change in European science and a rise in the importance of mechanical explanations.[46] This attitude appears to have improved the reception of *On the Mechanics of Animals*. The reviewer for the *Journal des sçavans* did not question the explanatory value of the machine analogy: "Since the causes of the actions of each organ are explained there [i.e., in the book] by the remarks regarding the particularities of their structure, and by comparisons with the artificial machines we are most familiar with, the author gave this treatise the title *On the Mechanics of Animals*." The review drew on this logic even when explaining details: on the movement of insects and similar animals, the reviewer noted that it took place "in accordance with the rules of mechanics, in order to provide the necessary strength and hardness to the small legs of insects."[47]

The third long-term project that shaped *On the Mechanics of Animals* was Claude's study of sound. Published as the second part of his *Essais de physique*, these reflections connected the physical movements that produce sounds to the types of objects that produce music.[48] He took up three topics he believed needed explaining: the percussive event that produces sound vibrations, the passage of these vibrations through the air, and the perception of these vibrations as sound.[49] Claude's method, based on analogies between the ear and other senses, demanded some anatomical knowledge. From the general understanding of sensation and the functions of the different parts of sensory organs, he inferred the function of the specific parts of the ear.[50]

The same skills that he would put to use in *Of the Mechanics of Animals* were crucial for Claude's work on sound. He supported his arguments, for instance, with drawings he had prepared himself, based on the dissections carried out at the Academy of Sciences. Explaining his approach, Claude wrote, "I plan to include in the description of this organ and in the figures I provide only what I distinctly saw and drew myself, so it would be clearer and more intelligible. The main reason communication becomes unclear is the dearth of knowledge about the subject under discussion, as it is impossible to explain to others what one does not understand."[51] Besides figures drawn from human dissection, Claude presented figures taken from the dissection of cows, turkeys, and lions (fig. 6.5).[52]

Of the Mechanics of Animals was possible because of a network of projects that Claude had developed over time. As we will see, the peculiar skills such projects demanded made Claude's mechanical theory of the natural world possible.

★

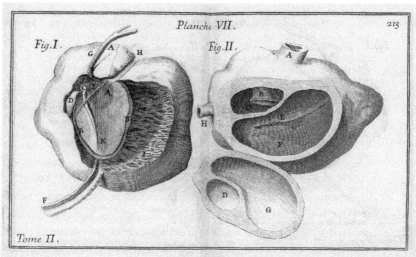

FIGURE 6.5.   Parts of the ear, based on the anatomy of cows and lions, from Claude Perrault's work on noise. FC6, P4263, 680e, Houghton Library, Harvard University.

I have noted that scholars who focus on the intellectual context for Claude's work usually trace his anatomical studies to his interest in mechanical philosophy, shaped in reaction to Descartes and to his modern position in the quarrel of the ancients and the moderns.[53] While I do not wish to belittle the importance of such inclinations, there is another way of connecting all these projects—a specific set of skills.

The most significant skill that benefited Claude was his ability to write eloquent memoirs, dedications, and translations. As we have seen in the previous chapter, after a dissection at the Academy of Sciences, Claude usually wrote an initial report. After some revision, these reports were published, becoming important elements of the academy's testament to the glory of its patron, Louis XIV. Claude's ability to write and publish and his connections to Colbert were instrumental in his appointment to the academy: the new institution needed writers like him to establish its reputation.[54]

In a similar manner, Claude's reputation as an architect rested on what he wrote—the translation of Vitruvius and his follow-up publication, *Ordonnance des cinq espèces de colonnes*—as much as on his designs for the Louvre or the academy's observatory. When he worked on the eastern façade of the Louvre, he presumably included theoretical components based on bookish knowledge, as well as visual ones. Claude was only one member of a committee that included the architects Louis Le Vau and the painter Charles Le Brun; it was a "profoundly collaborative work of architecture," and presumably Claude could contribute in theoretical as well as practical matters.[55] In both the academy and the world of architecture, Claude relied on his ability to write and get his writings published.

Claude could also draw—he boasted that in this area, he surpassed other architects—and this ability, too, played a significant role in his career. According to the philosopher Gottfried Leibniz, who lived in Paris from 1672 to 1676, Claude claimed to "draw in a nice and pleasing manner, unlike other architects of the day, who were not accomplished draftsmen and never finished [their drawings], satisfied with their lines and shadows made by wash painting."[56] The art collector and dealer Pierre-Jean Mariette certainly thought that Claude could have produced the drawings for his *Essais de physique* himself.[57] Claude could therefore flourish as a draftsman in the academy and rely on his skill as a scientific author. As the costs of publishing illustrations, especially given the requirements of natural history, proved prohibitive for many would-be authors in the seventeenth century, members of the Academy of Sciences enjoyed a remarkable privilege thanks to royal funding, in spite of its fluctuations. The years immediately preceding the publication of the *Mechanics of Animals* were in fact particularly difficult for scientific publishing in Paris, as the war with Holland made it hard for Colbert to finance the academy's publications.[58] And yet Claude could successfully bring to print several volumes of his essays, accompanied by detailed engravings that helped communicate his ideas.

Claude's skill in drawing was also useful in a number of other ways. His renderings of the academy's dissections were perhaps the most important feature of the luxurious editions meant to impress the public. In fact, one can still find some of his drawings in the archives of the Academy of Sciences.[59] While Claude lacked training in architecture and was not a recognized painter, his drawings and architectural plans show how he could contribute to building projects in ways that went beyond his work as a writer. He was adept at collecting information about the buildings and statues he encountered on his journeys, chronicled in his accurate drawings.[60]

Claude's skill as a draftsman distinguished him from many of the other academicians and from the judicial circles surrounding the Parlement of Paris. This is borne out by the usual context in which drawing and painting skills were acquired. In general, the training of painters and artists in France underwent a transformation during the seventeenth century. At the beginning of the century, an artisanal model dominated: this meant a period of apprenticeship in the workshop of an established painter. Later, especially after the foundation of the Academy of Painting in 1648, painters became more interested in abstract knowledge—geometry, arithmetic, and philosophy—as painting entered a more liberal, less artisanal phase. The Academy of Painting developed a more theoretical curriculum, while the workshops that had traditionally trained professional painters transmitted practices, with an emphasis on the use of color.[61]

The academies that trained young nobles for life at court devoted little time to painting, which was at best a hobby for one's leisure time. Such academies, which focused on the development of physical grace through classes in horsemanship, dancing, and fencing, rose in importance in the last quarter of the sixteenth century.[62] The magistrate Nicolas Pasquier sent his sons to such an academy, exhorting them to diligence in a "science that occupies the first place."[63] When the sons of notable families did draw or paint, it was part of their leisure activities, not aimed at practical results. More professional than the amateurs but lacking formal training, Claude was not an artist whose work can be attributed solely to the effects of a broad milieu, though perhaps his training as a doctor contributed: developments in the study of anatomy since the Renaissance depended on new techniques for visual representation.[64]

The two final components in the skill set that made possible *Of the Mechanics of Animals* were Claude's intimate familiarity with machines and his knowledge of anatomy. As I have already discussed, Claude's understanding of machines was unusual, even at a time of mechanical analogies, and related to his work in architecture. When Charles Perrault prepared Claude's posthumous book on machines for publication, the preface he composed implied that the sort of practical work on machines his brother had done was unusual among natural philosophers: "The ignorance of most men of letters [regarding machines] is proportional to their [knowledge of] literature. I have seen some so deeply erudite they could not distinguish a hammer from a mallet, a saw from a file, knowing such things only as tools used by artisans in their work. Most mathematicians have scant interest in these sorts of inventions, as they respect and admire only abstract and demonstrated truths."[65] In other words, mathematicians were not supposed to take an interest in practical inventions like the machines, whereas men of letters could not understand the technical principles behind them. Charles's text portrayed a situation quite different from the general belief in that machines could shed light on the working of the natural world.

Among all the academicians in seventeenth-century Paris, only François Blondel, author of *The Art of Throwing Bombs* and director of the Royal Academy of Architecture, showed a similar affinity for working with machines.[66] In fact, even though the Academy of Sciences took an interest in water pumps and established a collection of machines, most of the day-to-day work on the collection seems to have been handled by a junior member, the student Antoine de Niquet.[67] Blondel, Niquet, and Jean Richer—another junior member with an interest in machines—shared a background in military engineering; the latter two even served as military engineers during the French wars with the Netherlands in the 1670s. Familiarity with machines did not necessarily go hand in hand with drafting skills, and Colbert in fact scolded Richer for his poor draftsmanship.[68] Even mathematicians such as Huygens and Descartes, who spent considerable time working on the manufacture of lenses and pendulum clocks, had little esteem for craftsmen.[69] Under such circumstances, Charles's claims about Claude's unique interest in machines become more understandable.

Claude's knowledge of anatomy, on the other hand, related to his training as a doctor. The new philosophy of the seventeenth century emphasized direct observation of nature, and in spite of their aversion to manual labor, scholars came to prize dissection. Adrien Baillet, writing a biography of Descartes in 1691, explained that Descartes made daily visits to the butcher to see how he killed animals, in spite of having animal organs brought to his home so that he could examine them: "He [i.e., Descartes] did not believe that there was anything shameful in it for him, nothing unworthy of his condition in a practice that was innocent of itself, and which could have very useful results." In spite of this, Descartes was the target of mockery for his unusual interest, accused of "going to the villages to see pigs slaughtered."[70] Dissecting carried the risk of "status pollution."

This risk could be averted by membership in a recognized corporate body that handled dissection. For more than twenty years, before joining the Academy of Sciences, Claude was a member of the Parisian Faculty of Medicine. He practiced medicine and taught for several years; he was singled out for his eloquence as a lecturer, perhaps unsurprising in light of his involvement with the world of letters.[71] At the Faculty of Medicine professors attended anatomical dissections without having to participate in the physical and derogatory labor of dissection. The professors read or recited relevant classical passages or discussed medical fine points while surgeons or barbers, ignorant of the Latin being spouted around them, performed the dissections.[72]

His prior experience seems to explain Claude's appointment to the physical sciences section of the academy, as well as his avoidance of mathematical methods. Since Claude supervised the dissections carried out at the Academy of Sciences, the institution allowed him to transfer skills to a new context in which he produced his studies while maintaining a division of labor similar to that of the Faculty of Medicine. The continuity with the world of medicine was also evident among Claude's colleagues; as David Sturdy has argued in his discussion of the first generation of academicians, training in medicine "was more likely to be directly relevant to their later researches than that of their colleagues in the Académie."[73]

In comparison with a Descartes, Claude benefited from more thorough training in anatomy and from an institutional context that allowed him to draw on knowledge from dissection without posing a risk to his own status. In this manner, Claude's work on exotic animals probably only boosted his status in the eyes of patrons and other scholars. The academy's report to Colbert on the activities of the physical sciences section for the period between April 1678 and June 1679 noted that Claude had provided anatomical descriptions of "several rare animals, among them a tiger, a tigress, a white ibis, a salamander, and a marmot." In comparison, Du Verney's activities were consistently presented as "anatomical dissections," while Claude's were "descriptions."[74] The exotic animals appear to have resonated with the reviewer of *Mechanics of Animals* who wrote in the *Journal des sçavans*. The reviewer mentioned specifically the chameleon and porcupines, both animals exotic enough to be included in the 1676 edition of the *Memoirs of the Natural History of Animals*. In contrast, he used more generic categories, such as "birds," "insects," "frogs," and "turtles" for other types of animals.[75]

I see *Of the Mechanics of Animals* not as a product of a general sensitivity or of a practitioner's identity but as the intersection of very specific skills in several fields: writing, drawing, and knowledge of machines and anatomy. Not every academician could have produced this work; it was emphatically Claude's. Describing him as an academician or polymath does not help much, but when we take into account the interaction between Claude's skills and the projects and resources of the Academy of Sciences, we get a more complete and nuanced account.

Claude acquired the skills needed to produce his book within the context of his family's projects, and his family connected him to the networks that made his emergence as a creative subject possible. While I do not wish to argue that his brothers determined the specific content of Claude's work, the family strategy and the changes it underwent over the course of the century did produce structuring effects on Claude's science.

The literary projects he completed with his brothers made Claude a writer and an artist. An early work was a verse paraphrase of *The Aeneid*, and once Charles entered the world of letters more fully in the late 1650s, writing provided support for the financial career of his brother Pierre. These literary endeavors drew the attention of Colbert and led to Charles's appointment to the Petite académie. Some of Claude's surviving drawings appear in the description Corneillau wrote of a voyage to the Perrault country house in Viry (fig. 6.6). At least one of those drawings seems to anticipate those Claude would use in his scientific work.

The medical training that made all those dissections and the book *Of the Mechanics of Animals* possible reflected a family strategy. Such training required the support of patrons or a significant investment on the part of the family. As the five Perrault brothers received their degrees in the Paris area, where training was quite expensive, it is clear that economic considerations had an effect on their educational choices. While Jean and Pierre, the elders, as well as Charles, the youngest, obtained law degrees that allowed them to follow in their father's footsteps, Nicolas's training in theology and Claude's medical training represented attempts to diversify. In fact, many doctors belonged to medical families, meaning that Claude was not the typical graduate of a medical faculty. In many cases these families did not simply reproduce their professional identity: as L. W. B. Brockliss and Colin Jones claimed, medicine served as a "springboard to higher things"—certainly the case with Claude.[76]

Significantly, the family connected Claude to the networks that made his work possible. From the appointment to the Academy of Sciences to the architectural commissions for the Louvre façade, the observatory, and the

FIGURE 6.6. Depiction of a boat, from the frontispiece of "Voyage to Viry." British Library, MS, Add. 20087 © British Library.

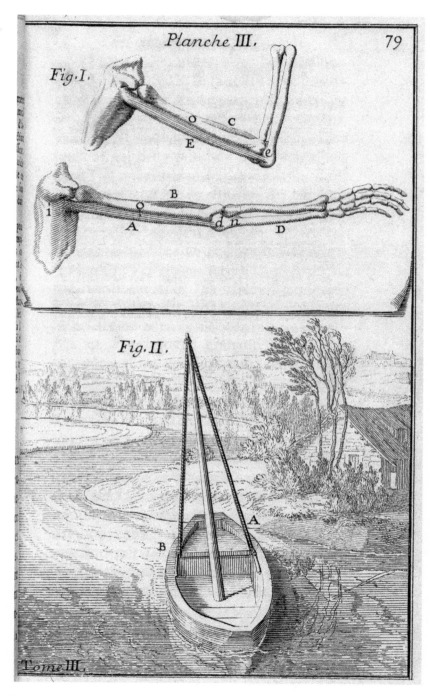

FIGURE 6.7. The structure of a boat as an analogy to muscles, from Claude Perrault's *Of the Mechanics of Animals*. FC6, P4263, 680e, Houghton Library, Harvard University.

work at Versailles, all depended on Charles's close relations to Colbert. For Claude, his family represented a structural hinge to other networks.[77]

Consider the journey Claude Perrault undertook to Bordeaux with his lawyer brother Jean and several others.[78] While Jean's presence raises the possibility that the purpose of this trip involved legal affairs, this is mere speculation. Nevertheless, Claude clearly had a specific goal in mind, as he used the trip to survey the architecture of interesting sites between Bordeaux and Paris. The travel diary he left includes not only descriptions of places seen and noteworthy events—most prominently the illness and death of Jean—but numerous drawings in his own hand. These drawings represent mostly architectural plans and interesting architectural features. For example, he drew a partial plan of the castle of Chambord and columns from the castle of Richelieu.[79] Claude also sketched other items of professional interest, such as a "monstrous birth" and instruments for working with stone.[80]

This "architectural tour" fit into plans made by Charles Perrault. It seems that during the late 1660s Charles was in charge of collecting information that could be used in Colbert's building projects. As we saw in chapter 4, in September 1668, just a short time before Claude's journey, Charles provided a recommended itinerary to the sculptor François Girardon, who traveled to southern France and from there to Italy. Girardon collected information much like that gathered by Claude; both were presumably working under Charles's guidance. In this case, as well as in others, the family provided a crucial direction for Claude's work.

Claude's case represents one type of nexus between kinship and institutions. In his case, the interaction between his kinship networks and the institutions he was involved in was based on a heterogeneous set of skills—which explains why his contemporaries view his skills as a unique combination—and led to involvement in a broad range of intellectual projects, from the Academy of Sciences to the reconstruction of the Louvre. The patronage relations that Charles cultivated served a crucial role in the broad range of appointments Claude held. This is a qualitatively different form of the way kinship could structure intellectual projects, as we can see by briefly looking at two other cases: the Blondel and Cassini families.

François Blondel was born in 1618 to a family of notables from Picardy. His mother came from a noble family, and through her, the family came to own two seigneuries. As a first-born son, Blondel developed a career suitable to the ambitions of a provincial notable: he went into military service, like all of his brothers. His military service, which coincided with France's entry into the Thirty Years' War, led him to become a client of Cardinal Richelieu. After the cardinal's death, he entered the service of Henri-Auguste de Loménie, comte de Brienne, longtime secretary of state. Thanks to his service to Brienne, which included diplomatic missions as well as accompanying his son on a four-year tour of European courts, the minister submitted a claim of nobility for Blondel's father in 1654. Two years later, Blondel was appointed professor of mathematics at the Royal College, where he lectured on many of the topics on which he would later publish, from architecture to the mechanics of artillery. In the late 1660s, Blondel became a client of Colbert and was rewarded with appointments as director of the Academy for Architecture and member of the Academy of Sciences.[81]

At first blush, Blondel's career seems similar to Claude's, with appointments and publications across a wide range of fields. However, I believe it is an example of a different type of relation between family strategies and institutions. In Blondel's case, the family strategy was based not on diversification but on concentration of efforts, and the result was a similar set of skills, at least for some of its sons. Specifically, Blondel's work reflects the training of a military engineer, which laid the foundation for his knowledge of mathematics. For Blondel, just as for other seventeenth-century architects, architecture was part and parcel of a broader interest in mathematics—Claude being a prominent exception to this rule.[82] The family strategy was also reflected in the careers of his other brothers: thanks to Brienne's support, his brother Antoine inherited his father's post as commander of the city of Ribemont and was destined to further diplomatic missions. Another brother, Méry, became an engineer of the order of St. John of Jerusalem.[83] In other words, in contrast with the Perraults, Blondel typifies a family strategy based on the concentration of efforts on a particular set of skills, which then—thanks to the games of patronage—was implemented in several institutions and social settings.

The Cassini family displays, in contrast to the preceding two, a case of a very tight fit between a family strategy and an institution. Giovanni Domenico Cassini (1625–1712) was the son of a distinguished Italian family who became— thanks to an early interest in astrology—one of Europe's most prominent astronomers in the middle of the seventeenth century. In 1669, he was lured to Paris and the newly founded Academy of Sciences by an extravagant pension of 9,000 livres. After having trouble in his first years in the capital—from difficulties coping with the French language to enduring the Parisian climate, harsher than the one in Bologna—he settled and founded a veritable dynasty of astronomers. His son, Jacques Cassini (1677–1755), grandson César-François Cassini de Thury (1714–84), and great-grandson Jean-Dominique Cassini (1748–1845) were all prominent astronomers who maintained the family's presence in the academy and its observatory. In their case, early training in astronomy, starting in the household, helped hone the skills that would allow them to maintain their dominance in the institution.[84] The Cassini family represents, therefore, a case of a family strategy invested in a highly specific skill, one that allowed it to maintain a symbiosis with one institution for more than a hundred years. Though they cannot be treated in detail here, all three families show that kinship had a structuring effect on scientific careers and that this effect could take different forms, with various degrees of fit between the family strategy and the institutional landscape in which it unfolded.

At the foundation of Claude Perrault's *On the Mechanics of Animals* stood a group of skills and a legacy of previous projects, which account for specific traits that would be obscured by approaches focused on social identities, philosophical commitments, or a putatively polymathic identity. Claude's skills and networks of projects help to account for a wide array of activities, explaining why contemporaries particularly appreciated his works. We lose touch with this when we view his career through our modern professional categories or when we seek to understand Claude's work simply in terms of its ideas.

Using this detailed case study to see how his work fitted into the broader institutional context of the Academy of Sciences also helps us understand the relations between kinship and formal cultural and intellectual institutions. The previous chapter allowed us to see how the *Natural History of Animals* project relied on a supply of animals from Versailles and contributed to establishing Claude at the Academy of Sciences. This chapter expanded the scope of this line of inquiry by setting Claude's work against the wider backdrop of the projects taken up at the academy between its foundation and Claude's death in 1688. This shows that Claude's work as an academician depended on an intersection of networks otherwise extraneous to the academy, among them the family of letters. The academy itself appears in a new light: instead of implementing a philosophical or political program, it offered resources that interacted in complex ways with skills and networks from outside the academy. Ultimately, to understand the academy's scientific projects we need to take into account the range of skills and networks the academicians brought to each project. Otherwise, the portrait of the academy, like the portrait of Versailles discussed in the previous chapter, remains narrow and rather one-sided.

Claude's place in a family network shaped both his skills and the creative work he did; kinship should not be seen as the ultimate explanation for Claude's scientific creativity, but it is indispensable for reconstructing it, as we could see by getting into the details of the origins and structure of one of Claude's projects. His death in 1688 put an end to his scientific work and left Charles as the sole living member of his generation. The epilogue examines what he and his children did to consolidate the family's fortunes, material and symbolic.

Epilogue (1690–1730)

Charles Perrault might have been describing his own situation when he concluded the moral to "Little Thumb": "Sometimes, though, it is the little brat who brings fortune to the entire family."[1] And the youngest of the brothers had much work to do. By 1690 the generation of Perraults who had made letters their profession was decimated. After Pierre's death around 1680 and Claude's in 1688, Charles alone was left alive. Of all his former functions under Colbert, he retained only his position in the Académie française. The next generation of Perraults was nearing adulthood, but since Pierre's children may have died by the early 1690s, only Charles's children—Charles, Charles-Samuel, Pierre, and Marie-Madeleine—stood to inherit the family's economic, social, and cultural capital.

Even though Charles cemented the identity of a family of letters in the 1690s, most of his children left the literary world behind. One son, Pierre d'Armancour, collaborated with him on the fairy tales. For Pierre, writing probably served as a springboard to a courtly and military career—it was not an end in itself. So the Perraults' family strategy shifted toward the court at the very same time it solidified the literary identity of the generation led by Charles and Pierre Jr.

Charles's children left no written records, and little is known about their lives. However, it is clear that, with the exception of Pierre's childhood contributions to his father's stories, this generation did not pursue literary careers. Almost nothing is known about Charles-Samuel and Marie-Madeleine; both appear to have died before their father's funeral in 1703, which they did not attend.[2] Their names occur in no records after that date, with one possible exception. Little is known about Marie-Madeleine beyond her role in the division of the Guichon inheritance (described in chapter 4) and her marriage to a page (*écuyer*) called Louis le Gentil.[3]

In 1702 Charles Jr. became a page in the service of the Duchesse de Bourgogne, a post that cost him at least 20,000 livres.[4] It was a strategic position, since the Duchesse de Bourgogne served as a link between the courtly clique of the Duc de Bourgogne—who was briefly heir to the throne—and the clique revolving around the Pontchartrain family and Madame de Maintenon. It was also directly built on the family strategy and his father's network—Nicolas Desmaretz, the comptroller general of finances, who had been a witness at Charles père's wedding in 1672, was a member of the duke's clique, like other heirs of Colbert.[5]

Since Charles Jr. maintained the title of "page of the late Dauphine" up to his death in late 1728 or early 1729, he never earned a more prestigious title. We also know that he maintained the same Parisian residence, on the rue Sainte-Anastase in Saint-Gervais. The only other records that shed light on him relate to the income from renting houses that had previously belonged to his parents and from the sale of some of this property (e.g., a house at Versailles was sold in 1714 for the sum of 14,000 livres).[6] It seems safe to conclude that Charles Jr. did not acquire a significant fortune, but it would be premature to assume that his economic status had simply declined. Though the sale of the house at Versailles seems to have been used for purchasing a rent (essentially, to repay a loan), Charles kept leasing other houses to tenants.[7] However, as far as the public was concerned, he remained in the shadow of his father: when his library was sold in May 1729, the books were advertised as belonging to Charles Sr., a "member of the Académie française." In fact, it is evident that many of the books in the library had been acquired by Charles Jr., since they had been published after his father's death in 1703.[8]

The most intriguing of Charles's children is the youngest, Pierre, born in 1678. It is unclear how the epithet "d'Armancour" came to be attached to his name.[9] As I pointed out in my discussion of manuscript circulation around Versailles (chapter 5), the initials "P. P." appear on the manuscript copy of Charles's tales in verse that was presented at the court, and Pierre was presented as the author of the tales in the publicity surrounding their publication. The question of who wrote the tales has been much discussed, and rather than return to a topic others have exhausted, I would like to consider how presenting Pierre as their author fits into a strategy focused on the court. His failure to write any other works stands in direct contrast to the high productivity of his father in this very period, suggesting that theirs was a very limited collaboration, serving mostly to raise Pierre's profile at court and in polite society.

The career he ultimately took up was military. In 1697 he fought a neighbor's son and, using the sword he carried, killed him. Charles had to pay 2,000 livres as compensation.[10] When he died in 1700, Pierre had been a lieutenant in the Regiment Dauphin.[11] He seems to have taken part in a wider process of seeking to establish nobility through the sword: in a trend that peaked in the 1680s, wealthy robe nobles "turned more and more to the sword for opportunities for their younger sons."[12] This was a risky strategy, as military service brought uncertain rewards and obvious risks. In many cases, turning to the sword led to the extinction of robe families.[13]

Charles did not possess the resources of a wealthy robe family, so it seems plausible that establishing connections at court through the dedication of the fairy tales was meant to promote his son, as court connections could make or break military careers. As we have seen, the lavish presentation manuscript of the tales, signed by Pierre, was presented to Elisabeth Charlotte d'Orléans, Louis XIV's niece. The publication of these details fits a range of other actions taken by family members. This means that the tales can be understood as part of the family's strategy, and attempts to identify their "individual author" are, to a certain extent, misleading.

In spite of the fragmentary evidence, a relatively clear picture emerges: Charles's children broke away from the life of letters to follow careers directly connected with the court, whether in the army or the service of the Duchesse de Bourgogne. Alas, this turn seems to have been premature. These careers did not develop, and by 1729, with the death of Charles, this branch of the Perrault family—and possibly the family as a whole—became extinct. We can trace this to the choices made by the Perraults, including, for example, late marriage, which meant Pierre and his brother Charles sired few children who lived to adulthood. "Every true story has an anticlimax," as John Updike once remarked, and the fate of Charles's children certainly seems like such an ending. Then how do we explain the strength of the literary identity of the Perraults and its persistence through the centuries?

By the 1690s Charles Perrault was the only living son of Pierre Perrault and Paquette Le Clerc. Instead of letting the memory of his brothers sink into oblivion, Charles expended considerable effort to shape it. The discourses surrounding the Perraults did not materialize out of thin air. The family proved

strong and meaningful enough to orient Charles's actions in the world of letters, and shaping its reputation required considerable effort on his part.

As with the publications surrounding Versailles, Charles used a combination of print and manuscript strategies. For the latter, he turned to two different technologies, writing out his *Mémoires* and assembling a manuscript
collection, as his contemporaries did in other cases.[14] The *Mémoires* communicated to his heirs and relatives information they might need to resolve disputes regarding the Perraults' authorship, their service to the crown, and the
dangers inherent in their association with Jansenism.[15]

But the *Mémoires* also refer the reader to other manuscripts, serving effectively as an index. For example, while discussing how he invented devices for
royal tapestries, Charles mentioned that "there is a collection of these, which
is to be found among my papers, following an essay on the devices."[16] And
while discussing proposed corrections to Claude's plans for a triumphal arch,
he explained, "I keep these two drawings in two gilded frames, as curiosities."[17]

Such references permit a partial reconstruction of the categories of documents Charles preserved: manuscripts and printed works by family members;
personal papers, probably related to his position as secretary of the Petite académie; architectural designs and notes on architectural theory by his brother
Claude; drawings Charles had made; and other prints.[18] He could not hold on
to everything that passed through his hands—he had to return papers, which he
would probably have preferred to keep, relating to his official position as *commis des bâtiments*.[19] Charles also obtained a manuscript copy of the journal by
Chantelou, who accompanied Bernini during his travels in France; he used that
document to describe the quarrels surrounding the designs for the Louvre.[20]

His *Mémoires* were only one component in the campaign Charles waged.
He used his access to print to name his brothers as authorities, publish them
anonymously, and publish them under their names. When we consider the
foregoing activities in the context of the *Mémoires*, we begin to see the potential blemishes that Charles sought to address, and how the interpretation of
the past presented in the *Mémoires* applied to concrete risks to the family reputation and to Charles's own standing.

Charles promoted his brothers by drawing on their theories and presenting
them as authorities. For example, in *Parallèle des anciens et des modernes*, which
champions modern art and forms of knowledge over the ancient, Charles
pointed his readers to Claude's work on ancient music, which demonstrated
the advantages of modern polyphony over the music of the ancients.[21] Charles
also referred his readers to Claude's treatise on architecture, the *Ordonnance
des cinq especes de colonnes*, treating it as an authoritative source on issues of
perspective.[22] He also published a short essay by Nicolas at the end of *Parallèle*,

omitting his brother's name. This fragment, entitled *Sentiment d'un Docteur de Sorbonne sur la doctrine des principes de connoissance de Descartes* (Reflections of a doctor from the Sorbonne on Descartes's doctrine of the principles of knowledge), is an attack on the relation between doubt and faith in Descartes.[23] Finally, Charles had works his brothers had not published during their lifetimes printed under their names. Three years before his death, he wrote the preface to Claude's *Recueil de plusieurs machines de nouvelle invention* (Collection of recently invented machines). He repeated the name of the Parisian Academy of Sciences in the introduction—praising its members and mentioning his role in founding the academy and Claude's place as a member—as if that might ensure the book a safe journey. Elaborate foldout engravings of machines must have demanded the talents of an unusually skillful printer and close supervision, and Charles employed the official printer of the Académie française, with whom he worked often. The privilege for publishing the book was first ceded by the Academy of Sciences to Boudot, its printer, who then associated himself with Coignard, the royal printer and the printer of the Académie française.[24]

These actions were reinforced in Charles's *Mémoires*, where he insisted that his family members get credit for their authorship. He devoted about a third of the book to the intrigues and upheavals surrounding the reconstruction of the Louvre, especially its eastern façade. The poet Nicolas Boileau, for example, had written to the theologian Antoine Arnauld, "[Claude Perrault] definitely did not create the Louvre façade, the observatory, or the Arc de triomphe."[25] Charles rejected such claims, stating that Claude was responsible for "the designs of the main façade of the Louvre, of the observatory, of the Arc de triomphe, of the chapel in Sceaux, and so on." He underscored these attributions by including buildings designed by Claude among the engravings on optics and mechanics in a collection of prints describing the arts.[26]

A controversy had in fact broken out in 1693, when the architect François d'Orbay disputed Claude's role in the creation of the Louvre's façade. D'Orbay argued that he and Louis Le Vau, who indeed collaborated with Claude on this project, were its real authors. Charles stated that he possessed strong proof that would refute such rumors. Such proofs presumably appeared in the collection of Claude's designs that Charles was preparing.[27] Unfortunately, Charles never dared to publish the collection, which would no doubt have revealed Colbert's clandestine machinations. In this decision he personified the essential tension between publication and disclosure, which characterized the relations between men of letters and the monarchy.[28]

In addition to policing his brothers' reputations, Charles made sure that his readers knew about the family's many talents. While building on the general trope of precocious childhood, he did not simply rehearse it in broad strokes.[29] For example, describing his own ability as a writer of verse, he wrote, "It is very true that this is a natural talent, evident since childhood."[30] In a similar manner, Charles defended Claude's credentials as a founding member of the Parisian Academy of Sciences, calling him "as talented as ten others."[31] Innate talent was an important consideration, as Claude did not have any formal training or much experience with natural history or natural philosophy prior to his appointment to the academy.

Charles also addressed the blemishes on his brothers' reputations, from Pierre's disgrace (as we have seen in chapter 4) to associations with Jansenism. He presented an intricate interpretation of Nicolas's relations with Jansenism. While the movement's champions professed unwavering doctrinal submission to the Catholic Church, many of their practices were viewed with anxiety by the temporal authorities, and Cornelius Jansenius, the father of the movement, had written the anti-French *Mars Gallicus* (1635). Louis XIV often mentioned how damaging Jansenists were—to the polity as well as to religion—because of the spirit of independence they spread.[32]

So Charles stressed the purely intellectual connection Nicolas had with the Jansenists. The defense of Arnauld Nicolas had mounted at the Sorbonne in 1655, emphasizing his religious orthodoxy, could have been seen as a link between the two, but Charles insisted that Nicolas had never exchanged a word with Arnauld. Nicolas liked to think that his opinions were the product of divine inspiration rather than of personal relations.[33] In other words, Charles wrote in order to reinterpret his brother's position in the social world, separating for future generations Nicolas's literary and intellectual connections to Jansenism from the political risks inherent in association with Port Royal.

As a member of a family of letters, Charles could not overlook how posterity would treat his deceased siblings. From the late 1690s to 1703 Charles shaped the family's reputation even as his children were struggling to establish themselves at court, using literature as a mere stepping-stone.

In early modern Europe, kinship served as a "'total' social phenomenon," to borrow a term from anthropologist Marcel Mauss, through which "all kinds of institutions are given expression at one and the same time."[34] This is why the Perraults offer a dazzling view of the changing social and cultural landscape of early modern France. Initially focused on social reproduction in the judicial milieu, the Perraults' strategy shifted to office holding and finance,

with Pierre's career coming to the foreground. However, as the political climate changed, Pierre's disgrace meant that the life of letters came to occupy
a central role for the family, with Charles and Claude holding office under
Colbert in the Petite académie, the Académie française, and the Parisian Academy of Sciences. Only after Colbert's death did Charles begin to publish as
a professional author, and later still he assumed the role of the Perraults'
reputational guardian.

The family provided the Perraults with a common name and an identity
familiar to their contemporaries. To refer to one often meant referring to his
brothers and to what contemporaries saw as a "house." This explains why
the Perraults' literary reputations could not be neatly separated and why
Charles expended considerable effort defending the standing of his family.
His reputation was ultimately dependent on the reputation of his brothers,
not least because of the objective overlap in their preoccupations and commitments. An intellectual feedback process was at work for this generation.
As one brother after the other became identified with a specific cause, their
commitments deepened. This would explain why Charles had to characterize Nicolas's support of Jansenism so carefully in his *Mémoires*. The family
strategy of the Perraults yoked the fates of four brothers together as the family's center of gravity moved from the parish of Saint-Etienne-du-Mont to
the fashionable districts of midcentury Paris. In contrast to the situation of
authors who collaborated with each other on an ad hoc basis, the duration of
the relations among the Perraults meant that they were always at least loosely
bound together. The bounded nature of these relations ultimately means that
the entire notion of an individual "career" for early modern men of letters
needs to be reconsidered.

The prominence of kinship in early modern culture means that its functions varied in interaction with a broad range of social institutions; its
importance cannot be reduced to the scale of the household or domestic
space.[35] So rather than starting, as is usual, from the formal definitions of
groupings such as academies or salons and asking how these definitions
structured the literary or scientific work done under their aegis, I started
with the Perraults and then asked how they drew on their connections with
these institutions. This question, in turn, allowed us to see what effects
membership in these institutions had on the Perraults' works. Clearly it had
an important function as a marker of status even when no perceptible relation existed between the institution and the works. As was saw in chapter 1,
Claude was consistently identified as a member of the Faculty of Medicine,
which took pride in his architectural achievements, although these were
unrelated to his training as a doctor.

Institutions are often viewed as providing strict models of conduct for their members, and the academies of the seventeenth century were supposed to impose "monastic and courtly codes of dullness" on their members.[36] Rather than subjugating their creative projects to these models, the Perraults drew on institutions for their own goals through the use of the written word. While politeness and civility have been attributed to the influence of salons and the court, radiating from Paris and Versailles throughout Europe, chapters 3 and 5 show that the Perraults themselves generated images of literary sociability, or of Versailles itself, in relation to their family strategy.

While the court was a center of power and court capitalism an important context for understanding what writers did, the social import of the court was realized in the context of the dynamic society of Paris. The court integrated the economy of office holding with networks surrounding the ministers, powerful courtiers, and dignitaries of the royal household. This was as true of Charles's career as it was of his children's, who sought positions directly at the court.

Family strategies are based on choices of family members but also on their reactions to changing circumstances. Planning is meaningful when it is oriented toward socially significant paths for success: even opportunities have a structure. So changing relations between the court and Parisian society recast the paths available to the Perraults, in terms of both their positions in the services of grandees and their office holding. Chapters 2 and 4 demonstrate how the monarchy's thirst for cash created paths of mobility for officeholders and opportunities to speculate on tax revenues and loans to the king. There was no sharp break between these economic opportunities and the writing careers pursued by the Perraults. Just as Charles's literary career started while advancing Pierre's career as a financier, Charles's service to Colbert furthered Claude's career and probably motivated Pierre's literary and philosophical endeavors. Pierre's literary criticism and his work on springs put him in a position to benefit from Charles's new status in the world of letters after Pierre was forced to sell his office, plunging into debt. Literary scholars and intellectual historians will appreciate how this case connects studies of court capitalism to literary careers, adding capitalism to the usual focus on the court as a cultural institution. Social and economic historians will appreciate the very real impact the life of letters had on social networks and economic fortunes, adding the court to their usual interest in capitalism.

At a broader level, I have tried to convey the importance of studying the cultural and intellectual institutions of seventeenth-century Paris as nodes in the intersection of numerous networks and not as clearly defined bodies creating a sense of autonomy for science and literature. Claude's work on the mechanics of animals is an illuminating example. It shows the benefits of examining the projects of the Academy of Sciences as a result not of the professionalization of science but of networks of many sorts, not least family networks and the skills and professional training not addressed by this formal institution. Other studies have claimed that the transition between private patronage and formal academies was not a neat or orderly process.[37] Through an examination of the networks that underwrote patronage systems and royal institutions, this book has begun to show why this was so.

Claude's achievement in the Parisian Academy of Sciences shows that at that time intellectual projects did not necessarily arise from a unified habitus or a monolithic persona. We need not fall back, though, on the familiar device of labeling early modern writers and scholars polymaths. Rather, we can trace the particular traits of intellectual works to the encounter between different sets of skills, acquired through immersion in a potentially wide range of contexts. For example, we have seen that Charles began to cultivate a fashionable literary style while working as Pierre's aide, and that skill proved useful in his service to Colbert. However, the opportunities opened by his role as an advisor to Colbert allowed him to work on projects that would have been out of his grasp otherwise, from writing descriptions of the gardens of Versailles to work on coins glorifying Louis XIV. This work for Colbert led to Charles's appointment to the Académie française and his participation in the quarrel of the ancients and the moderns.

A tight focus on a specific set of social actors reveals how kinship, patronage, and sociability—key concepts for a range of studies of early modern Europe—worked in practice. We may need to consider refining how we think of such concepts. Patronage is most illuminating in this sense. Whereas Sharon Kettering has presented patronage and kinship as diametrically opposed logics—the former an "informal, voluntary, often impermanent relationship between participants who were unequal in status," the latter an involuntary relation based on birth, between people of similar status and related by formal blood ties—the Perraults show how kinship and patronage readily interacted.[38]

A brief look at a few examples establishes the wide range of phenomena covered by the concept of patronage. The Perraults certainly served Colbert, but they also acted as local patrons in their parish (chapter 2). In addition, Charles patronized artists working on the Royal Building projects (chapter 4). Claude built his reputation on his translation of Vitruvius, a work dedicated to Louis XIV (chapter 1). While all these forms of patronage conform to Kettering's definition, each one of them differs considerably from the others and deviates from contemporaries' descriptions of the Perraults' relation to Colbert.

In each case, the networks were activated in a different context. In the first case, physical proximity in a tightly knit quarter connected the Perraults to clients in their parish. In the second case, Charles served as a patron thanks to his position in the Royal Buildings. The third case represents a classic form of literary patronage. Scrutinizing the formal and informal networks that constituted patronage relations does much to differentiate types of patronage and the way they happened in practice. Since patronage was a multifaceted phenomenon, only by teasing out its different forms rather than subsuming them under a broad umbrella term can we understand its functioning in early modern society.

For the Perraults, kinship may have been as influential in their careers as patronage. Charles's career provides the clearest evidence. The link between Charles and Colbert ensured his appointment to the Petite académie and transformed his literary career as well as his social networks. Yet there were limits to this relation, from Charles's inability to help Pierre after his disgrace to the way Charles's career revolved around alternatives to ministerial patronage after the early 1680s. Often Charles turned to his family for guidance, from his entry to the world of letters through his uses of Versailles to his probable role in facilitating Claude's appointment to the Academy of Sciences. In other words, even in the extreme case of Charles's service to Colbert, kinship still provided a structuring element.

An analysis in terms of family strategy underscores the interactions between the Perraults' individual histories and the changing paths they could take. And the Perraults certainly reacted to changes of differing dynamics. They were influenced both by linear changes related to political developments and by cyclical changes related to the circulation of power cliques at the highest echelons of the monarchy. The Perraults arrived at Paris at an inopportune moment for socially ambitious families. They found themselves in the trough between two significant shifts in the ranks of office-holding families, the first in the late sixteenth century and the second in the middle decades of the seventeenth. The first consisted of families such as the Séguiers, Harlays, and de Thous; they came to the capital from Tours (like the Perraults) or Orléans in the early decades of the sixteenth century.[39] These families achieved notable status in municipal offices and in the Paris Parlement. In the 1590s, after Henri IV famously "pacified the kingdom" and established the Bourbon dynasty, these families aligned themselves with the new dynasty and rose to prominent positions. Pierre Séguier, for example, served as chancellor for four decades before his death in 1672.

While the Perraults arrived in Paris too late to achieve the splendid success of these "great servants of state," as Denis Richet called them, they were also, at first, too early to align themselves with Colbert. That future statesman entered the world of finance in the 1630s and quickly developed a network of supportive relatives and friends. In the 1660s Colbert reorganized the financial council by assigning places to the members of that network. Once Pierre forfeited his post, the office went to a member of this clan—evidently Colbert was just cleaning house, and Pierre was merely a casualty of a new clique.[40]

The paramount importance of timing explains why Charles was involved mainly with cultural matters during his time in the kings' buildings. He and Colbert were simply never close enough to collaborate on other issues; that was why the minister could turn a deaf ear to appeals regarding Pierre. Acting on such appeals would have lessened his commitment to his own network of relatives and associates. In other words, the fortunes of the Perraults were shaped by the cycle of rising and declining family networks and cliques, a cycle on which the monarchy itself was dependent.

In addition, the family's trajectory intersected with a range of cultural, scientific, and intellectual developments, each with its own unique logic. And here, too, linear processes combined with developments that had a different form and rhythm, and all fed into the available strategies at any given moment. For example, new royal academies offered the Perraults unprecedented opportunities to engage in intellectual projects. The quarrel of the ancients and the moderns, to take a less concrete example, ran its course rather steadily in seventeenth-century France, with occasional salvos exchanged. It was Charles's intervention toward the end of the century that permanently improved his visibility in the world of letters. Other processes of intellectual change had such a wide sweep that they cannot explain the particular choices made by the Perraults. The rise of mechanical principles as part of the new philosophy is particularly instructive. Claude certainly drew on these principles, but his unique combination of skills made possible *Of the Mechanics of Animals*. Viewing such sweeping changes in terms of changing strategies and shifting networks allows for connecting disparate phenomena with each other and, perhaps more important, with the ambitions of the actors that made them as they reacted to their changing environment.

An examination of the strategies at play in the seventeenth century reveals the different logics of social distinction and intellectual choices. Rather than tracing all forms of dignity back to the king, as the fount of an orderly social hierarchy, the Perraults could seek notability through finance, through the creation of a circle of rural sociability, and through literary and scientific careers. This was a complex world, and reducing it to the values of a "culture of absolutism" or the logic of a "courtly society" eliminates much of that complexity.[41] On the other hand, simply claiming that these phenomena were complex would not add much to our understanding: we need ways to articulate the specific dynamics that underwrote the changes of the seventeenth century. Networks shaped by family strategies offer a way out of the fuzziness of broad notions of culture and the contingent particularities of social and political dynamics, for several reasons. The family was highly valued by contemporaries, it bridged formal and informal institutions, and it was not fleeting—family strategies unfolded over decades, sometimes even centuries, as in the case of the Godefroy family studied by Caroline Sherman.[42]

Although informal networks were crucial in the early modern period, in the long run the formal institutions won. We can view Charles Perrault as a literary author or Claude Perrault as a scientist since the institutions to which they belonged are still with us. The images of science and letters created during that period effectively rewrote personal networks out of the picture, in spite of the importance of such networks to the authors the institutions enshrine. Versailles, very much present today as a museum, diverts our gaze from the connections that made possible the construction of the palace and the propagation of its image.

This makes it easier for us to see early modern authors as the vanguard in a process of individualization: their signatures, self-images, and institutional roles combined to portray them as almost free-floating individuals. Indeed, the Perraults took an active part in this process, with Charles describing the gifts of genius as a special "heat" or a "divine flame" in the soul that effortlessly lights the "obscure night in which secretive nature hides from us."[43] This language, which seems to prefigure Romantic notions of the author as a lonely and heroic genius, emerged, however, in the framework of the family networks that made Charles Perrault into a putatively unique talent.

In my mind, family strategies help to explain the specific dynamics of the seventeenth century, particularly the relations among individuals, kinship, and cultural change. Indeed, we still live in a world of Kennedys, Clintons, and Bushes; of Francis Ford, Sofia, and Roman Coppolas. Our intellectual world has families like the Mertons, whose Robert K. developed the sociology of science into a mature intellectual pursuit, while his son, Robert C., became a Nobel laureate in economics for a model that made the trade in financial derivatives possible. If we choose to look at the early twentieth century, we will encounter Sigmund, Anna, and Lucian Freud, recalling the relations between intellectual and artistic projects that we saw in the Perrault family. Kinship networks are still with us. But they are embedded in a different social, cultural, and institutional landscape. A Kennedy, a Coppola, and a Merton had to deal with mass media and politics; with the rise of the university as the central locus of intellectual life; with the emergence of the social sciences as a distinct field of inquiry; and, most important for kinship, with different understandings of public and private spheres. The transformations of the seventeenth century, in contrast, related to the venality of office, to royal finance and its relation to political elites, to the cultural model of the academy, and to the reaction to Cartesian philosophy. Only when we go beyond the household and properly note these differences does the intellectual family resume its place at the heart of the cultural and intellectual revolution of early modern France.

🍎 APPENDIX

Family Trees

Note: when known, the years of birth and death, offices, or titles for family members are listed on the page following each family tree.

Family Tree 1: Pierre and Pacquette

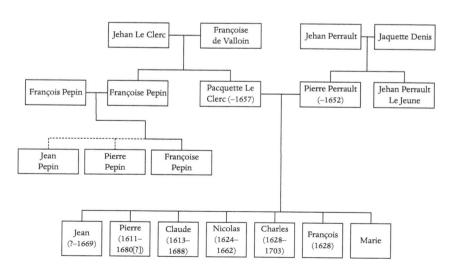

Jehan Perrault, brodeur du roi, Tours

Jacquette Denis

Pierre Perrault (?–1652), avocat, Paris

Jehan Perrault le jeune, brodeur du roi, Tours

Pacquette Le Clerc (?–1657)

Jehan Le Clerc, printer?

Françoise de Valloin

Françoise Pepin (elder)

François Pepin, royal councillor

Françoise Pepin (younger)

Pierre Pepin, noble homme; conseiller du roi et élu en l'élection de Paris

Jean Pepin, écuyer conseiller, secrétaire du roi

Jean Perrault (?–1669), avocat

Pierre Perrault (1611–80 [?]), receveur général, author of two pieces
of literary critique (on *Don Quixote* and *Alceste*), which remained in
manuscript form, and of a treatise "on the origins of fountains"

Claude Perrault (1613–88), doctor of medicine, architect, translator of
Vitruvius and author of a treatise on architecture, founding member
of the Académie Royale des Sciences, in charge of the zoological
dissection project, author of a four-volume treatise on "physics"

Nicolas Perrault (1624–62), doctor of theology at the Sorbonne, defended
Antoine Arnauld during the Jansenist controversy, author of a polemical
anti-Jesuit work

Charles Perrault (1628–1703), literary author, member of the Académie
française and the Petite Académie, commis des bâtiments under
Colbert

François Perrault (1628), Charles's twin brother, died at the age of six
months

Marie Perrault (died at the age of thirteen)

Family Tree 2: Charles and Marie

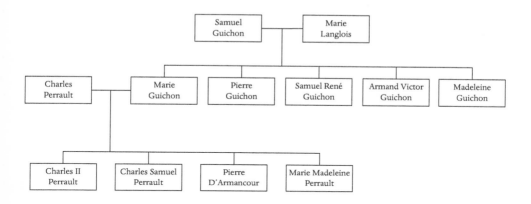

Samuel Guichon, Seigneur de Rozieres et Vilaines, conseiller du roi
   receveur, et payeur des rentes de l'hôtel de ville de Paris assignée sur
   les cinq grosses fermes

Marie Langlois

Marie Guichon (1653–1678)

Pierre Guichon, écuyer conseiller du roi, trésorier général de fortifications
   de France (1685), sieur de Rozieres et Villaine (later documents)

Samuel René Guichon, prestre, chanoine de l'église cathédrale de Verdun

Armand Victor Guichon, prieur commanditaire de prieuré de Saint Ayoul
   de Provins et de saint Serin de la Selle (1685), chanoine de l'église de
   Paris (1703)

Madeleine Guichon

Charles-Samuel Perrault (1675–c. 1729), écuyer of the Duchesse de Bourgogne

Charles Perrault

Pierre d'Armancour (1678–1700), lieutenant in the Régiment Dauphin

Marie-Madeleine Perrault (1674–1701)

Family Tree 3: Pierre and Catherine

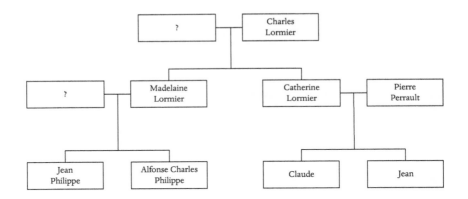

Catherine Lormier

Charles Lormier, conseiller, Cour des aides

Claude Perrault (1658–?)

Jean Perrault (1661–?)

Madeleine Lormier, Catherine Lormier's sister, involved in finance

Jean Philippe, avocat en Parlement

Alfonse Charles Philippe, sieur de la Buissonnière

For more details on the Lormier family, see Bennini, *Conseillers*.

❧ Notes

Introduction

1. Bruno Bettelheim, *The Uses of Enchantment: The Meaning and Importance of Fairy Tales* (New York: Vintage, 1989), 236.

2. Bettelheim noted, while discussing the division of Cinderella-type stories into two groups—father or mother as antagonist—that in the second "mother and daughters are so closely identified with each other that one gets the feeling that they are one unit split into different groups." Ibid., 248.

3. Charles Perrault, *Les Contes de Perrault dans tous leurs états*, ed. Annie Collognat and Marie-Charlotte Delmas (Paris: Omnibus, 2007), 721.

4. Ibid., 724.

5. Ibid., 727–28.

6. David Warren Sabean and Simon Teuscher, "Kinship in Europe: A New Approach to Long Term Development," in *Kinship in Europe: Approaches to Long-Term Development (1300–1900)*, ed. David Warren Sabean, Simon Teuscher, and Jon Mathieu (New York: Berghahn, 2007), 1.

7. On the need for such an approach, see Robert A. Schneider, "Political Power and the Emergence of Literature: Christian Jouhaud's Age of Richelieu," *French Historical Studies* 25, no. 2 (2002): 357–58. To borrow a definition discussed by William Sewell, I use "culture" as the "institutional sphere devoted to the making of meaning." This is a highly structured symbolic meaning, bringing together literature, science, architecture, and poetry. This definition clearly draws on the concept of culture as "high culture," but I do not wish to attribute any sense of superiority to the texts and practices I study. While Sewell sees the narrow range of meanings covered by this concept as a problem, I would like to claim that it has an enormous practical advantage: it allows us to work on a clearly defined and highly delineated corpus of objects and to avoid seeing culture as a homogeneous whole, or a broad and undifferentiated set of normative conceptions. William H. Sewell, "The Concept(s) of Culture," in *Logics of History: Social Theory and Social Transformation* (Chicago: University of Chicago Press, 2005), 158–59.

8. Brad S. Gregory, "Is Small Beautiful? Microhistory and the History of Everyday Life," *History and Theory* 38, no. 1 (1999): 100–110.

9. No major biographical study has appeared on the Perraults in the past thirty years. I am much indebted to the previous work by Paul Bonnefon, who edited numerous texts by the Perraults in the late nineteenth and early twentieth centuries (see bibliography); and more recently, to Marc Soriano, *Le Dossier Perrault* (Paris: Hachette, 1972); Jean-Luc Gautier, "Charles Perrault, premières œuvres, 1649–1675" (Thèse de doctorat, Paris-X, 1978); Jacques Barchilon and Peter Flinders, *Charles Perrault* (Boston:

Twayne Publishers, 1981); Antoine Picon, *Claude Perrault, 1613–1688, ou, la curiosité d'un classique* (Paris: Picard, 1988).

10. These problems can stem from the conflation of institutions as formal organizations (as a type of collective actor) with institutions as socially recognized ways of doing things. See Florence Hsia, "Mathematical Martyrs, Mandarin Missionaries, and Apostolic Academicians: Telling Institutional Lives," in *Institutional Culture in Early Modern Society*, ed. Anne Goldgar and Robert I. Frost (Leiden: Brill, 2004), 12, and the preceding historiographical discussion; Jon Elster, *Explaining Social Behavior: More Nuts and Bolts for the Social Sciences* (Cambridge: Cambridge University Press, 2007), 427–28.

11. A. N. Whitehead, *Science and the Modern World* (New York: Free Press, 1967), chap. 3.

12. See the different overviews in John Martin, "Inventing Sincerity, Refashioning Prudence: The Discovery of the Individual in Renaissance Europe," *American Historical Review* 102, no. 5 (1997): 1309–42; Geoff Baldwin, "Individual and Self in the Late Renaissance," *Historical Journal* 44, no. 2 (2001): 341–64; Moshe Sluhovsky, "Discernment of Difference, the Introspective Subject, and the Birth of Modernity," *Journal of Medieval & Early Modern Studies* 36, no. 1 (2006): 169–99; Gregory S. Brown, "Am 'I' a 'Post-Revolutionary Self'? Historiography of the Self in the Age of Enlightenment and Revolution," *History and Theory* 47, no. 2 (2008): 229–48.

13. Darrin M. McMahon, *Divine Fury: A History of Genius* (New York: Basic Books, 2013); Charly Coleman, *The Virtues of Abandon: An Anti-Individualist History of the French Enlightenment* (Stanford: Stanford University Press, 2014).

14. This approach, and much else in this book, is indebted to the argument on the autonomy of authors vis-à-vis political power in Christian Jouhaud, *Les pouvoirs de la littérature: Histoire d'un paradoxe* (Paris: Gallimard, 2000).

15. Claire Dolan, "Anachronisms or Failures? Family Strategies in the Sixteenth Century, as Drawn from Collective Biographies of Solicitors in Aix-En-Provence," *Journal of Family History* 33, no. 3 (2008): 291–303; Leslie Page Moch et al., "Family Strategy: A Dialogue," *Historical Methods* 20, no. 3 (1987): 113–25; Pier Paolo Viazzo and Katherine A. Lynch, "Anthropology, Family History, and the Concept of Strategy," *International Review of Social History* 47, no. 3 (2002): 423–52.

16. There is no doubt that in the early modern period, families, at least those above utter poverty, did engage in conscious planning of their collective future. Natalie Zemon Davis, "Ghosts, Kin, and Progeny: Some Features of Family Life in Early Modern France," *Daedalus* 106, no. 2 (1977): 87–114; Christophe Duhamelle, "The Making of Stability: Kinship, Church, and Power among the Rhenish Imperial Knighthood, Seventeenth and Eighteenth Centuries," in Sabean, Teuscher, and Mathieu, *Kinship in Europe*, 125–44.

17. Michel de Certeau, *The Practice of Everyday Life* (Berkeley: University of California Press, 1984), 34–42, esp. 37. See also Certeau's discussion of Bourdieu's concept of strategy on 52–56.

18. Caroline R. Sherman, "The Genealogy of Knowledge: The Godefroy Family, Erudition, and Legal-Historical Service to the State" (PhD diss., Princeton University, 2008), 5; Caroline R. Sherman, "The Ancestral Library as an Immortal Educator," *Proceedings of the Western Society for French History* 35 (2007): 41–54.

19. For the broad hypotheses, see Gadi Algazi, "Scholars in Households: Refiguring the Learned Habitus, 1480–1550," *Science in Context* 16, no. 1–2 (2003): 9–42; "Eine gelernte Lebensweise: Figurationen des Gelehrtenlebens zwischen Mittelalter

und Früher Neuzeit," *Berichte zur Wissenschaftsgeschichte* 30 (2007): 107–18, and other works by Algazi listed in the bibliography.

20. Alix Cooper, "Homes and Households," in *The Cambridge History of Science*, vol. 3, *Early Modern Science*, ed. Katharine Park and Lorraine Daston (Cambridge: Cambridge University Press, 2006), 224–37; Cooper, "Picturing Nature: Gender and the Politics of Natural-Historical Description in Eighteenth-Century Gdańsk/Danzig," *Journal for Eighteenth-Century Studies* 36, no. 4 (2013): 519–29.

21. Deborah Harkness, "Managing an Experimental Household: The Dees of Mortlake and the Practice of Natural Philosophy," *Isis* 88, no. 2 (1997): 247–62. See also her "Maps, Spiders, and Tulips: The Cole-Ortelius-L'Obel Family and the Practice of Science in Early Modern London," in *From Strangers to Citizens: The Integration of Immigrant Communities in Britain, Ireland, and Colonial America, 1550–1750*, ed. Randolph Vigne and Charles Littleton (London: Huguenot Society of Great Britain and Ireland and Sussex Academic Press, 2001), 184–96.

22. Paula Findlen, "Masculine Prerogatives: Gender, Space, and Knowledge in the Early Modern Museum," in *The Architecture of Science*, ed. Peter Galison and Emily Thompson (Cambridge, MA: MIT Press, 1999), 37.

23. Sarah Gwyneth Ross, *The Birth of Feminism: Woman as Intellect in Renaissance Italy and England* (Cambridge, MA: Harvard University Press, 2009).

24. Meghan K. Roberts, *Sentimental Savants: Philosophical Families in Enlightenment France* (Chicago: University of Chicago Press, 2016).

25. Dániel Margócsy, *Commercial Visions: Science, Trade, and Visual Culture in the Dutch Golden Age* (Chicago: University of Chicago Press, 2014).

26. Katherine A. Lynch, "The Family and the History of Public Life," *Journal of Interdisciplinary History* 24, no. 4 (1994): 665–84.

27. But see Paula Findlen, "Ereditare un museo. Collezionismo, strategie familiari e pratiche culturali nell'Italia del XVI secolo," *Quaderni Storici* 115, no. 1 (2004): 45–81. In thinking on the family and the limits of institutions, I have found extremely helpful Sabina Loriga, *Soldats: Un laboratoire disciplinaire: L'Armée piémontaise au XVIIIᵉ siècle*, 2nd ed. (Paris: Belles Lettres, 2007).

28. Paul-André Rosental, "Les liens familiaux, forme historique?," *Annales de démographie historique* 100, no. 2 (2000): 49–81.

29. Sarah Hanley, "Engendering the State: Family Formation and State Building in Early Modern France," *French Historical Studies* 16, no. 1 (1989): 4–27; for Colbert's explicitly pronatalist policies, see Leslie Tuttle, *Conceiving the Old Regime: Pronatalism and the Politics of Reproduction in Early Modern France* (New York: Oxford University Press, 2010); Suzanne Desan and Jeffrey Merrick, introduction to *Family, Gender, and Law in Early Modern France*, ed. Suzanne Desan and Jeffrey Merrick (University Park: Penn State University Press, 2009), xii–xxvi.

30. David Warren Sabean, *Kinship in Neckarhausen, 1700–1870* (Cambridge: Cambridge University Press, 1998), 6, 398–99.

31. Sabean and Teuscher, "Kinship in Europe," esp. 14–15; and paraphrasing Gadi Algazi, "Bringing Kinship (Back) In," *Mediterranean Historical Review* 25, no. 1 (2010): 86; Mario Biagioli, "Plagiarism, Kinship, and Slavery," *Theory, Culture & Society* 31, no. 2–3 (2014): 65–91. On the uses of kinship terminology in scholarly context, see Carol Pal, *Republic of Women: Rethinking the Republic of Letters in the Seventeenth Century* (Cambridge: Cambridge University Press, 2012), 78–109; Françoise Waquet, *Les*

Enfants de Socrate: Filiation intellectuelle et transmission du savoir, XVIIᵉ–XXIᵉ siècle (Paris: Albin Michel, 2008), 77–81, 169–203.

32. Peter N. Miller, *Peiresc's Europe: Learning and Virtue in the Seventeenth Century* (New Haven: Yale University Press, 2000), 2.

33. For a summary, see Oded Rabinovitch, "Rethinking the Center-Periphery Nexus in the Early Modern Period: The Paris-Province Relation in Villiers's *Entretiens sur les contes de fées,*" *Proceedings of the Western Society for French History* 38 (2010): 63–65.

34. See the starting points in Andrew Trout, *City on the Seine: Paris in the Time of Richelieu and Louis XIV* (New York: St. Martin's, 1996); Orest A. Ranum, *Paris in the Age of Absolutism: An Essay,* rev. and expanded ed. (University Park: Penn State University Press, 2002); Colin Jones, *Paris: Biography of a City* (New York: Viking, 2005).

35. Pierre Bourdieu, *The Rules of Art: Genesis and Structure of the Literary Field* (Stanford: Stanford University Press, 1996).

36. See, even in a modern and hence post-Romantic context, Casper Andersen, Jakob Bek-Thomsen, and Peter C. Kjærgaard, "The Money Trail: A New Historiography for Networks, Patronage, and Scientific Careers," *Isis* 103, no. 2 (2012): 310–15.

37. My work builds on approaches that highlight the social impact of practices of writing and the social role of men of letters in French society. In this world, even "publication" was understood to publish the reputation of the author as well as the circulation of texts. See Christian Jouhaud and Alain Viala, eds., *De la publication: Entre Renaissance et Lumières* (Paris: Fayard, 2002); Grihl, *Écriture et action: XVIIᵉ–XIXᵉ siècle, une enquête collective* (Paris: Éditions de l'École des hautes études en sciences sociales, 2016), and the references to works by Jouhaud, Schapira, Ribard, and Viala in the bibliography.

38. For an overview, see Élie Haddad, "Noble Clienteles in France in the Sixteenth and Seventeenth Centuries: A Historiographical Approach," *French History* 20, no. 1 (2006): 75–109, and in the literary context, Peter Shoemaker, *Powerful Connections: The Poetics of Patronage in the Age of Louis XIII* (Newark: University of Delaware Press, 2007); Katia Béguin, *Les Princes de Condé: Rebelles, courtisans et mécènes dans la France du Grand Siècle* (Seyssel: Champ Vallon, 1999).

39. James B. Collins, *The State in Early Modern France,* 2nd ed. (Cambridge: Cambridge University Press, 2009), esp. 75–82, 146–50.

40. Alain Génetiot, *Le Classicisme* (Paris: PUF, 2005), 79.

41. For basic works, see Roger Hahn, *The Anatomy of a Scientific Institution: The Paris Academy of Sciences, 1666–1803* (Berkeley: University of California Press, 1971); Alice Stroup, *A Company of Scientists: Botany, Patronage, and Community at the Seventeenth-Century Parisian Royal Academy of Sciences* (Berkeley: University of California Press, 1990); D. J. Sturdy, *Science and Social Status: The Members of the Académie des Sciences 1666–1750* (Woodbridge, UK: Boydell Press, 1995).

42. See chap. 3. For the broad framework for these studies, see Marc Fumaroli, *L'âge de l'éloquence: Rhétorique et "res literaria" de la Renaissance au seuil de l'époque classique* (Paris: A. Michel, 1994); Fumaroli, *Trois institutions littéraires* (Paris: Gallimard, 1994); Carolyn C. Lougee, *Le paradis des femmes: Women, Salons, and Social Stratification in Seventeenth-Century France* (Princeton: Princeton University Press, 1976).

43. See the discussion in chapter 5. For an example of a study stressing the court as a source of taste and inspiration, see Jean-François Solnon, *La Cour de France* (Paris: Fayard, 1987), 373–417.

44. See, among many possible references, Pierre Bourdieu, "Le champ littéraire," *Actes de la recherche en sciences socials* 89 (1991): 3–46, and *Rules of Art*, esp. chap. 3 "The Market for Symbolic Goods."

45. Alain Viala, *Naissance de l'écrivain: Sociologie de la littérature à l'âge classique* (Paris: Minuit, 1985); Jean-Philippe Genet, "La mesure et les champs culturels," *Histoire & Mesure* 2, no. 1 (1987): 137–53; Christian Jouhaud, "Histoire et histoire littéraire: Naissance de l'écrivain," *Annales: E.S.C.* 43, no. 4 (1988), 849–66; and see chap. 3.

46. For a clear exposition, see Charles Wetherell, "Historical Social Network Analysis," supplement, *International Review of Social History* 43 (1998): 126–27, on which I rely in this paragraph; Mustafa Emirbayer and Jeff Goodwin, "Network Analysis, Culture, and the Problem of Agency," *American Journal of Sociology* 99, no. 6 (1994): 1411–54; Claire Lemercier, "Analyse de réseaux et histoire de la famille: Une rencontre encore à venir?," *Annales de démographie historique* 109, no. 1 (2005): 7–31. At its roots, network analysis drew on urban anthropology and did not stress the formal modeling common today. See, for example, Elizabeth Bott, *Family and Social Network: Roles, Norms, and External Relationships in Ordinary Urban Families*, 2nd ed. (New York: Free Press, 1971).

47. John Mohr and Harrison White, "How to Model an Institution," *Theory and Society* 37, no. 5 (2008): 485–512.

48. Giulia Calvi and Carolina Blutrach-Jelín, "Sibling Relations in Family History: Conflicts, Co-Operation and Gender Roles in the Sixteenth to Nineteenth Centuries. An Introduction," *European Review of History/Revue europeenne d'histoire* 17, no. 5 (2010): 695–704; Christopher H. Johnson and David Warren Sabean, eds., *Sibling Relations and the Transformations of European Kinship, 1300–1900* (New York: Berghahn, 2011).

49. E.g., Michael Bennett, "Note-Taking and Data-Sharing: Edward Jenner and the Global Vaccination Network," *Intellectual History Review* 20, no. 3 (2010): 415–32, and the critical discussion in Peter Dear, "Historiography of Not-So-Recent Science," *History of Science* 50, no. 2 (2012): 203–5.

50. Beyond Emirbayer and Goodwin, "Network Analysis," see the classic John F. Padgett and Christopher K. Ansell, "Robust Action and the Rise of the Medici, 1400–1434," *American Journal of Sociology* 98, no. 6 (1993): 1259–1319.

51. On the need to differentiate uses of different types of kin and acquaintances, see Wetherell, "Historical Social Network Analysis," 142–43.

52. Kristen Neuschel, *Word of Honor: Interpreting Noble Culture in Sixteenth-Century France* (Ithaca: Cornell University Press, 1989), 23.

53. Claude Lévi-Strauss, *The View from Afar* (New York: Basic Books, 1985), chap. 3, esp. 44; see further the discussion in Élie Haddad, *Fondation et ruine d'une maison: Histoire sociale des comtes de Belin, 1582–1706* (Limoges: Presses universitaires de Limoges, 2009), esp. 137–46; Jonathan Dewald, *Status, Power, and Identity in Early Modern France: The Rohan Family, 1550–1715* (University Park: Penn State University Press, 2015), and for a slightly later period, Christopher H. Johnson, *Becoming Bourgeois: Love, Kinship, and Power in Provincial France, 1670–1880* (Ithaca: Cornell University Press, 2015).

1. Representing a Family of Letters

1. Perrault, *Contes*, 587–91.

2. BN, MS, Cabinet d'Hozier, 266.

3. Adrien Baillet, *Jugemens des savans sur les principaux ouvrages des auteurs* (Paris: Charles Moette, Charles le Clerc, Pierre Morisset, Pierre Prault, Jacques Chardon, 1722), 5:499 (original edition 1685–86).

4. For important signposts and overviews, see Christine Haynes, "Reassessing 'Genius' in Studies of Authorship," *Book History* 8 (2005): 287–320; Geoffrey Turnovsky, *The Literary Market: Authorship and Modernity in the Old Regime* (Philadelphia: University of Pennsylvania Press, 2010); Martha Woodmansee, "The Genius and the Copyright: Economic and Legal Conditions of the Emergence of the 'Author,'" *Eighteenth-Century Studies* 17, no. 4 (1984): 425–48; Adrian Johns, *The Nature of the Book: Print and Knowledge in the Making* (Chicago: University of Chicago Press, 1998).

5. This contrasts with the notion that in Europe, family members "participated as individuals in the public sphere." Jan de Vries, *The Industrious Revolution: Consumer Behavior and the Household Economy, 1650 to the Present* (Cambridge: Cambridge University Press, 2008), 19.

6. Michel Foucault, "What Is an Author?," in *Language, Counter-Memory, Practice: Selected Essays and Interviews*, ed. Donald F. Bouchard (Ithaca: Cornell University Press, 1977), 113–38; Roger Chartier, "Foucault's Chiasmus: Authorship between Science and Literature in the Seventeenth and Eighteenth Centuries," in *Scientific Authorship: Credit and Intellectual Property in Science*, ed. Mario Biagioli and Peter Galison (New York: Routledge, 2003), 13–31.

7. David Saunders and Ian Hunter, "Lessons from the 'Literary': How to Historicise Authorship," *Critical Inquiry* 17, no. 3 (1991): 482–83.

8. Alain Viala, *La France galante: Essai historique sur une catégorie culturelle, de ses origines jusqu'à la Révolution* (Paris: Presses Universitaires de France, 2008), 170–73.

9. Nick Wilding, *Galileo's Idol: Gianfrancesco Sagredo and the Politics of Knowledge* (Chicago: University of Chicago Press, 2014), 137.

10. Peter N. Miller, "The 'Man of Learning' Defended: Seventeenth-Century Biographies of Scholars and an Early Modern Ideal of Excellence," in *Representations of the Self from the Renaissance to Romanticism*, ed. Patrick Coleman, Jayne Lewis, and Jill Kowalik (Cambridge: Cambridge University Press, 2000), 39–40.

11. Chartier, "Foucault's Chiasmus," 20; Dinah Ribard, *Raconter, vivre, penser: Histoire(s) de philosophes, 1650–1766* (Paris: Éditions de l'École des hautes études en sciences sociales–Vrin, 2003); Jean-Luc Chappey, *Ordres et désordres biographiques: Dictionnaires, listes de noms, réputation des Lumières à Wikipedia* (Seyssel: Champ Vallon, 2013).

12. Anthony Grafton, "The World of the Polyhistors: Humanism and Encyclopedism," in *Bring Out Your Dead: The Past as Revelation* (Cambridge, MA: Harvard University Press, 2001), 166–80; Francine Wild, *Naissance du genre des ana (1574–1712)* (Paris: Honoré Champion, 2001).

13. Maria Lúcia Pallares-Burke, "'The Spectator,' or the Metamorphoses of the Periodical: A Study in Cultural Translation," in *Cultural Translation in Early Modern Europe*, ed. Peter Burke and R. Po-chia Hsia (Cambridge: Cambridge University Press, 2007), 143–46; Jean-Pierre Vittu, "Du *Journal des savants* aux *Mémoires pour l'histoire des sciences et des beaux-arts*: L'esquisse d'un système européen des périodiques savants," *XVIIe siècle* 57 (2005): 527–45.

14. Dewald, *Status, Power, and Identity*, 26–36, 178; Chappey, *Ordres*, 88–91, 101–5; and for a case study based on this dictionary, see Yasushi Noro, "Un littérateur face

aux événements du 17ᵉ siècle: Amable Bourzeis et les événements dans sa biographie" (PhD diss., Université Blaise Pascal—Clermont-Ferrand II, 2006).

15. Baillet, *Jugemens des savans*, 6:284–350; Martin Mulsow, "Practices of Unmasking: Polyhistors, Correspondence, and the Birth of Dictionaries of Pseudonymity in Seventeenth-Century Germany," *Journal of the History of Ideas* 67, no. 2 (2006): 219–50.

16. J. B. Shank, *The Newton Wars and the Beginning of the French Enlightenment* (Chicago: University of Chicago Press, 2008), 165–73; Charles B. Paul, *Science and Immortality: The Éloges of the Paris Academy of Sciences (1699–1791)* (Berkeley: University of California Press, 1980); David A. Bell, *The Cult of the Nation in France: Inventing Nationalism, 1680–1800* (Cambridge, MA: Harvard University Press, 2001), esp. 108–19.

17. Ann Blair, *Too Much to Know: Managing Scholarly Information before the Modern Age* (New Haven: Yale University Press, 2010); Françoise Waquet, "Conserver et transmettre le savoir à l'époque classique," in *Tisser le lien social*, ed. Alain Supiot (Paris: Éditions de la Maison des sciences de l'homme, 2004), 275–85.

18. Estienne Pasquier, "Epigrammata," in *Œuvres d'Estienne Pasquier*...(Amsterdam: Aux depens de la Compagnie des libraires associez, 1723), 1:1125–222; this work was originally published in 1582. On the importance of Diogenes Laertius, see Ribard, *Raconter*, 59–69.

19. Thevet's work was voluminous, with high-quality illustrations, and used Greek and Hebrew type. André Thevet, *Les vrais pourtraits et vies des hommes illustres grecz, latins et payens, recueilliz de leurs tableaux, livres, médalles antiques et modernes* (Paris: La Vesve Kervert et Guillaume Chaudière, 1584).

20. Antoine Teissier, *Éloges des hommes savans, tirez de l'histoire de M. de Thou, avec des additions contenans l'Abrégé de leur vie, le jugement, & le Catalogue de leurs Ouvrages* (Geneva: Jean-Herman Widerhold, 1683).

21. Louis Moréri, *Le grand dictionnaire historique*...(Paris: J. Vincent, 1732 and 1759), s.v. "Perrault, Charles" and "Perrault, Claude" (hereafter cited as Moréri 1732 and Moréri 1759).

22. *Journal des sçavans*, March 10, 1704, 174–76; Abbé Tallemant, "Éloge funèbre de Mr. Perrault," in *Recueil des harangues prononcées par messieurs de l'Académie française dans leurs réceptions, & en d'autres occasions différentes, depuis l'establissement de l'Académie jusqu'à présent* (Amsterdam: Aux dépens de la Compagnie, 1709), 2:591–602; Evrard Titon du Tillet, *Le Parnasse françois, dedié au roi* (Paris: Jean-Baptiste Coignard fils, 1732–34), 496–98.

23. *Journal des sçavans*, February 28, 1669, 80–81; Bernard le Bovier de Fontenelle, eulogy of Claude Perrault, in *Mercure galant* (1688), as reproduced in Fontenelle, *Œuvres completes*, ed. Alain Niderst (Paris: Fayard, 1989), 7:269–72; *Histoire des ouvrages des Savans*, November 1688, 310–14; Charles Perrault, *Les Hommes illustres, avec leurs portraits au naturel*, ed. D. J. Culpin (Tübingen, Ger.: Gunter Narr, 2003), 175–78.

24. See the list of sources, which Culpin has described as partial, in Perrault, *Hommes illustres*, 513–15; Birgit Bernard, "*Les Hommes illustres*: Charles Perraults Kompendium der 100 berühmtesten Männer des 17. Jahrhunderts als Reflex der Colbertschen Wissenschaftspolitik," *Francia* 18, no. 2 (1991): 23–46.

25. Quoted in Robert Descimon, "La vénalité des offices et la construction de l'État dans la France moderne: Des problèmes de la représentation symbolique aux problèmes du coût social du pouvoir," in *Les figures de l'administrateur: Institutions, réseaux, pouvoirs en Espagne, en France, et au Portugal, 16ᵉ–19ᵉ siècle*, ed. Robert

Descimon, Jean-Frédéric Schaub, and Bernard Vincent (Paris: Éditions de l'École des hautes études en sciences sociales, 1997), 78. Descimon further stresses the ambiguities surrounding venal offices while outlining the ideology that supported them.

26. See, for example, Fontenelle's eulogy, in *Œuvres completes*, 7:269–72.

27. Perrault, *Hommes illustres*, 177–78. "Physics" here meant Claude's work on natural history and machines.

28. Dom Clemencet, *Histoire littéraire de Port-Royal*, Bibliothèque Mazarine, MS 4534, 8ᵉ pièce, fol. 1.

29. Charles Perrault also made this claim in his *Mémoires de ma vie*, ed. Antoine Picon (Paris: Macula, 1993), 115–16.

30. William Doyle, *Jansenism: Catholic Resistance to Authority from the Reformation to the French Revolution* (New York: St. Martin's, 2000), 27–28.

31. Two clean copies of this translation survive today in Parisian libraries; I have consulted Mazarine MS 2475, fols. 1–31.

32. AN, MC, LXIX 110, 2 November 1682; AN, MC, C 260, 22 April 22 1660.

33. AN, MC, XCV 49, 22 March 1698.

34. AN, MC, LXXVIII 493, 18 April 18 1702. Amonton was the son of a lawyer from Normandy who had moved to Paris. Sturdy, *Science and Social Status*, 291, 299.

35. AN, MC, CXII 367, 10 November 1673.

36. Antoine Furetière, *Dictionnaire Universel*...(The Hague: A. and R. Leers, 1690), s.v. "auteur."

37. For these lists in an English translation of Moréri, see Richard Yeo, "Alphabetical Lives: Scientific Biography in Historical Dictionaries and Encyclopaedias," in *Telling Lives in Science: Essays on Scientific Biography*, ed. Michael Shortland and Richard Yeo (Cambridge: Cambridge University Press, 1996), 143–44.

38. Darrin M. McMahon, *Divine Fury: A History of Genius* (New York: Basic Books, 2013), 69–70.

39. Germain Brice, *Description nouvelle de la ville de Paris*...(Paris: Nicolas Le Gras, Nicolas Le Clerc, and Barthelemy Girin, 1698), 1:26–27, and see Gilles Chabaud, "Images de la ville et pratiques du livre: Le genre des guides de Paris (XVIIᵉ–XVIIIᵉ siècles)," *Revue d'histoire moderne et contemporaine* 45, no. 2 (1998): 340–41.

40. Mazarine MS 4534, fol. 13; Moréri 1759, s.v. "Perrault, Claude."

41. The 1759 edition of the Moréri at the John Hay Library, Brown University (Hay Transfer 2-size D9.M8 1759) includes a marginal notation to Charles's entry, probably from the later eighteenth century, which attributed the tales to Charles and his son.

42. For example, Charles-Athanase Walckenaer, *Lettres sur les contes de fées. Mémoires sur les abeilles solitaires. Notices biographiques* (Paris: Firmin Didot frères, fils et cie, 1862); Marc Soriano, *Les Contes de Perrault, culture savante et traditions populaires* (Paris: Gallimard, 1968), 35–71; Soriano, *Dossier Perrault*, 346.

43. Brice, *Description nouvelle*, 1:350.

44. Daniella J. Kostroun, *Feminism, Absolutism, and Jansenism: Louis XIV and the Port-Royal Nuns* (Cambridge: Cambridge University Press, 2011).

45. Perrault, *Hommes illustres*, 190–91.

46. Charles Ancillon, *Mémoires concernant les vies et les ouvrages de plusieurs modernes célèbres dans la République des Lettres* (Amsterdam: Les Wetsteins, 1709), 7; on Conrart's skill as a writer, see 11–12, 84–87.

47. Ibid., 43; Nicolas Schapira, *Un Professionnel des lettres au XVIIe siècle: Valentin Conrart, une histoire sociale* (Seyssel: Champ Vallon, 2003).

48. Perrault, *Hommes illustres*, 195.

49. Jay M. Smith, *The Culture of Merit: Nobility, Royal Service, and the Making of Absolute Monarchy in France, 1600–1789* (Ann Arbor: University of Michigan Press, 1996), 57–60.

50. Moréri 1759.

51. Moréri 1732.

52. Tallemant, "Éloge funèbre de Mr. Perrault, " 597.

53. *Mercure galant*, May 1703, 233–35.

54. Perrault, *Hommes illustres*, 141.

55. Ibid., 397; Anthony Grafton, *Joseph Scaliger: A Study in the History of Classical Scholarship* (Oxford: Clarendon, 1983), 1:102.

56. Perrault, *Hommes illustres*, 50, 150.

57. Jacques Véron, "L'Académie Française et la circulation des élites: Une approche démographique," *Population* 40, no. 3 (1985): 462. In Alain Viala's sample of 550 literary authors, the percentage of those born in Paris (18%) is even smaller. *La naissance des institutions de la vie littéraire en France au XVIIe siècle (1643–1665): Essai de sociopoétique* (Lille: A.N.R.T., 1983), 235. Still, the chances of developing a literary career in Paris were higher than in the provinces. At the Academy of Sciences, most original members seem to have had strong Paris connections. Yet of the group of twenty-six academicians appointed between 1669 and 1698 whose origins are known, Paris and its region accounted for ten, a ratio very close to the one noted for the Académie française. Sturdy, *Science and Social Status*, 138–39, 170.

58. Mazarine MS 4534, 8e pièce, fol. 1; Moréri 1732.

59. Perrault, *Hommes illustres*, 181.

60. Ibid., 199.

61. Ibid., 141.

62. Ibid., 148.

63. Jean de la Quintinie, *Instruction pour les jardins fruitiers et potagers*... (Paris: C. Barbin, 1690); on the success of La Quintinie's work, see Perrault, *Hommes illustres*, 458–59.

64. Vincent Voiture, *Les œuvres de Monsieur de Voiture* (Paris: A. Courbé, 1650).

65. Gilberte Périer, "La vie de Monsieur Pascal, écrite par Madame Périer, sa sœur," in Blaise Pascal, *Œuvres complètes*, ed. Jacques Chevalier (Paris: Gallimard, 1954), 3–34, followed by a biography written by her daughter, Marguerite Périer. "Mémoire sur la vie de M. Pascal, écrit par mademoiselle Marguerite Périer, sa nièce," 35–41.

66. Perrault, *Hommes illustres*, 403.

67. Davis, "Ghosts, Kin, and Progeny," esp. 92–96.

68. Perrault, *Hommes illustres*, 53. This was not the only example of delivering remains to Port-Royal; see Elizabeth A. R. Brown, "Authority, the Family, and the Dead in Late Medieval France," *French Historical Studies* 16, no. 4 (1990): 831–32. On the handling of remains in the French royal family, see Jean-Marie Apostolidès, *Le Roi-Machine: Spectacle et politique au temps de Louis XIV* (Paris: Minuit, 1981), 15.

69. Perrault, *Hommes illustres*, 177–78.

70. Ibid., 121.

71. Brice, *Description nouvelle*, 2:182–84.

72. Marc Fumaroli, "Les abeilles et les araignées," in *La Querelle des Anciens et des Modernes, XVIIᵉ–XVIIIᵉ siècles*, ed. Anne-Marie Lecoq (Paris: Gallimard, 2001), 52–59.

73. On translations in the Perrault family, see more broadly Emmanuel Bury, "Théorie et pratique de la traduction chez les frères Perrault," *XVIIᵉ siècle* 66 (2014): 447–66.

74. Perrault, *Hommes illustres*, 129. Literary kin were not always happy. Peiresc did have to cede books and an apartment in the family house to his brother's "worthless" son. Miller, *Peiresc's Europe*, 176n150.

75. Tallemant, "Éloge funèbre de Mr. Perrault," 599.

76. Perrault, *Hommes illustres*, 53.

77. While dedications did play an important role in connecting authors to patrons, patronage was complex, and the mechanisms that drove it were various. For an example of the ways dedications fit into a scholarly career, see the discussion of Pierre de Marca's dedication of a book to the chancellor Séguier and the publication of a work supporting Richelieu in Perrault, *Hommes illustres*, 32.

78. Tallemant, "Éloge funèbre de Mr. Perrault," 596.

79. Mazarine MS 4534, 8ᵉ pièce, fol. 1.

80. Tallemant, "Éloge funèbre de Mr. Perrault," 592.

81. Ibid., 597.

82. Mario Biagioli, *Galileo, Courtier: The Practice of Science in the Culture of Absolutism* (Chicago: University of Chicago Press, 1993), 323–29.

83. Perrault, *Hommes illustres*, 142.

84. Gadi Algazi, "*Exemplum* and *Wundertier*: Three Concepts of the Scholarly Persona," *BMGN—Low Countries Historical Review* 131, no. 4 (2016): 8–32; compare Ribard, *Raconter*, 147–57.

85. Clemencet, *Histoire littéraire*.

86. [Alexandre Varet], "Avertissement sur la publication de cet ouvrage," in Nicolas Perrault, *La Morale des Jésuites, extraite fidèlement de leurs livres imprimez avec la permission et l'approbation des supérieurs de leur compagnie, par un docteur de Sorbonne* (Mons: La veuve Waudret, 1667), n.p.

87. Perrault, *Hommes illustres*, 393–95.

88. For a broad overview, see Emmanuel Bury, *Littérature et politesse: L'Invention de l'honnête homme, 1580–1750* (Paris: Presses universitaires de France, 1996).

89. Robert A. Schneider, "Friends of Friends: Intellectual and Literary Sociability in the Age of Richelieu," in *Men and Women Making Friends in Early Modern France*, ed. Lewis C. Seifert and Rebecca M. Wilkin (Farnham, UK: Ashgate, 2015), 154–55.

90. Turnovsky, *Literary Market*, 45–50.

91. Philippe Fortin de la Hoguette, *Testament ou conseils fidèles d'un bon père à ses enfants* (Paris: P. Le Petit, 1656), 265.

92. Nicolas Faret, *L'Honneste-homme, ou l'art de plaire à la court* (Paris: Toussaincts du Bray, 1630), 214.

93. Lewis C. Seifert, *Manning the Margins: Masculinity and Writing in Seventeenth-Century France* (Ann Arbor: University of Michigan Press, 2009).

94. *Journal des sçavans*, July 11, 1701, 315. The journal also ran an epitaph of Scudéry by Vertron in the June 27 issue of the same year, p. 290.

95. Joan DeJean: "Lafayette's Ellipses: The Privileges of Anonymity," *PMLA* 99, no. 5 (1984): 884–902.

96. Moréri 1759, s.v. "Fayette, Marie-Magdeléne [sic] Pioche de la Vergne, comtesse de la." La Fayette, Scudéry, and five other female authors were also eulogized in François de Callières, "Éloges de sept dames illustres françoises," in *De la Science du monde, et des connoisances utiles à la conduite de la vie* (Paris: Étienne Ganeau, 1717), 304–10.

97. *Journal des sçavans*, December 1734, 832–36; Moréri 1759, s.v. "Heritier de Villandon (Marie-Jeanne l')."

98. *Journal des sçavans*, December 1734, 833.

99. See, for example, Titon du Tillet, *Le Parnasse françois*, 459–60 (on Mademoiselle des Houlières); 483–86 (on Scudéry).

100. Jean de La Forge, introduction to *Le cercle des femmes sçavantes* (Paris: Jean-Baptiste Loyson, 1663), n.p.

101. Antoine Baudeau de Somaize, *Le grand dictionnaire des précieuses*, reprinted by Roger Duchêne, in *Les précieuses, ou comment l'esprit vint aux femmes* (Paris: Fayard, 2001).

102. Charles Loyseau, *Traité des ordres et simples dignitez* (Paris, 1620), 122. On the sixteenth-century forms of writing on "illustrious men," see Patricia Eichel-Lojkine, "Les Vies d'hommes illustres," *Nouvelle revue du XVIe siècle* 12, no. 1 (1994): 63–77.

103. See, for example, Viala, *Naissance*, chap. 4.

104. Joan E. DeJean, *Tender Geographies: Women and the Origins of the Novel in France* (New York: Columbia University Press, 1991); Henri-Jean Martin, *Livre, pouvoirs et société à Paris au XVIIe siècle (1598–1701)*, 3rd ed. (Geneva: Droz, 1999), 544–51.

105. Ribard, *Raconter*, 10–17; Jean-Pierre Cavaillé, "'Le plus éloquent philosophe des derniers temps': Les stratégies d'auteur de René Descartes," *Annales: Histoire, sciences sociales* 49, no. 2 (1994): 349–67.

106. Miller, "'Man of Learning' Defended"; Anne Goldgar, *Impolite Learning: Conduct and Community in the Republic of Letters, 1680–1750* (New Haven, CT: Yale University Press, 1995).

107. Jean le Rond d'Alembert, "Éloge de Charles Perrault," in *Œuvres de d'Alembert* (Paris: A. Belin, Bossange père et fils, Bossange frères, 1821), 2:230.

108. I am deeply indebted to Denis Richet's insight regarding royal functionaries, who should be seen less as individuals than as members of families and lineages. *La France moderne: L'Esprit des institutions* (Paris: Flammarion, 1973), 80.

2. Finance and Mobility

1. Perrault, *Contes*, 337–38.

2. John Lough, *Writer and Public in France: From the Middle Ages to the Present Day* (Oxford: Clarendon, 1978); Viala, in *Naissance*, 57–59, showed that ecclesiastical benefices, obtained from patrons, could bring authors more income than gratifications or sales of books. He still stressed, though, an orientation toward commercial genres such as the theater or the novel in the careers of authors who follow the audacious "strategy of success" (chap. 7, 217–38).

3. Turnovsky, *Literary Market*.

4. For examples, see Lough, *Writer and Public*, 99–100 and passim; Viala, *Naissance*; Shoemaker, *Powerful Connections*, chap. 1; Turnovsky, *Literary Market*, 25–28. As far as the numbers used in this chapter go, I am interested mostly in stressing the different scales they imply and the general portrait that they help in producing. In many

cases, the actual numbers in notarial documents can be misleading. For example, the sums of dowries in marriage contracts have on occasion been artificially inflated in order to project an image of riches beyond the actual means of the bride's family; even probate records could be falsified in many ways: from the simple omission of property to the keeping of double records of inventories. Contemporaries indeed recognized that not all the financial documents left by financiers were useful in determining the actual wealth of the deceased, since in many cases the documents concealed as much as they clarified. See Daniel Dessert, *Argent, pouvoir et société au Grand Siècle* (Paris: Fayard, 1984), 111–27.

5. David D. Bien, "Manufacturing Nobles: The Chancelleries in France to 1789," *Journal of Modern History* 61, no. 3 (1989): 446–86.

6. Robert Descimon, "Chercher de nouvelles voies pour interpréter les phénomènes nobiliaires dans la France moderne. La noblesse, 'essence' ou rapport social?," *Revue d'histoire moderne et contemporaine* 46, no. 1 (1999): 5–21; Descimon, "Élites parisiennes entre XVᵉ et XVIIᵉ siècle: Du bon usage du Cabinet des titres," *Bibliothèque de l'École des chartes* 155 (1997): 607–44, and most broadly, Descimon, "Conclusion: Nobles de lignage et noblesse de service: Sociogenèses comparées de l'épée et de la robe (XVᵉ–XVIIIᵉ siècle)," in *Épreuves de noblesse: Les expériences nobiliaires de la robe parisienne (XVIᵉ–XVIIIᵉ siècle)*, ed. Robert Descimon and Élie Haddad (Paris: Belles lettres, 2010), 277–302. On the limits of legal definitions of nobility, see also Ellery Schalk, "Ennoblement in France from 1350 to 1660," *Journal of Social History* 16, no. 2 (1982): 101–10.

7. The following discussion is based on Descimon, "Élites parisiennes," 631–44.

8. Élie Barnavi and Robert Descimon, *La Sainte Ligue, le juge et la potence: L'Assassinat du président Brisson (15 novembre 1591)* (Paris: Hachette, 1985), 69–71; Barbara Diefendorf, "The Catholic League: Social Crisis or Apocalypse Now?," *French Historical Studies* 15, no. 2 (1987): 332–44.

9. Myriam Yardeni, "L'Ordre des avocats et la grève du barreau parisien en 1602," *Revue d'histoire économique et sociale* 44, no. 4 (1966): 481–507; Robert Descimon, "The Birth of the Nobility of the Robe: Dignity versus Privilege in the Parlement of Paris, 1500–1700," in *Changing Identities in Early Modern France*, ed. Michael Wolfe (Durham, NC: Duke University Press, 1996), 95–123.

10. In what follows, I have drawn on Françoise Bayard, *Le monde des financiers au XVIIᵉ siècle* (Paris: Flammarion, 1988); Dessert, *Argent*. See also Daniel Dessert, "The Financier," in *Baroque Personae*, ed. Rosario Villari (Chicago: University of Chicago Press, 1995), 57–81, and Marie-Laure Legay, *La banqueroute de l'État royal: La gestion des finances publiques de Colbert à la Révolution* (Paris: Éditions de l'École des hautes études en sciences sociales, 2011).

11. Dessert, "Financier," 71; David D. Bien, "Offices, Corps, and a System of State Credit: The Uses of Privilege under the Ancien Regime," in *The French Revolution and the Creation of Modern Political Culture*, vol. 1, *The Political Culture of the Old Regime*, ed. Keith Michael Baker (Oxford: Pergamon, 1987), 89–114.

12. Gail Bossenga, "Markets, the Patrimonial State, and the Origins of the French Revolution," *1650–1850: Ideas, Aesthetics, and Inquiries in the Early Modern Era* 11 (2005): 443–509; George V. Taylor, "Types of Capitalism in Eighteenth-Century France," *English Historical Review* 79 (1964): 478–97, esp. 487–92.

13. Bossenga, "Markets, the Patrimonial State," 462–63.

14. André Hallays, *Les Perrault* (Paris: Perrin et cie, 1926), 243–46, and Gautier, "Charles Perrault," 937.

15. Pierre Leveel, *Histoire de la Touraine*, 2nd ed. (Paris: Presses universitaires de France, 1967), 60–61, 73–76, 92–93 and passim; see also the broad-stroke survey in Jean-Pierre Surrault, "La Touraine des temps modernes (1515–1789)," in *L'Indre-et-Loire: La Touraine des origines à nos jours*, ed. Claude Crubois (Saint-Jean-d'Angély: Éditions Bordessoules, 1982), 195–285. Since the region remained loyal to the monarchy, some residents moved to Paris after receiving nominations to Parisian positions as a reward for their loyalty. For an example, see Martine Bennini, *Les conseillers à la cour des aides (1604–1697): Étude sociale* (Paris: H. Champion, 2010), 272.

16. Augustin Jal, *Dictionnaire critique de biographie et d'histoire; errata et supplément pour tous les dictionnaires historiques, d'après des documents authentiques inédits*, 2nd ed. (Paris: H. Plon, 1872), 1321. Unfortunately, the parish records Jal used were destroyed in 1871, during the fires of the Paris commune. Therefore, it is impossible to know why Jean is not mentioned—Jal thought, wrongly, that he was an uncle—and what his exact date of birth was.

17. John Bossy, "Godparenthood: The Fortunes of a Social Institution in Early Modern Christianity," in *Religion and Society in Early Modern Europe, 1500–1800*, ed. Kaspar von Greyerz (Boston: Allen & Unwin, 1984), 194–201.

18. Perrault, *Mémoires*, 109.

19. On churchwardens as local notables, see David Garrioch, *The Formation of the Parisian Bourgeoisie, 1690–1830* (Cambridge, MA: Harvard University Press, 1996), 48–54.

20. For the donations, see AN, MC, XVIII 187, 18 January 1632; AN, MC, XVIII 186, 23 November 1631; AN, MC, XVIII 189, 10 February 1633.

21. Théophile Lavallée, *Histoire de Paris depuis les temps des Gaulois jusqu'à nos jours*, 2nd ed. (Paris: Michel Lévy frères, 1857), 2: 299–306.

22. AN, MC, VI 236, 13 October 1644; AN, MC, X 97, 10 March 1648.

23. Gautier, "Charles Perrault," 938, 1005–6. Henri-Jean Martin identified a Jean Le Clerc who was active as an engraver at the end of the sixteenth century: *Livre, pouvoirs et société*, 165.

24. AN, MC, LXXIII 195, 7 November 1626; Robert Descimon, "Un langage de la dignité," esp. 84–85 for the use of "honorable homme" as a designation for bourgeois in Paris.

25. These rents (sometimes translated as "annuities") were a legal fiction allowing for lending money at interest without violating the religious injunctions regarding usury. One side—the lender—gave the other side a lump sum in return for a rent, to be paid over a number of years defined by both sides. The borrowing party returned the original sum of money at a time of his or her choice (this differentiated rents from loans with interest). Effectively, the yearly rent was the interest paid on the original loan. Philip T. Hoffman, Gilles Postel-Vinay, and Jean-Laurent Rosenthal, *Priceless Markets: The Political Economy of Credit in Paris, 1660–1870* (Chicago: University of Chicago Press, 2000), 14–25.

26. In Roland Mousnier's scheme of Parisian social hierarchy in the seventeenth century, Pierre and Paquette fit the third stratum of the "notables," who could expect dowries

of 20,000–100,000 livres (the upper echelons of this stratum) or 3,000–10,000 livres (the lower echelons). For a summary, see René Pillorget, *Paris sous les premiers Bourbons, 1594–1661* (Paris: Association pour la publication d'une histoire de Paris, 1988), 122–34.

27. Christiane Klapisch-Zuber, *Women, Family, and Ritual in Renaissance Italy* (Chicago: University of Chicago Press, 1985). For a more nuanced view of patriarchy within the French context, see Julie Hardwick, *The Practice of Patriarchy: Gender and the Politics of Household Authority in Early Modern France* (University Park: Penn State University Press, 1998), and especially Hardwick's *Family Business: Litigation and the Political Economies of Daily Life in Early Modern France* (Oxford: Oxford University Press, 2009).

28. Some witnesses took part in both networks, and some are unidentified, explaining why the percentages do not add up to 100 percent.

29. Scarlett Beauvalet and Vincent Gourdon, "Les liens sociaux à Paris au XVIIe siècle: Une analyse des contrats de mariage de 1660, 1665 et 1670," *Histoire, économie et société* 17, no. 4 (1998): 596–601.

30. Ibid., 598–99. For this phenomenon in the Séguier family, see Denis Richet, "Une famille de robe: Les Séguier avant le chancelier," in *De la Réforme à la Révolution: Études sur la France moderne* (Paris: Aubier, 1991), 157–72.

31. Charles Perrault, *Mémoires*, 109. On women and education in the Godefroy family, see Sherman, "Genealogy of Knowledge," 177–95.

32. [Varet], "Avertissement sur la publication de cet ouvrage."

33. Perrault, *Mémoires*, 117–18, 120.

34. Ibid., 122.

35. The social origins of financiers were diverse, but a judicial background was common. See Bayard, *Monde des financiers*, 277–78.

36. For examples of diversification of family strategies among different family branches (between commerce and office holding), see Robert Descimon, "The 'Bourgeoisie Seconde': Social Differentiation in the Parisian Municipal Oligarchy in the Sixteenth Century, 1500–1610," *French History* 17, no. 4 (2003): 388–424.

37. Perrault, *Mémoires*, 110–11.

38. Ibid., 120–22, quote on 121. On the lax standards at Orléans, see L. W. B. Brockliss, *French Higher Education in the Seventeenth and Eighteenth Centuries: A Cultural History* (Oxford: Clarendon, 1987), 78–79.

39. Picon, *Claude Perrault*, 30–33.

40. BN, FF 24714, 108.

41. Gérard Namer, *L'abbé Le Roy et ses amis; essai sur le Jansénisme extrémiste intramondain* (Paris: S.E.V.P.E.N., 1964), 42–66 (which suffers from chronological inexactitudes); Jean Lesaulnier, "Nicolas Perrault, théologien de Port-Royal 1624–1661," *XVIIe siècle* 66 (2014): 417–27.

42. L. W. B. Brockliss, "Patterns of Attendance at the University of Paris, 1400–1800," *Historical Journal* 21, no. 3 (1978): 529–31; Brockliss, *French Higher Education*, 55; Brockliss and Colin Jones, *The Medical World of Early Modern France* (Oxford: Clarendon Press, 1997), 213.

43. *Catalogue des partisans contre lesquels on doit agir pour la contribution aux dépenses de la Guerre* (n.p., 1649), 13, 17 (Bibliothèque de l'Arsenal, 8-H-7830[13]).

44. Charles Perrault, *Mémoires*, 217–18, gives 1654 as the date for the purchase of this office, and Gautier follows him (945). However, in 1654 Claude was still Housset's aide, as can be seen in *Lettres Patentes pour la décharge des comptes des exercices &*

maniemens faits tant par le sieur Housset, Tresorier des Parties Casuelles, que par Maistre Pierre Perrault, commis par le Roy à l'exercice de ladite Charge en l'année 1654. & à la reddition & appuremens de ses comptes, BN F-5001 (250), n.p. In 1654, Pierre replaced Housset as a treasurer of the parties casuelles for the duration of the year. AN, P 2374, fols. 477–81. Pierre bought the office in 1657, though he might have exercised some of its functions early as Housset's aide—see AN, E 371b, fols. 329–31, 28 May 1664. For the relation between Housset and Claude, see Vte de Montbas, "Un manuscrit inédit de Claude Perrault," *Revue de l'art ancien et moderne* 51 (1927): 331–33. On the Bonneau family, see Daniel Dessert, *L'Argent du sel, le sel de l'argent* (Paris: Fayard, 2012).

45. Daniel Dessert, "Finances et société au XVIIe siècle: À propos de la chambre de justice de 1661," *Annales: E.S.C.* 24, no. 4 (1974): 847–81; John F. Bosher, "'Chambres de Justice' in the French Monarchy," in *French Government and Society 1500–1850: Essays in Memory of Alfred Cobban,* ed. John Bosher (London: Athlone, 1973), 19–40.

46. There were exceptions: Colbert's associates were treated less severely by the chambre. See Dessert, *Argent,* 340.

47. For Pierre's file, see BN, 500 Colbert 234, fol. 291r–v. The sums represented here are higher than the ones in the d'Ormesson collections: AN, 144AP62, dossier 24 and AN, 144AP65, dossier 3. Dessert published the list of 248 individuals taxed at more than 100,000 livres, representing the upper strata of this social group in "Finances et société," not including Pierre. Dessert did include him in his later and more comprehensive study, without stating the amount he was fined. See Dessert, *Argent,* 669.

48. Dessert, "Finances et société," 850.

49. Ibid., 877.

50. Ibid., 851–52. Dessert possibly overestimated the number of nobles by taking for granted that the titles they claimed indeed reflected noble status.

51. Dessert, *Argent,* 108.

52. Boris Noguès, *Une archéologie du corps enseignant: Les professeurs des collèges parisiens aux XVIIe et XVIIIe siècles* (Paris: Belin, 2006), 53–60. L. W. B. Brockliss also points to the great variance in salaries among the professoriate. Brockliss, *French Higher Education,* 44.

53. Brockliss and Jones, *Medical World,* 320–28 (323 for Renaudot).

54. BN, FF 7723, fols. 67, 73.

55. They were worth 30,000 livres. See marriage contract of Charles Lormier's son, AN, MC, CX 100, 17 December 1640; marriage contract of Madeleine Lormier, AN, MC, LI 154, 3 September 1628; marriage contract of Catherine Lormier, AN, MC, LI 190, 19 September 1638; division of inheritance between Charles Lormier's children, AN, MC, LI 226, 31 May 1649; sale of property between brothers, AN, MC, LI 529, 30 January 1652. For these references, I am indebted to Bennini, *Les conseillers,* 451.

56. See the transactions in AN, MC LI 535, 10 July 1654; AN, MC, LI 537, 5 June 1655; AN, MC, LI 537, 22 March 1655; AN, MC, LI 538, 2 August 1655; AN, MC, LI 538, 17 July 1655; AN, MC, LI 539, 9 March 1656; AN, MC, LI 540, 1 August 1656; AN, MC, LI 540, 2 June 1656; AN, MC, LI 541, 3 October 1656. On Sébastien Hardy's involvement in finance, see Bayard, *Le monde,* 271.

57. AN, MC, LII 119, 28 July 1688. Contemporaries knew that the figures in such documents could be inflated. Dessert, *Argent,* 111–27. Even if this sum is inflated, it seems likely that Catherine's financial contribution had been of the utmost importance to Pierre's career.

58. For the sale of office (which also included the office of an aide and a third of the office of the quadrennial receiver-general in the generality of Paris), see AN, MC, XLVI 70, 2 May 1657. In other cases, this office in the generality of Paris was sold for 173,000 livres in 1654, and by the early 1670s its price had soared to about 360,000 livres; see Dessert, *Argent*, 150. On Catherine's house, AN, MC, LI 540, 2 June 1656, and on the division of her father's property, AN, MC, LI 226, 31 May 1649.

59. Jal, *Dictionnaire critique*, 1321.

60. Bennini, *Conseillers*, 325. This average age of the French population at large was under thirty: see Scarlett Beauvalet-Boutouyrie, *La population française à l'époque moderne (XVIᵉ–XVIIIᵉ siècle): Démographie et comportements*, 2nd ed. (Paris: Belin, 2008), 138–41.

61. Dessert, *Argent*, 46–48.

62. *Plaise au Roi et à Nosseigneurs de son conseil, en jugeant le procès pour René Souchu, . . . demandeur, contre maître Pierre Perrault et Claude Coquille, . . . défendeurs, avoir la bonté de prendre lecture du placet qui est présenté en forme d'état sommaire, servant d'instruction, et de conserver en justice le bon droit dudit Souchu* [BN, FOL-FM-15848, n.p.]; and *Plaise à Monsieur . . . avoir pour recommandé en justice le bon droit pour maître Pierre Perault, ci-devant receveur général des finances à Paris, . . . contre François Maillot, ci-devant son commis . . .* [BN, 4-FM-25439].

63. AN, MC, LII 119, 28 July 1688.

64. According to the judicial brief, the total value of the taxes Perrault and Coquille contracted for in these years in the election of Meaux was around 300,000 livres in each year. *Plaise au Roi et à Nosseigneurs de son conseil*.

65. Dessert, *Argent*, 562–63, 441–42. The Marin family held the office of triennial receiver general, which was later held by Pierre de la Croix.

66. Ibid., 340.

67. The Pepins continued to live in Saint-Étienne-du-Mont. See the transactions in MC, XLIX 344, 22 February 1659; and for another deal struck in the parish, see AN, MC, XVI 119, 4 May 1659.

68. Jal, *Dictionnaire critique*, 1321.

69. AN, MC, XCV 49, 22 March 1698.

70. Perrault, *Mémoires*, 118.

71. Ibid., 119.

72. AN, MC, LXV 32, 25 January 1654.

73. Perrault, *Mémoires*, 122–23. Charles was still living there in September 1663: AN, MC, XC 227, 28 September 1663.

74. The list is based on AN, MC, LII 107, 30 June 1684. On the development of these areas, see Trout, *City on the Seine*, 94–95, 98–99.

75. Perrault, *Mémoires*, 122.

76. This was not a rare phenomenon, since family milieus were also central for the establishment of Descartes's posthumous reputation. See Stéphane van Damme, *Descartes: Essai d'histoire culturelle d'une grandeur philosophique* (Paris: Presses de Sciences Po, 2002), 47–53.

77. Scarron was paralyzed by an accident and lost the use of his legs, and he used the expression "cul de jatte" ("bowl-assed") to describe himself. See Paul Scarron, *La relation véritable de tout ce qui s'est passé en l'autre monde . . .* (Paris: Toussaint Quinet, 1648), "To the reader" (n.p.).

78. Perrault, *Mémoires*, 113–14; Marc Soriano, "Burlesque et langage populaire de 1647 à 1653: Sur deux poèmes de jeunesse des frères Perrault," *Annales: E.S.C.* 24, no. 4 (1969): 949–75; Soriano, *Dossier Charles Perrault*, 48–58.

79. Orest Ranum, *The Fronde: A French Revolution, 1648–1652* (New York: Norton, 1993), 60–81, 92–114.

80. La Rochefoucauld, *Maxims*, trans. Leonard Tancock (Harmondsworth, UK: Penguin, 1959), 44.

3. The Perraults in the Countryside

1. Perrault, *Contes*, 577–78.

2. For a much broader take on credit and appearances in a slightly later period, see Clare Crowston, *Credit, Fashion, Sex: Economies of Regard in Old Regime France* (Durham, NC: Duke University Press, 2013).

3. Nicolas Schapira, "Écrivains et élites urbaines au XVIIᵉ siècle: Peut-on se passer du modèle du salon?," in *La Ville et l'esprit de société*, ed. Katia Béguin and Olivier Dautresme (Tours: Presses universitaires François Rabelais, 2004), 17–32; Schapira, *Professionnel des lettres*, esp. 243–44; Stéphane van Damme, "La sociabilité intellectuelle. Les usages historiographiques d'une notion," *Hypothèses* (1997): 121–32; and especially Antoine Lilti, *Le monde des salons: Sociabilité et mondanité à Paris au XVIIIᵉ siècle* (Paris: Fayard, 2005), 10–12.

4. For a succinct summary of the prevalent views, see Joan DeJean, "The Salons, 'Preciosity,' and the Sphere of Women's Influence," in *A New History of French Literature*, ed. Denis Hollier (Cambridge, MA: Harvard University Press, 1989), 297–303. The major traits of DeJean's synthesis appear in recent work: for example, Faith Beasley, *Salons, History, and the Creation of Seventeenth-Century France: Mastering Memory* (Aldershot, UK: Ashgate, 2006), 28. The only competing institution, according to most scholars, was the Académie française; for differing views on its importance for codifying the status of men of letters, compare Marc Fumaroli, "La Coupole," in *Trois institutions littéraires* (Paris: Gallimard, 1994), with Jouhaud, *Pouvoirs de la littérature*, 11–17. For a brief comparison of seventeenth- and eighteenth-century salons, see Roger Chartier, "The Man of Letters," in *Enlightenment Portraits*, ed. Michel Vovelle (Chicago: University of Chicago Press, 1997), 158.

5. For the most explicit formulation of this assumption, see Julie Campbell, *Literary Circles and Gender in Early Modern Europe: A Cross-Cultural Approach* (Aldershot, UK: Ashgate, 2006), 9–10.

6. Compare Joan DeJean, *Tender Geographies: Women and the Origins of the Novel in France* (New York: Columbia University Press, 1991), 18–42, with the analysis in Myriam Maître, *Les Précieuses: Naissance des femmes de lettres en France au XVIIᵉ siècle* (Paris: H. Champion, 1999), 132–93.

7. Compare Carolyn C. Lougee, *Paradis des Femmes*, and Anne E. Duggan, *Salonnières, Furies, and Fairies: The Politics of Gender and Cultural Change in Absolutist France* (Newark: University of Delaware Press, 2005), 121–64.

8. Compare Lougee, *Paradis des Femmes*, and Benedetta Craveri, *The Age of Conversation* (New York: New York Review Books, 2005).

9. Schapira, "Écrivains et élites urbaines," 25. Certain sources offer glimpses of conversations. See, for example, Jean Orcibal, "Descartes et sa philosophie jugés à

l'hôtel Liancourt," in *Descartes et le cartésianisme hollandais. Études et documents*, ed. E. J. Dijksterhuis (Paris: Presses universitaires de France, 1950), 87–107.

10. Lilti, *Monde des salons*, 120–21.

11. BL, MS, Additional (Add.) 20087.

12. BN, MS FF 15125.

13. The first plot was estimated at 4.5 arpents (approx. 4 acres); the other plots were considerably smaller. This document is cited in Gautier, "Charles Perrault," 1017–18. As the exact dating of the building of different parts of Viry is problematic, this document at least shows that the fountain already existed in 1641.

14. J. C. Nemeitz, *Séjour de Paris*...(Leiden, Neth.: Jean van Abcoude, 1727), 170; Pillorget, *Paris*, 34.

15. Françoise Bayard, "Manière d'habiter des financiers de la première moitié du XVIIe siècle," *XVIIe Siècle* 41 (1989): 53.

16. Joseph di Corcia, "*Bourg, Bourgeois, Bourgeois de Paris* from the Eleventh to the Eighteenth Century," *Journal of Modern History* 50, no. 2 (1978): 222.

17. Schapira, *Professionnel des lettres*, 244–46.

18. Pierre Bayle, *Dictionnaire historique et critique* (Rotterdam, Neth.: R. Leers, 1697), 5.

19. James S. Ackerman, *The Villa: Form and Ideology of Country Houses* (Princeton: Princeton University Press, 1990), 9–10.

20. Paraphrasing Katia Béguin, *Princes de Condé*, 337–40. For English parallels, see Sukanya Dasgupta, "'Of Polish'd Pillars, or a Roofe of Gold': Authority and Affluence in the English Country-House Poem," in *Contested Spaces of Nobility in Early Modern Europe*, ed. Matthew P. Romaniello and Charles Lipp (Farnham, UK: Ashgate, 2011), 189–212.

21. Bernard Beugnot, *Le discours de la retraite au XVIIe siècle: Loin du monde et du bruit* (Paris: Presses universitaires de France, 1996), 39–53.

22. Schneider, "Friends of Friends," 136–37.

23. BL, MS, Add. 20087.

24. Bernard le Bovier de Fontenelle, *Conversations on the Plurality of Worlds*, trans. H. A. Hargreaves (Berkeley: University of California Press, 1990), 7.

25. BL, MS, Add. 20087, fol. 4r. Similarly, Madeleine de Scudéry described the voyage to Conrart's country house in one of her novels: *Clélie, histoire romaine* (Paris: Augustin Courbé, 1654–60), 2.2: 796–805, esp. 797.

26. Bayard, *Monde des financiers*, 394–95.

27. Madeleine Jurgens and Pierre Couperie, "Le logement à Paris au XVIe et XVIIe siècles: Une source, les inventaires après décès," *Annales: E.S.C.* 17, no. 3 (1962): 500.

28. BL, MS, Add. 20087, fol. 4v.

29. Ibid. At least in a later period in his life (1672 at the latest), Charles Perrault in fact possessed a minor work attributed to Michelangelo (see chapter 4).

30. Their taste is said to have been closer to that of the old sword nobility than to the robe nobility. Antoine Schnapper, *Curieux du Grand Siècle* (Paris: Flammarion, 1994), 407; Bayard, "Manière d'habiter."

31. BL, MS, Add. 20087, fol. 10r.

32. Krzysztof Pomian, *Collectors and Curiosities: Paris and Venice 1500–1800* (Cambridge: Polity Press, 1990), 36–37.

33. The mention of the grotto could also serve as evidence for later rewriting of the poem, as Charles claimed to have built it in the late 1650s—though he could have meant a simple reconstruction.

34. BL, MS, Add. 20087, fol. 8v.

35. Trout, *City on the Seine*, 58–59. For an anecdote on access to the garden of the Palais-Royal, see Christiaan Huygens, *Œuvres complètes* (The Hague, Neth.: M. Nijhoff, 1888–1950), 7:170–72.

36. Pierre Le Muet, *Manière de bien bastir pour toutes sortes de personnes*... (Paris: François Jollain, 1681), 14–15.

37. BL, MS, Add. 20087, fol. 10v.

38. Daniel Riou, "Naissance du roman moderne au XVIIe siècle—idéologie, institution, réception," in *Histoire de la France littéraire*, vol. 2, *Classicismes, XVIIe–XVIIIe siècle*, ed. Jean-Charles Darmon and Michel Delon (Paris: Quadrige / PUF, 2006), 665.

39. An addition at the end of the manuscript explains that "this poem is the first, but it is much augmented by the same author and the images are made by my brother the doctor [*médecin*] M. Perrault." BL, MS, Add. 20087, fol. 14r.

40. While a selection of them was published in 1907, the sections relevant to the Perraults remain in manuscript. See Frédéric Lachèvre, ed., *La Chronique des chapons et des gélinottes du Mans d'Étienne Martin de Pinchesne* (Paris: H. Leclerc, 1907).

41. Gautier, "Charles Perrault," 872–73. More precisely, Gautier situates three such dinners in September 1662; see further Gautier's excellent chronology for the years 1628–62, on pp. 937–59.

42. BN, FF 15125, fols. 118r–120v (two folios in this section are paginated as 120, but I follow the original pagination).

43. Schneider, "Friends of Friends," 141–42; eighteenth-century salons' sociability also attributed particular importance to codes of hospitality. Lilti, *Monde des Salons*, 62–65.

44. Michel de Marolles, *Le livre des peintres et graveurs*, ed. Georges DuPlessis (Paris: Paul Daffis, 1872), 25; Perrault, *Hommes illustres*, 240–43.

45. BN, FF 15125, fol. 3v.

46. BN, FF 15125, fols. 205r–206r.

47. BN, FF 15125, fols. 119r–125v.

48. BN, FF 15125, fols. 3r–29v.

49. The identity of the last two remains uncertain. See Gautier, "Charles Perrault," 872, 875.

50. BN, FF 15125, fol. 25r.

51. BN, FF 15125, fol. 16r.

52. See, for example, Lewis Seifert, *Fairy Tales, Sexuality, and Gender in France, 1690–1715: Nostalgic Utopias* (Cambridge: Cambridge University Press, 1996), 93–94.

53. BN, FF 15125, fols. 195r–206r. For the exact chronology, see Gautier, "Charles Perrault," 953–54.

54. According to Charles's *Mémoires* (p. 120), Pierre was in contact with Vitart as early as 1656. Their relationship was probably related to their Jansenist sensibilities: Pierre supposedly communicated to Port Royal through Vitart Nicolas Perrault's support of Arnauld.

55. Gautier, "Charles Perrault," 954. Jean Racine, letter to the Abbé le Vasseur, 13 September 1660, in *Œuvres complètes*, ed. Raymond Picard (Paris: Gallimard, 1966), 2:383–86.

56. Perrault, *Mémoires*, 123.

57. Ibid., 123–24.

58. Bibliothèque de l'Arsenal, MS 5422, fols. 359–66; MS 5131, fols. 207–13, 215–218, 219–55 (also includes Charles's translation of a letter by the sixteenth-century chancellor Michel de l'Hôpital); MS 5418, fols. 709–15; MS 5131, fols. 131–52; MS 5418, fols. 1207–16. See Schapira, *Professionnel des lettres*, 414–23.

59. Viala, *France galante*, 286.

60. On Huygens and his family, see A. G. H. Bachrach, "The Role of the Huygens Family in Seventeenth-Century Dutch Culture," in *Studies on Christiaan Huygens*, ed. H. J .M. Bos et al. (Lisse, Neth.: Swets & Zeitlinger, 1980), 27–52; Cornelis Dirk Andriesse, *Huygens: The Man behind the Principle* (Cambridge: Cambridge University Press, 2005); see further Roger Hahn, "Huygens and France," in Bos et al., *Studies on Christiaan Huygens*, 53–55.

61. In 1675, for example, Huygens expressed his desire to meet the Perraults at Viry as soon as possible, since the leaves were starting to turn yellow. Huygens, *Œuvres*, 7:497–98.

62. Huygens, *Œuvres*, 8:185, 8:192.

63. Huygens met Nanteuil on 18 December 1660. Henri L. Brugmans, ed., *Le séjour de Christian Huygens à Paris et ses relations avec les milieux scientifiques français; suivi de son journal de voyage à Paris et à Londres* (Paris: E. Droz, 1935), 138.

64. Huygens, *Œuvres*, 4:414.

65. Ibid., 7:349; Jacques Barchilon, "Les frères Perrault à travers la correspondance de Christian Huygens," *XVIIᵉ siècle* 56 (1962): 19–36.

66. Perhaps a relative of an Utrecht pastor who had connections to Huygens's father; see Huygens, *Œuvres*, 5:60.

67. Ibid., 7:112–13.

68. Ibid., 8:107.

69. Ibid., 7:112–113; 8:507–509; 8:314; 8:320–21. It is hard to give an exact estimate for this length, since the aune of Paris differed from the aune of Amsterdam.

70. Ibid., 7:170.

71. Ibid., 10:323. On high-society life as a foundation for scientific work, see Geoffrey V. Sutton, *Science for a Polite Society: Gender, Culture, and the Demonstration of Enlightenment* (Boulder: Westview Press, 1995).

72. Huygens, *Œuvres*, 19:372–73. On the Parisian soundscape, see David Garrioch, *The Making of Revolutionary Paris* (Berkeley: University of California Press, 2002), 18–20, 22–23.

73. Fokko Jan Dijksterhuis, *Lenses and Waves: Christiaan Huygens and the Mathematical Science of Optics in the Seventeenth Century* (Dordrecht, Neth.: Kluwer Academic Publishers, 2004), 77–92.

74. Huygens, *Œuvres*, 7:321; see Nicole Howard, "Marketing Longitude: Clocks, Kings, Courtiers, and Christiaan Huygens," *Book History* 11 (2008): 81.

75. This and the following paragraphs are based on Perrault, *Mémoires*, 120–25.

76. Titon du Tillet, *Parnasse françois*, 255–56.

77. Lachèvre, *La chronique*, 158–60, quote on 158.

78. BN, FF 15125, fols. 118r–119r.

79. Lougee, *Paradis des Femmes*.

80. Somaize, *Grand dictionnaire des précieuses*, reprinted by Roger Duchêne, in *Les précieuses ou comment l'esprit vint aux femmes* (Paris: Fayard, 2001), 455.

81. Ibid., 526.

82. Ibid., 498, 477.

83. Robert Descimon, "L'exemplarité sociale des *Historiettes* de Tallemant des Réaux," in *Construire l'exemplarité: Pratiques littéraires et discours historiens, XVIe–XVIIIe siècles*, ed. Laurence Giavarini (Dijon: Éditions universitaires de Dijon, 2008), 181–95.

84. Gédéon Tallemant des Réaux, *Historiettes*, ed. Antoine Adam (Paris: Gallimard, 1967), 1:407, 2:845, 873–74.

85. Jean de La Forge, *Le cercle des femmes sçavantes* (Paris: J.-B. Loyson, 1663), entry on "Cleon," n.p.

86. Titon du Tillet, *Parnasse françois*, 489.

87. For other examples, see Robert Darnton, "The Devil in Holy Water: Political Libel in Eighteenth-Century France," *Proceedings of the British Academy* 151 (2007): 387–422, esp. 396; Blair, *Too Much to Know*, 173–229; Roger Chartier, "From Court Festivity to City Spectators," in *Forms and Meanings: Texts, Performances, and Audiences from Codex to Computer* (Philadelphia: University of Pennsylvania Press, 1995), 43–81.

88. *Poesies meslées du Sieur de Pinchesne, dediées à Monseigneur le Duc de Montausier* (Paris: André Cramoisy, 1672).

89. Ibid. The introduction also describes the collection as a *guirlande* (bouquet of flowers), recalling the "guirlande de Julie," the most famous collection of poetry written in the Rambouillet circle. Delphine Denis, *Le Parnasse galant: Institution d'une catégorie littéraire au XVIIe siècle* (Paris: Champion, 2001).

90. Viala, *Naissance*, 164.

91. Nemeitz, *Séjour de Paris*, 133, and on the author, see Chabaud, "Images de la ville," 343–44.

92. Cf. Daniel Gordon, "'Public Opinion' and the Civilizing Process in France: The Example of Morellet," *Eighteenth-Century Studies* 22, no. 3 (1989): 302–28.

93. Nicolas Schapira, "Le 'Salon' écrit par les professionnels des Lettres (France, XVIIe siècle)," *Papers on French Seventeenth Century Literature* 38 (2011): 315–28.

94. Molière, "Les précieuses ridicules," in *Œuvres complètes* (Paris: Gallimard, 1956), vol. 1.

95. Ibid., scene IV.

96. Ibid., scene IX, quote on 231–32.

97. Antoine Furetière, *Le Roman bourgeois* (Paris: Gallimard, 1981), 34–40.

98. Ibid., 117, 139–40.

4. Failure in Finance and the Rise of Charles Perrault

1. Perrault, *Contes*, 641.

2. Richard Bonney, "The Fouquet-Colbert Rivalry and the 'Revolution' of 1661," in *Ethics and Politics in Seventeenth-Century France*, ed. Keith Cameron and E. Woodrough (Exeter, UK: University of Exeter Press, 1996), 107–18.

3. [Charles Perrault], *Ode sur la Paix* (Paris: Charles de Sercy, 1660), privilege.

4. Pierre Clément, ed., *Lettres, instructions et mémoires de Colbert* (Paris: Imprimerie impériale, 1861–73), 1: 422.

5. Ibid., 1:423, 440.

6. The literature on these events is vast. For recent views, see Jérôme Janczukie-wicz, "La prise du pouvoir par Louis XIV: La construction du mythe," *XVIIe siècle* 57 (2005): 243–64; Vincent J. Pitts, *Embezzlement and High Treason in Louis XIV's France: The Trial of Nicolas Fouquet* (Baltimore: Johns Hopkins University Press, 2015), 6–8, 44–60.

7. Perrault, *Mémoires*, 126–27. Chapelain's letter to Colbert on the Petite acadé-mie, dated 18 November 1662, appears in Jean Chapelain, *Lettres de Jean Chapelain, de l'Académie française*, ed. Philippe Tamizey de Larroque (Paris: Imprimerie nationale, 1880), 2:272.

8. Perrault, *Mémoires*, 127.

9. Ibid., 127–30.

10. Gautier, "Charles Perrault," 960–61.

11. Perrault, *Mémoires*, 134.

12. Clément, *Lettres, instructions, et mémoires*, 5:458.

13. Ibid.

14. In a previous letter, dated 12 March 1670, Chapelain described Perrault as the person who helped Chapelain obtain things for Heinsius. Chapelain, *Lettres de Jean Chapelain*, 414–15; Chapelain, *Les lettres authentiques à Nicolas Heinsius (1649–1672): Une amitié érudite entre France et Hollande*, ed. Bernard Bray (Paris: Champion, 2005), 534, 538.

15. Perrault, *Mémoires*, 189.

16. Huygens, *Œuvres*, 7:123–24.

17. Perrault, *Mémoires*, 191–99.

18. BN, Mélanges Colbert 120 bis, fol. 926, 23 May 1664; BL, MS Add. 24210, fol. 13, 31 July 1672.

19. BN, Mélanges Colbert 121, 21 June 1664.

20. BN, Mélanges Colbert 130, fol. 336, 22 June 1665; fol. 440, 27 June 1665; BN, FF 22081, fol. 22, 24 October 1679.

21. Huygens, *Œuvres*, 7:213–14.

22. Ibid., 6:67.

23. Ibid., 8:28.

24. Ibid., 7:57.

25. Ibid., 8:479–80, 8:507–9, 8:531–32, 9:99–100. Charles probably performed a similar function in the Académie Française; he updated Pierre-Daniel Huet on events in the Parisian academy while Huet was out of town. BN, FF 15189, fols. 64ff, June–July 1684.

26. Huygens, *Œuvres*, 7:36.

27. Ibid., 8:405–6, 495.

28. Ibid., 6:203–4, 8:139, 147, 151, 154–55, 225–28.

29. Ibid., 7:224, 8:507–9.

30. Ibid., 7:80, 84, 86, 100–101. The dispute between the Carcavy and Perrault families also related to the inappropriate manner in which Carcavy presented a family member to the Perraults.

31. Dessert, *Argent*, 330–31.

32. Perrault, *Mémoires*, 218.

33. Ibid., 220.

34. Ibid., 220–23.

35. *Plaise au Roi et à Nosseigneurs de son conseil.* For the possible sale of the office, AN, MC, LII 119, 28 July 1688.

36. In some cases, the differences could depend on personal interest. In comparison with his brother, Louis XIII, Gaston d'Orléans showed a much greater interest in science. Claude K. Abraham, "The French Royal Family: Patrons of Science in the Age of Louis XIII," *French Review* 37, no. 2 (1963): 206–12.

37. This discussion is based mostly on the succinct survey in Shoemaker, *Powerful Connections*, 30–36; see also Déborah Blocker and Élie Haddad, "Protections et statut d'auteur à l'époque moderne: Formes et enjeux des pratiques de patronage dans la querelle du Cid (1637)," *French Historical Studies* 31, no. 3 (2008): 381–416. On Théophile de Viau, see Stéphane van Damme, *L'Épreuve libertine: Morale, soupçon et pouvoirs dans la France baroque* (Paris: CNRS, 2008).

38. See the list of men of letters Chapelain suggested to Colbert in his *Opuscules critiques* (Paris: E. Droz, 1936), 341–64.

39. Mark Bannister, "The Crisis of Literary Patronage in France, 1643–1655," *French Studies* 39, no. 1 (1985): 18–30; Richard Maber, "Colbert and the Scholars: Menage, Huet and the Royal Pensions of 1663," *Seventeenth-Century French Studies* 7 (1985): 106–14; Georges Couton, "Effort publicitaire et organisation de la recherche: Les gratifications aux gens de lettres souls Louis XIV," in *Le XVIIᵉ siècle et la recherche: Actes du 6ème Colloque de Marseille* (Marseille: A. Robert, 1976), 41–55, and Viala, *Naissance*.

40. All the figures here and in the next paragraphs are based on the first three volumes of Jules Guiffrey, ed., *Comptes des bâtiments du roi sous le règne de Louis XIV* (Paris: Imprimerie Nationale, 1881–1901), and on the lists of gratifications published in Clément, *Lettres, instructions et mémoires*, 5:466–98.

41. Over this period, there are two years that stand out as extraordinary: in 1669, Charles is not listed as receiving an income as an aide, and in 1676 he is listed as receiving income only as part of the gratifications for men of letters. In light of the consistency of his earnings over this entire period, covering nearly twenty years, it seems probable that these are lacunae in the evidence (rather than conscious attempts to decrease Charles's salary).

42. These do not include the sums I assume Charles earned in 1669 and 1676 but were simply not documented. If these sums are included, Charles's overall income in this period would amount to 106,000 livres.

43. This estimate is based on Viala, *Naissance*, 113; see also the discussion in Turnovsky, *Literary Market*, 26–27.

44. Claudine Nédelec and Jean Leclerc, "Pierre Perrault critique littéraire," *XVIIᵉ siècle* 66 (2014): 429–45; Maurice Bardon, *Critique du livre de Dom Quichotte de la Manche* (Paris: Les Presses Modernes, 1930).

45. AAS, PV, vol. 4, fols. 123v–125r. See also Jacques Sircoulon, "Pierre Perrault, précurseur de l'hydrologie moderne," *Europe* 68, no. 739–40 (1990): 40–47.

46. [Pierre Perrault], *De l'origine des fontaines* (Paris: Jean and Laurent d'Houry, 1678) (originally published 1674). Huygens indeed took notes regarding at least the preface of Pierre's work. Huygens, *Œuvres*, 22:102–3. For the broad interest in this topic, see, for example, the discussion in the popularization of Gassendi's philosophy in François Bernier, *Abrégé de la philosophie de Gassendi* (Lyon: Anyson and Posuel, 1678), 5:41–73.

47. Perrault, *Mémoires*, 223–24.

48. AN, MC, LXXXVIII 224, 26 April 1672. Jacques Barchilon has published the list of Charles's property, leaving in manuscript the marriage contract itself. "Charles Perrault à travers les documents du Minutier Central des Archives Nationales. L'inventaire de ses meubles en 1672," *XVIIe siècle* 65 (1964): 3–15.

49. Scarlett Beauvalet, François-Joseph Ruggiu, and Vincent Gourdon, "Réseaux et mobilités à Paris au milieu du XVIIe siècle," *Histoire, économie et société* 17 (1998): 547–60, and Beauvalet and Gourdon, "Les liens sociaux."

50. Beauvalet, Ruggiu, and Gourdon, "Réseaux et mobilités," quote on 550.

51. Claire Lemercier, "Analyse de réseaux et histoire de la famille: Une rencontre encore à venir?," *Annales de démographie historique* 109, no. 1 (2005): 10.

52. I have not included in this number Pierre Perrault and Pierre Pepin, even though they signed as "noble homme." Even if their claim to nobility did not necessarily have a formal approval, their willingness to assert it in the ceremony is in itself a testament to the ambitions in Charles's milieu.

53. Slightly more than 7 percent (7.1) of the marriage contracts included a total of fifteen to twenty witnesses, and only 3.8 percent included more than twenty witnesses. Beauvalet and Gourdon, "Les liens sociaux," 588.

54. Ibid., 595.

55. Ibid., 597.

56. There are other examples for cases in which the wife of a notable signed without the husband's being present, even though the husband was a patron or protector of the person getting married. See, for example, the contract for the second marriage of François Blondel in AN, MC, XXIV 447, 28 January 1660.

57. Beauvalet and Gourdon, "Les liens sociaux," 597.

58. Sarah Chapman, *Private Ambition and Political Alliances: The Phélypeaux de Pontchartrain Family and Louis XIV's Government, 1650–1715* (Rochester, NY: University of Rochester Press, 2004), esp. 37, 49–50, 109–10; Thierry Sarmant and Mathieu Stoll, *Régner et gouverner: Louis XIV et ses ministres* (Paris: Perrin, 2010), 215–20.

59. See chap. 2.

60. Jal, *Dictionnaire critique*, 1321.

61. Perrault, *Mémoires*, 223.

62. Ibid.

63. [René Cerveau], *Supplément au nécrologe de plus célebres defenseurs et confesseurs de la verité des dix-septieme et dix-huitieme siecles...* (n.p., 1763) (unpaginated list of dates); [René Cerveau], *Nécrologe de plus célebres defenseurs et confesseurs de la verité du dix-huitieme siecle... première partie* (n.p., 1760), 171–72.

64. Perrault, *Contes*, 210.

65. This house was left to Marie by the late M. Morrand, who decreed that his sister, Mme. Molé, should benefit from the rent. For all the details of the dowry, see AN, MC, LXXXVIII 224, 26 April 1672.

66. In order to assess the relation between dowry and status, historians have routinely used data provided in Antoine Furetière's novel *Le Roman bourgeois*. As a woman with a dowry of between 45,000 and 75,000 livres, Marie would have been expected to marry a councillor at the court of aides (*cour des aides*) or the Grand Council, relatively high judicial and financial offices but not the highest. For a richer woman, one with a dowry falling between 75,000 and 150,000 livres, the appropriate

match was a councillor at Parlement or a *maître des comptes*. Given that Marie's dowry was very close to the upper boundary of the first category, her marriage appears to have happened at an intersection of social strata, which agrees with the other data on this marriage. Furetière, *Le Roman bourgeois*, 47–48; Madeleine Alcover, "Furetière et la stratification sociale: Le 'tariffe des mariages,'" *Papers on French Seventeenth Century Literature* 8 (1981): 75–93; Laurence Croq, "Des titulaires à l'évaluation sociale des qualités: Hiérarchie et mobilité collective dans la société parisienne du XVIIᵉ siècle," in *Dire et vivre l'ordre sociale en France sous l'Ancien Régime*, ed. Fanny Cosandey (Paris: Éditions de l'École des hautes études en sciences sociales, 2005), esp. 156–57; Craig Moyes, "Juste(s) titre(s): L'Économie liminaire du *Roman bourgeois*," *Études françaises* 45, no. 2 (2009): 25–45.

67. Marriage contracts of Molière, AN, MC, XLII 152, 23 January 1662, Rés [reserve] 386; of Racine, AN, MC, LXXVI 62, 30 May 1677, Rés 447; of Quinalt, AN, MC, C 260, 22 April 1660; of Conrart, AN, MC, XXI 124, 19 February 1634; of Scarron, AN, MC, LXIV 93, 4 April 1652, Rés 495; and of Donneau de Visé, AN, MC, XV 232, 20 July 1671.

68. Françoise d'Aubigné herself demonstrates the swings of fortune that could happen in this milieu: the granddaughter of Agripa d'Aubigné, the most renowned Huguenot author of the late sixteenth and early seventeenth centuries, she would secretly marry Louis XIV and impose her will on the court as Madame de Maintenon. Mark Bryant, "Partner, Matriarch and Minister: The Unofficial Consort, Mme de Maintenon of France, 1669–1715," in *Queenship in Europe 1660–1815: The Role of the Consort*, ed. Clarissa Campbell Orr (Cambridge: Cambridge University Press, 2004), 77–106.

69. Annik Pardailhé-Galabrun, *The Birth of Intimacy: Privacy and Domestic Life in Early Modern Paris* (Philadelphia: University of Pennsylvania Press, 1991), 153–56; Philip Benedict, "Toward the Comparative Study of the Popular Market for Art: The Ownership of Paintings in Seventeenth-Century Metz," in *The Faith and Fortunes of France's Huguenots, 1600–85* (Aldershot, UK: Ashgate, 2001), 193–94; Antoine Schnapper, "Probate Inventories, Public Sales and the Parisian Art Market in the Seventeenth Century," in *Art Markets in Europe, 1400–1800*, ed. Michael North and David Ormrod (Aldershot, UK: Ashgate, 1998), 131–41.

70. Schapira, *Professionnel*, 369–72, and Conrart's testament on 500–504.

71. The comparison regarding the amount and value of books owned cannot be made in detail, since Charles's inventory did not even detail what kinds of books he owned. Further, even though the dates of the documents are fairly close (1672 and 1674), a simple comparison does not take into account a strong "life-cycle" effect: Charles was at the beginning of his career as a literary author, while Conrart had been at the heart of Parisian literary life for about forty years.

72. Pardailhé-Galabrun, *Birth of Intimacy*, 147–53.

73. Philippe Minard, *La fortune du colbertisme: État et industrie dans la France des Lumières* (Paris: Fayard, 1998), 15–20. The classic study remains Charles W. Cole, *Colbert and a Century of French Mercantilism* (New York: Columbia University Press, 1939), 2: 132–362.

74. On Le Brun's stature, see Perrault, *Hommes illustres*, 228–231, and Bénédicte Gady, *L'Ascension de Charles Le Brun: Liens sociaux et production artistique* (Paris: Éditions de la Maison des sciences de l'Homme, 2010).

75. BN, FF 390, fols. 11r–12r.

76. AN, MC, XX 341, 17 April 1676; AN, MC, LXV 97, 10 February 1678; AN, MC, XCI 408, 25 April 1678; AN, MC, LXIX 102, 9 February 1681. In 1701, long after he had left Colbert's service, Charles agreed to act as the godfather of a royal painter's daughter. Jal, *Dictionnaire critique*, 957.

77. Schnapper, *Curieux*, 410ff.

78. Ralph E. Giesey, "Rules of Inheritance and Strategies of Mobility in Prerevolutionary France," *American Historical Review* 82, no. 2 (1977): 271–89.

79. George V. Taylor, "Noncapitalist Wealth and the Origins of the French Revolution," *American Historical Review* 72, no. 2 (1967): 469–96, esp. 486–87; Taylor's notion that the rents constituted a safe investment needs to be critically reexamined following the discussion in Katia Béguin, *Financer la guerre au XVIIᵉ siècle: La dette publique et les rentiers de l'absolutisme* (Seyssel: Champ Vallon, 2012).

80. Huygens, *Œuvres*, 7:153.

81. Perrault, *Mémoires*, 232–33.

82. In accordance with the inheritance practices, Charles's marriage contract treated the charge as property belonging to the lineage, which had to revert to it after Charles's death. AN, MC, LXXXVIII 224, 26 April 1672.

83. AN, MC, LXXXVIII 239, 14 April 1676; AN, MC, LXXXVIII 291, 31 August, 1691. Charles also received compensation on rent owned on a house in this street, but since it is not included in the archives of the Guichon's notaries, it could be unrelated. AN, MC, LI 601, 7 March 1681.

84. To make matters more confusing, Charles also paid for properties in other parts of the city, such as a house on the rue de Thorigny, where the family also owned a house. See AN, MC, III 720, 11 September 1686; AN, MC, III 729, 9 and 31 August 1688; AN, MC, CII 142, 7 November 1687; AN, MC, XLIII 233, 18 November 1697; AN, MC, III 730, 24 September 1688. For the most informed discussion of the Perraults' houses, see Alexandre Gady, "Les maisons de Claude et Charles Perrault, à l'Estrapade (5e arr. actuel)," *Commision du vieux Paris: Procès-verbaux* (1997): 11–22 (procès-verbal de la séance du 3 juin).

85. AN, MC, XCIV 47, 29 September 1677; AN, MC, XV 267, 14 August 1678.

86. For Louis XIV's decree, see Clément, *Lettres, instructions, et mémoires,* 5:529; for Charles's property in Versailles, see AN, O¹ 19, fols. 262v–263r; AN, O¹ 25, fols. 174r–175r; AN, MC, C 497, 16 November 1714. See also Gautier, "Charles Perrault," 1059–60, for a transcription of one of the king's gifts in AN, O¹ 19, fols. 262v–263r.

87. For example, in 1691 Charles lodged a complaint against tenants in a house in the Rue Saint-Jacques. BN, FF 21725, fol. 130r–v. The annual rent, 72 livres, is much lower than other rents on houses Charles handled and seems to suggest that he divided properties into smaller apartments or that he owned apartments as well as buildings.

88. Huygens, *Œuvres*, 7:153, 8:122. Huygens seems to be a little off on the date of birth.

89. For the boys, see Jal, *Dictionnaire critique*, 1321. So far, the only evidence for the birth of Charles Perrault's daughter has been a dedication to "Mademoiselle Perrault" in Mlle. L'Héritier's *Œuvres meslées* (Paris: Jean Guignard, 1696), 1. I have found evidence for her in the documents relating to the succession of Samuel Guichon's property (Marie Guichon's father). The notary's marginal notation identified her as "Damoiselle Marie Magdeleine Perault," but her own signature at the bottom of the page is "Marie Madeleine Perrault," and I follow this spelling. See AN, MC, LXXXVIII 267, 5 April 1685.

90. Jal, *Dictionnaire critique*, 1321.

91. AN, MC, LXXXVIII 224, 26 April 1672.

92. Perrault, *Mémoires*, 231–32; Jacob Soll, *The Information Master: Jean-Baptiste Colbert's Secret State Intelligence System* (Ann Arbor: University of Michigan Press, 2009), 153–59.

93. AN, MC, LXXXVIII 267, 5 April 1685, where it also stipulated that the sum was half of what Marie received as an advance in her marriage contract.

94. Jal, *Dictionnaire critique*, 957. The register of Saint-Benoist seems to have been signed by Victor Armand Guichon (Jal transcribed the name as Hector hermand Guichon), Charles, and two of his sons, Charles and Pierre. *Mercure galant*, May 1703, 250–51.

95. Charles Perrault, *La Chasse. A Monsieur de Rosieres* (Paris: La Veuve de Jean Bapt. Coignard and Jean Baptiste Coignard Fils, 1692).

96. Charles Perrault and François Boutard, *Sur L'embrasement de l'Eglise de Troyes. Ode* (Troyes: Edme Prevost, 1692).

97. Tallemant, "Éloge funèbre de Mr. Perrault," 2:598.

98. Nicolas Boileau-Despréaux, *Œuvres complètes*, ed. Antoine Adam (Paris: Gallimard, 1966),781–82. In comparison, Charles's poem did not provoke strong reactions by other supporters of the ancients, who were not as personally hostile to him. Pierre-Daniel Huet, one of the most renowned scholars in France at the time, criticized Charles's support of the moderns while still describing him as his friend. Huet, *Mémoires (1718)*, ed. Philippe Joseph Salazar (Toulouse: Société de Littératures Classiques, 1993), 79, 117–18.

99. Charles wrote an elaborate manuscript titled "Christian Thoughts," which can be probably dated to the period 1685–1703 and was never published in his lifetime. BN, FF 25575.

100. *Mercure galant*, December 1698, 126–34; Charles Perrault, *Portrait de Messire Benigne Bossuet, evêque de Meaux, au Serenissime Prince Cosme III, Grand Duc de Toscane* (Paris: Jean-Baptiste Coignard, 1698).

101. On Charles's aesthetic, see further Larry Norman, "La pensée esthétique de Charles Perrault," *XVIIᵉ siècle* 66 (2014): 481–92.

102. This manuscript copy is bound with a printed version of the French poem, with the Latin translation facing the French original [BN, RES-YE-72]. On the importance of translations into Latin, see Peter Burke, "Translations into Latin in Early Modern Europe," in *Cultural Translation in Early Modern Europe*, ed. R. Po-chia Hsia and Peter Burke (Cambridge: Cambridge University Press, 2007), 65–80.

103. Mazarine, MS 3933. As would be fitting for a worldly poet, Charles underscored the "natural purity" and elegance of Santeul's Latin poetry in *Hommes illustres*, 293.

104. *Leo aeger, vulpes et lupus, fabula. Le Lion malade, le renard et le loup, fable traduite du latin de M. Du Périer* (Paris: A. Cramoisy, 1686); *Traduction des fables de Faerne* (Paris: J.-B. Coignard, 1699).

105. Yvonne Bézard, "Autour d'un éloge de Pascal: Une affaire de censure tranchée par Louis XIV en 1696," *Revue d'histoire littéraire de la France* 33 (1926): 215–24.

106. BN, FF 24346, 24350, and for a later copy, BN, FF 9297.

107. Charles Perrault, *Le Génie, épistre à M. de Fontenelle* (Paris: J.-B. Coignard, 1688); Charles Perrault, *À M. le président Rose. Épître* (Paris: J.-B. Coignard, 1691); Charles Perrault, *A monsieur de La Quintinye, sur son livre De l'instruction des jardins fruitiers & potagers* (1690?); Charles Perrault, *À Mgr le Dauphin sur la prise de Philisbourg, ode*

(Paris: J.-B. Coignard, 1688); Charles Perrault, *Pour le roi de Suède, ode* (Paris: J.-B. Coignard, 1702); *Au Roy Philippe V allant en Espagne, ode* [Latin by F. Boutard and French by Charles Perrault] (Paris: J.-B. Coignard, 1701). For the connections between Charles and the Swedes, see Soriano, *Dossier Charles Perrault,* 339–40.

108. See most prominently the classic article by Robert Darnton, "The High Enlightenment and the Low-Life of Literature in Pre-Revolutionary France," *Past and Present* 51 (1971): 81–115, but see in addition the discussion in Turnovsky, *Literary Market.* For a discussion on a much broader scale, see Roger Chartier, "Time to Understand: The Frustrated Intellectuals," in *Cultural History: Between Practices and Representations* (Ithaca: Cornell University Press, 1988), 127–50.

5. The Perraults and Versailles

1. Perrault, *Contes,* 203–4.

2. Huygens, *Œuvres,* 7:172–73. On the Carons, Huygens's relatives, see ibid., 6:76.

3. Jean de La Fontaine, *L'Amour de Psyché et de Cupidon* [1669], book 1, in *Œuvres de J. de La Fontaine,* ed. Henri Regnier (Paris: Hachette, 1892), 8:31.

4. Huygens, *Œuvres,* 7:173.

5. Jacques Barchilon even suggested that the wealth of details on characters and architecture in Perrault's tales is based on the characters and the architecture of Versailles. *Perrault's Tales of Mother Goose, the Dedication Manuscript of 1695 Reproduced in Collotype Facsimile with Introduction and Critical Text* (New York: Pierpont Morgan Library, 1956), 89–90.

6. Frédéric Tiberghien, *Versailles: Le chantier de Louis XIV, 1662–1715* (Paris: Perrin, 2002); Richard Bonney, "Vindication of the Fronde? The Cost of Louis XIV's Versailles Building Programme," *French History* 21, no. 2 (2007): 205–25; Jeroen Duindam, *Vienna and Versailles: The Courts of Europe's Major Dynastic Rivals, 1550–1780* (Cambridge: Cambridge University Press, 2003), 45–89.

7. For the complexities and range of actors in another royal project, see Chandra Mukeri, *Impossible Engineering: Technology and Territoriality on the Canal du Midi* (Princeton: Princeton University Press, 2009).

8. Norbert Elias, *The Court Society* (Oxford: Blackwell, 1983); Elias, *The Civilizing Process* (Oxford: Blackwell, 1994). For a penetrating critique, see Jeroen Duindam, *Myths of Power: Norbert Elias and the Early Modern European Court* (Amsterdam: Amsterdam University Press, 1994). For Versailles as a source of inspiration, see, among many possible examples, Solnon, *Cour de France,* 373–417.

9. Emmanuel Le Roy Ladurie, *Saint-Simon and the Court of Louis XIV* (Chicago: University of Chicago Press, 2001), 349–52; William Beik, "A Social Interpretation of the Reign of Louis XIV," in *L'Etat ou le Roi: Les fondations de la modernité monarchique en France (XIVᵉ–XVIIᵉ siècles),* ed. Neithard Bulst, Robert Descimon, and Alain Guerreau (Paris: Éditions de la Maison des Sciences de l'Homme, 1996), 147–53; Leonhard Horowski, "'Such a Great Advantage for My Son': Office-Holding and Career Mechanisms at the Court of France, 1661 to 1789," *Court Historian* 8 (2003): 125–75.

10. For an overview, see Duindam, *Vienna and Versailles,* 3–20. However, this view is far from being an orthodoxy, and the impact of the old terminology can still be felt, especially in studies of art and culture. For example, see Georgia Cowart, *The*

Triumph of Pleasure: Louis XIV and The Politics of Spectacle (Chicago: University of Chicago Press, 2008), 45.

11. Giora Sternberg, *Status Interaction during the Reign of Louis XIV* (Oxford: Oxford University Press, 2014).

12. Peter Burke, *The Fabrication of Louis XIV* (New Haven: Yale University Press, 1992), esp. 86–91 and passim, for the importance of Colbert's "machine." Gérard Sabatier claimed that Versailles became part of "Louis XIV's strategy as a complete mechanism. Even better: it became the most effective instrument of absolutism," in his *Versailles, ou la figure du roi* (Paris: A. Michel, 1999), 41. Cf. Chandra Mukerji, *Territorial Ambitions and the Gardens of Versailles* (Cambridge: Cambridge University Press, 1997).

13. Jeroen Duindam, "Early Modern Court Studies: An Overview and a Proposal," in *Historiographie an europäischen Höfen (16.–18. Jahrhundert)*, ed. Markus Völkel and Arno Strohmeyer (Berlin: Duncker & Humblot, 2009), 38.

14. Abby E. Zanger, *Scenes from the Marriage of Louis XIV: Nuptial Fictions and the Making of Absolutist Power* (Stanford: Stanford University Press, 1997), esp. 70 for the argument that propaganda efforts were the results of collaborations between Mazarin, Louis XIV, and literary actors who did not share identical interests but could cooperate to their mutual benefit; Richard Cleary, *The Place Royale and Urban Design in the Ancien Régime* (Cambridge: Cambridge University Press, 1999); Claire Goldstein, *Vaux and Versailles: The Appropriations, Erasures, and Accidents That Made Modern France* (Philadelphia: University of Pennsylvania Press, 2008); and Elizabeth Hyde, *Cultivated Power: Flowers, Culture, and Politics in the Reign of Louis XIV* (Philadelphia: University of Pennsylvania Press, 2005), 137–96. However, of these works, only Goldstein's focuses explicitly on Versailles, and it employs a different approach than mine.

15. Éric Soullard, "Les eaux de Versailles sous Louis XIV," *Hypothèses*, no. 1 (1997): 108.

16. Solnon, *Cour de France*, 279–81.

17. Primi Visconti, *Mémoires sur la Cour de Louis XIV, 1673–1681*, ed. Jean-François Solnon (Paris: Perrin, 1988), 152.

18. Tiberghien, *Versailles*, 33–39.

19. BN, Mélanges Colbert 176 bis, fol. 742; BN, Mélanges Colbert 153 bis, fol. 784; see also Tiberghien, *Versailles*, 51–52.

20. Isaac Benserade and Charles Perrault, *Le labyrinthe de Versailles* (Paris: De l'imprimerie royale, 1679), as well as Charles Perrault, *Recueil des divers ouvrages en prose et en vers* (Paris: Jean-Baptiste Coignard, Guillaume de Luyne et Jean Guignard, 1675), 225–68. Marc Soriano doubts Charles's involvement in the project with Benserade, arguing that Charles tried to claim this work to his credit by composing other versions of the fables. This interpretation only reinforces the portrait of Charles as a "creative poacher" suggested here. Soriano, *Dossier Charles Perrault*, 168–69.

21. Charles Perrault et al., *Courses de testes et de bague faites par le Roy et par les princes et seigneurs de sa cour en l'année M.DC.LXII* (Paris: Imprimerie Royale, 1670).

22. Huygens, *Œuvres*, 7:172–73.

23. Charles Perrault, *Parallèle des Anciens et des Modernes...* (Paris: Jean Baptiste Coignard, 1688–97).

24. Ibid., 1:110. Perrault used the word *pièce* in a wide sense, to include not only a room but also courts and other enclosed spaces.

25. Ibid., 1: 110–26.

26. Ibid., 1:122.

27. Charles Perrault, *Saint Paulin, Évêque de Nole* (Paris: Jean Baptiste Coignard, 1686).

28. Ibid., 39–45.

29. R. J. Howells, "The Uses of Versailles in the 'Parallèle des anciens et des modernes,'" *Newsletter of the Society for Seventeenth-Century French Studies* 5 (1983): 70–77. More generally, see (among many possible references) April G. Shelford, *Transforming the Republic of Letters: Pierre-Daniel Huet and European Intellectual Life, 1650–1720* (Rochester, NY: University of Rochester Press, 2007); Larry F. Norman, *The Shock of the Ancient: Literature and History in Early Modern France* (Chicago: University of Chicago Press, 2011).

30. Perrault, *Parallèle,* 1:10.

31. Ibid., 1:109–10.

32. Rabinovitch, "Rethinking the Center-Periphery Nexus."

33. Perrault, *Parallèle,* 2:2–3.

34. Ibid., 1:161–66.

35. Ibid., 3:31.

36. Ibid., 4:84–87.

37. Ibid., 4:285–92, and see Howells, "Uses of Versailles," 75–76; Simon Werrett, *Fireworks: Pyrotechnic Arts and Sciences in European History* (Chicago: University of Chicago Press, 2010), 126–29.

38. Perrault, *Parallèle,* 1:126–45. Cf. Fontenelle's claim that since nature remains the same, it produces the same products, and consequently, the moderns are not inferior in comparison with the ancients. Bernard Le Bovier de Fontenelle, "Digression sur les Anciens et les Modernes," in *La Querelle des Anciens et des Modernes, XVIIᵉ–XVIIIᵉ Siècles,* ed. Anne-Marie Lecoq (Paris: Gallimard, 2001), 295–98.

39. For starting points, see Harold Love, *Scribal Publication in Seventeenth-Century England* (Oxford: Clarendon Press, 1993), and the forum "How Revolutionary Was the Print Revolution?," *American Historical Review* 107, no. 1 (2002): 84–128.

40. Bontemps was one of the four *premier valets de chambre.* The manuscript copy is in Bibliothèque du château de Chantilly, MS 442.

41. Pierre de Nolhac, *Les bibliothèques du château de Versailles* (Paris: Le Livre contemporain, 1906), 6; Simone Balayé, *La Bibliothèque nationale, des origines à 1800* (Geneva: Droz, 1988), 199n. For the differences between the king's private collections and the Royal Library, see Roger Chartier, "Le Prince, la bibliothèque et la dédicace," in *Le Pouvoir des bibliothèques: La mémoire des livres en Occident,* ed. Marc Baratin and Christian Jacob (Paris: A. Michel, 1996), 204–23; see also Simone Balayé, "La Bibliothèque du Roi, première bibliothèque du monde, 1664–1789," in *Histoire des bibliothèques françaises,* vol. 2, *Les bibliothèques sous l'Ancien Régime, 1530–1789,* ed. Claude Jolly (Paris: Promodis-Éditions du Cercle du librairie, 1988), 209–33. Gallois described dozens of French libraries, and especially Parisian ones, in Pierre le Gallois, *Traité des plus belles bibliothèques de l'Europe* (Paris: E. Michallet, 1680), 121–37. This and the next paragraphs rely on Oded Rabinovitch, "Anonymat et institutions littéraires au XVIIᵉ siècle: La revendication des œuvres anonymes dans la carrière de Charles Perrault," *Littératures classiques* 80 (2013): 87–104.

42. Perrault, *Recueil;* Sabatier, *Versailles,* 444, for Le Laboureur; Gautier, "Charles Perrault," 32.

43. Perrault, *Recueil*, épître, n.p.

44. Ibid.

45. Charles Perrault, *Critique de l'opéra, ou examen de la tragédie intitulée Alceste, ou le Triomphe d'Alcide* (Paris: Claude Barbin, 1674); *Le Banquet des dieux, pour la naissance de Monseigneur le Duc de Bourgogne* (Paris: J.-B. Coignard, 1682).

46. This table omits pirated editions printed outside France and the first publication, in 1691, of "Griselidis," as part of a collection of poetry and orations read at the Académie française. See Catherine Velay-Vallantin, "Tales as a Mirror: Perrault in the Bibliothèque Bleue," in *The Culture of Print: Power and the Uses of Print in Early Modern Europe*, ed. Roger Chartier (Princeton: Princeton University Press, 1989), 93–97.

47. Soriano, *Contes de Perrault*, 54–71; Gérard Gélinas, *Enquête sur les Contes de Perrault* (Paris: Imago, 2004); Monique Brosseau, with the contribution of Gérard Gélinas, "Du nouveau dans le dossier Perrault," *Papers on French Seventeenth Century Literature* 36 (2009): 267–76.

48. See, for example, Pierre de Villiers, *Entretiens sur les contes de fées et sur quelques autres ouvrages du temps, pour servir de préservatif contre le mauvais gout* (Paris: Jacques Collombat, 1699), 108–10. Jacques Barchilon showed the changes made between the manuscript and the printed version in Barchilon, *Perrault's Tales of Mother Goose*.

49. E.g., the satirical suggestions that Blaise Pascal was helped by his father in Gabriel Daniel, *Voyage du monde de Descartes* (Paris: Nicolas Pepie, 1702), 262–63.

50. Guy Rowlands, *The Dynastic State and the Army under Louis XIV: Royal Service and Private Interest, 1661–1701* (Cambridge: Cambridge University Press, 2002), 169, and Hervé Drévillon, *L'Impôt du sang: Le métier des armes sous Louis XIV* (Paris: Tallandier, 2006), esp. chaps. 5 and 6.

51. Filippo de Vivo, *Information and Communication in Venice: Rethinking Early Modern Politics* (Oxford: Oxford University Press, 2007), 12.

52. Gustave Loisel, *Histoire des ménageries de l'antiquité à nos jours* (Paris: Ocatve Doin et fils, 1912), 2:102–83. On the importation of exotic animals, see also Louise Robbins, *Elephant Slaves and Pampered Parrots: Exotic Animals in Eighteenth-Century Paris* (Baltimore: Johns Hopkins University Press, 2002).

53. These paragraphs draw on my broader discussion of the Academy of Science in Oded Rabinovitch, "Chameleons between Science and Literature: Observation, Writing, and the Early Parisian Academy of Sciences in the Literary Field," *History of Science* 51, no. 1 (2013): 33–62, which also provides further references (esp. notes 6 and 13).

54. Guy Meynell, "The Académie des sciences at the rue Vivienne, 1666–1699," *Archives internationales d'histoire des sciences* 44 (1994): 22–37. In 1699, the academy moved to the Louvre.

55. Marianne Grivel, "Le Cabinet du Roi," *Revue de la Bibliothèque nationale* 18 (1985): 36–57, and Anita Guerrini, *The Courtiers' Anatomists: Animals and Humans in Louis XIV's Paris* (Chicago: University of Chicago Press, 2015), 147–51.

56. On the limits of the academy's ability to provide the monarchy with useful technology, see Robin Briggs, "The Académie Royale des Sciences and the Pursuit of Utility," *Past & Present* 131 (1991): 38–88. Contrast Roger Hahn, "Louis XIV and Science Policy," in *Sun King: The Ascendancy of French Culture during the Reign of Louis XIV*, ed. David L. Rubin (Washington, DC: Folger Shakespeare Library, 1992), 195–206.

57. Sturdy, *Science and Social Status*, 86–87.

58. The memoir on lime was presented in 1667, AAS, PV (Archives de l'Académie de sciences, procès-verbaux), vol. 1, fols. 308–28, published in the fourth volume of Claude Perrault's *Essais de physique* (Paris, 1688); on the academy's decision regarding the circulation of sap and the critiques of this project see AAS, PV, vol. 4, fols. 98r–99v, and, for a different interpretation, see Alice Stroup, *A Company of Scientists: Botany, Patronage, and Community at the Seventeenth-Century Parisian Royal Academy of Sciences* (Berkeley: University of California Press, 1990), 131–44.

59. Peter Sahlins, "The Beast Within: Animals in the First Xenotransfusion Experiments in France, ca. 1667–68," *Representations* 129 (2015): 25–55.

60. The most detailed analysis of the purely anatomical aspects of this project is the dated F. J. Cole, *A History of Comparative Anatomy, from Aristotle to the Eighteenth Century* (London: Macmillan, 1944), 393–434, now superseded by Guerrini, *Courtiers' Anatomists*.

61. *Mémoires pour servir à l'histoire naturelle des animaux* (Paris: Imprimerie royale, 1676).

62. Sutton, *Science for a Polite Society*, 126–29; Erica Harth, *Ideology and Culture in Seventeenth-Century France* (Ithaca: Cornell University Press, 1983), 261–64; E. C. Watson, "The Early Days of the Académie des Sciences as Portrayed in the Engravings of Sébastien Le Clerc," *Osiris* 7 (1939): 556–87.

63. Guerrini, *Courtiers' Anatomists*, 148–49; Picon, *Claude Perrault*, 54–74.

64. AAS, dossier Claude Perrault.

65. *Mémoires pour servir à l'histoire naturelle des animaux* (Paris: Imprimerie royale, 1676), frontispiece and preface. On the distribution of credit among practitioners in such projects, see Guerrini, *Courtiers' Anatomists*, 105–9.

66. I discuss this episode in a fuller manner in "Chameleons between Science and Literature."

67. AAS, PV, vol. 4, fol. 227.

68. *Description anatomique d'un caméléon, d'un castor, d'un dromadaire, d'un ours et d'une gazelle* (Paris: Léonard, 1669), 47.

69. AAS, PV, vol. 4, fols. 229–94, passim.

70. Peter Sahlins, "The Royal Menageries of Louis XIV and the Civilizing Process Revisited," *French Historical Studies* 35, no. 2 (2012): 237–67.

71. Loisel, *Histoire de ménageries*, 2:297.

72. C. A. Bayly, "'Archaic' and 'Modern' Globalization in the Eurasian and African Arena, ca. 1750–1850," in *Globalization in World History*, ed. A. G. Hopkins (New York: Norton, 2002), 50–52.

73. For this and other details, I am indebted to Nicholas Dew, "Species as Specimens: Louis XIV's Menagerie and the Académie des Sciences" (unpublished manuscript, 1998).

74. The *pochettes des séances* for the years 1667–76, preserved in the academy's archives, include notes on the dissections of several common animals, such as pigeons, dogs, and ducks.

75. AAS, dossier J. G. Duverney.

76. *Mémoires pour servir à l'histoire naturelle des animaux* (1676), 186.

77. Justel to Oldenburg, 3 October 1666, in Henry Oldenburg, *Correspondence*, ed. A. Rupert and Marie Boas Hall (Madison: University of Wisconsin Press, 1965), 3:240; Vernon to Oldenburg, 2 June 1669, in Oldenburg, *Correspondence*, 6:6.

78. Cf. Sahlins, "Royal Menageries."

79. Tiberghien, *Versailles*, 45–49, 98.

80. Le Roy Ladurie, *Saint-Simon*, chap. 4, esp. 150.

81. Jouhaud, *Pouvoirs de la littérature*, 20–21, 368.

82. Even letters of dedication reveal a wide range of motivations and of relations between writers and their protectors. Wolfgang Leiner, *Der Widmungsbrief in der französischen Literatur (1580–1715)* (Heidelberg: Winter, 1965), 131–57.

83. Compare the stress on Colbert's state projects in Soll, *Information Master*, 153–59, with the importance of family elements in John C. Rule and Ben S. Trotter, *A World of Paper: Louis XIV, Colbert de Torcy, and the Rise of the Information State* (Montreal: McGill-Queen's University Press, 2014), 226–76.

84. Huygens, *Œuvres*, 7:193. On Huygens's anxiety about the war, see ibid., 7:173 and especially 7:195.

85. Rowlands, *Dynastic State*, and Chapman, *Private Ambition*.

86. William Beik, "The Absolutism of Louis XIV as Social Collaboration," *Past & Present* 188 (2005): 196–97, for the distinction between the "practice of governance" and the "theory of absolutism."

6. Claude Perrault and the Mechanics of Animals

1. Alberto Tenenti, "Claude Perrault et la pensée scientifique française dans la seconde moitié du XVIIᵉ siècle," in *Éventail de l'histoire vivante, hommage à Lucien Febvre offert par l'amité d'historiens, linguistes, géographes, économistes, sociologues, ethnologues* (Paris: A. Colin, 1953), 2:303–16.

2. Claude's eulogy in *Mercure galant*, reproduced in Fontenelle, *Œuvres complètes*, 7:269–71.

3. See the classic study, Hahn, *Anatomy of a Scientific Institution*; Stroup, *Company of Scientists*, and the summary in James E. McClellan III, "L'Académie royale des sciences (1666–1793)," in *Lieux de savoir*, vol. 1, *Espaces et communautés*, ed. Christian Jacob (Paris: A. Michel, 2007), 716–36.

4. For an attempt to define and work through this problem, see J. B. Shank, "Making Science and State (Or the Other Way Around) in Louis XIV's France" (unpublished manuscript, 2012).

5. Claude Perrault, *De la mécanique des animaux*, vol. 3 of *Essais de physique, ou recueil de plusieurs traitez touchant les choses naturelles* (Paris: Jean-Baptiste Coignard, 1680–88).

6. For the importance of heterogeneous contexts in the creation of skills and attitudes, I am indebted to Bernard Lahire, "De la théorie de l'habitus à une sociologie psychologique," in *Le Travail sociologique de Pierre Bourdieu: Dettes et critiques*, ed. Bernard Lahire (Paris: La Découverte, 2001), 121–52.

7. The major difference between Claude Perrault's thinking and that of Descartes resided in Claude's reliance on the concepts of hardness (*dureté*) and spring (*ressort*). For Descartes, the cohesion of bodies stemmed from the effort necessary to separate their constituent parts. Claude used these concepts, in turn, to explain why body parts move: "The fibers in muscles or membranes move since they are naturally tense, just like a bone is naturally hard and cartilage is naturally flexible." Picon, *Claude Perrault*, 76; François Azouvi, "Entre Descartes et Leibniz: L'Animisme dans les *Essais de physique* de Claude Perrault," *Recherches sur le XVIIᵉ siècle* 5 (1982): 9–19.

8. Claire Salomon-Bayet, *L'Institution de la science et l'expérience du vivant: Méthode et expérience à l'Académie royale des sciences, 1666–1793* (Paris: Flammarion, 1978), 72.

9. Guerrini, *Courtiers' Anatomists*, quote on 156.

10. Domenico Bertoloni Meli, *Mechanism, Experiment, Disease: Marcello Malpighi and Seventeenth-Century Anatomy* (Baltimore: Johns Hopkins University Press, 2011), 12–16, 280–306 for discussion of differing approaches.

11. Perrault, *Mécanique*, 1–2.

12. Ibid., 7–8. The French term *expérience* could designate both experience and experiments.

13. Ibid., 68–118.

14. Ibid., 303.

15. Ibid., 296–302.

16. Marin Cureau de La Chambre, *Nouvelles conjectures sur la digestion* (Paris: Pierre Rocolet, 1636), esp. 15–19 for a discussion of digestion in terms of changes induced in the food.

17. Bernier, *Abrégé de la philosophie de Gassendi*, 7:600–623.

18. Christoph Lüthy, "Where Logical Necessity Becomes Visual Persuasion: Descartes's Clear and Distinct Illustrations," in *Transmitting Knowledge: Words, Images, and Instruments in Early Modern Europe*, ed. Sachiko Kusukawa and Ian Maclean (Oxford: Oxford University Press, 2006), 103.

19. Perrault, *Mécanique*, 4–5.

20. I have used the (posthumous) edition of René Descartes, *L'Homme et un traité de la formation de fœtus* (Paris: Charles Angot, 1664).

21. Perrault, *Mécanique*, 79, 255, 270.

22. Joseph Du Verney, *Traité de l'organe de l'ouïe . . .* (Paris: Estienne Michallet, 1683).

23. Howard E. Gruber, "The Evolving Systems Approach to Creative Work," in *Creative People at Work: Twelve Cognitive Case Studies*, ed. Doris B. Wallace and Howard E. Gruber (New York: Oxford University Press, 1989), 3–24; Frederic L. Holmes, *Investigative Pathways: Patterns and Stages in the Careers of Experimental Scientists* (New Haven: Yale University Press, 2004).

24. Gerd Gigerenzer, "Where Do New Ideas Come From?," in *Dimensions of Creativity*, ed. Margaret A. Boden (Cambridge, MA: MIT Press, 1994), 54–55.

25. See the detailed discussion in Adrian Mallon, "Science and Government in France, 1661–1699: Changing Patterns of Scientific Research and Development" (PhD diss., Queen's University Belfast, 1983), chap. 2.

26. Ibid., 90–92.

27. Stéphane Schmitt, "Studies on Animals and the Rise of Comparative Anatomy at and around the Parisian Royal Academy of Sciences in the Eighteenth Century," *Science in Context* 29, no. 1 (2016): 13–17.

28. Claude Perrault, *Mémoires pour servir à l'histoire naturelle des animaux*; Denis Dodart, *Mémoires pour servir à l'histoire des plantes* (Paris: Imprimerie royale, 1676).

29. Stroup, *Company of Scientists*, esp. 89–102.

30. Mallon, "Science and Government," 92–130 for an overview; Nicholas Dew, "*Vers la ligne*: Circulating Measurements around the French Atlantic," in *Science and Empire in the Atlantic World*, ed. James Delbourgo and Nicholas Dew (New York: Routledge, 2008), 53–57; Nicholas Dew, "Scientific Travel in the Atlantic World: The French

Expedition to Gorée and the Antilles, 1681–1683," *British Journal for the History of Science* 43, no. 1 (2010): 1–17; Florence Hsia, *Sojourners in a Strange Land: Jesuits and Their Scientific Missions in Late Imperial China* (Chicago: University of Chicago Press, 2009).

31. Perrault, *Mécanique*, 95, 124, 147.

32. Ibid., 5. Perrault recruited du Verney to the academy after the death of Gayant and Pecquet, his collaborators on animal dissections: Sturdy, *Science and Social Status*, 189–92; Guerrini, *Courtiers' Anatomists*, 12–15 and chapters 5–6.

33. Charles-Antoine Jombert, *Catalogue raisonnée de l'œuvre de Sébastien Le Clerc, chevalier romain, dessinateur et graveur du cabinet du Roi . . .* (Paris: Chez l'auteur, 1774), 1:lxxxii, 270–73.

34. Watson, "Early Days"; Oded Rabinovitch, "A Learned Artisan Debates the System of the World: Le Clerc versus Mallemant de Messange," *British Journal for the History of Science* 50, no. 4 (2017): 603–36.

35. Jombert, *Catalogue*, 1:lxxxi.

36. AAS, PV, vol. 10, fol. 112r–v. No such volume appeared in the seventeenth century; for the legacy of the project, see Guerrini, *Courtiers' Anatomists*, 247–54.

37. See, for example, Daniel Garber, "On the Frontlines of the Scientific Revolution: How Mersenne Learned to Love Galileo," *Perspectives on Science* 12, no. 2 (2004): 135–63.

38. The quotations here are from the classic E. J Dijksterhuis, *The Mechanization of the World Picture* (Princeton: Princeton University Press, 1986), 498, 495.

39. Mallon, "Science and Government," 76–81; Dennis Des Chene, "Mechanisms of Life in the Seventeenth Century: Borelli, Perrault, Régis," *Studies in History and Philosophy of Biological and Biomedical Sciences* 26, no. 2 (2005): 245–60.

40. Stroup, *Company of Scientists*, 49.

41. AAS, PV, vol. 8, fols. 64r, 196v.

42. AAS, PV, vol. 11, fol. 35r.

43. AAS, PV, vol. 7, fols. 245r–v, 109v–110r.

44. Huygens, *Œuvres*, 9:99–100.

45. On promised improvements on Claude's translation, see Huygens, *Œuvres*, 9:448; on the ancient machine that perhaps served as an inspiration for a vacuum pump, see ibid., 19:241.

46. E.g., Domenico Bertoloni Meli, *Thinking with Objects: The Transformation of Mechanics in the Seventeenth Century* (Baltimore: Johns Hopkins University Press, 2006), 161–65.

47. *Journal des sçavans*, August 12, 1680, 217–22, quotes on 217, 219.

48. Claude Perrault, *Du bruit*, vol. 2 of *Essais de physique*; see Veit Erlmann, *Reason and Resonance: A History of Modern Aurality* (New York: Zone Books, 2010), 69–109.

49. Perrault, *Bruit*, 5.

50. Ibid., 217–18.

51. Ibid., 187–88.

52. For example, ibid., 213.

53. Beyond the works discussed above, see Picon, *Claude Perrault*, 103–14.

54. On Du Hamel, see Sturdy, *Science and Social Status*, 82–86.

55. Robert W. Berger, *The Palace of the Sun: The Louvre of Louis XIV* (University Park: Penn State University Press, 1993), 25–40, 83–86, quote on 85; Michael Petzet,

Claude Perrault und die Architektur des Sonnenkönigs: Der Louvre König Ludwigs XIV. und das Werk Claude Perraults (Munich: Deutscher Kunstverlag, 2000), 158–82.

56. Gottfried Wilhelm Leibniz, "Note de Leibniz sur l'achèvement du Louvre," *Revue des sociétés savantes* 3 (1857): 595.

57. Pierre-Jean Mariette, *Abecedario et autres notes inédites sur les arts et les artists*, ed. Ph. de Chennevières and A. de Montaiglon (Paris: J.-B. Dumoulin, 1856), 3:106.

58. Mallon, "Science and Government," 135–37; Stroup, *Company of Scientists*, 80; Tara Nummedal and Paula Findlen, "Words of Nature: Scientific Books in the Seventeenth Century," in *Thornton and Tully's Scientific Books, Libraries and Collectors: A Study of Bibliography and the Book Trade in Relation to the History of Science*, 4th ed., ed. Andrew Hunter (Brookfield, VT: Ashgate, 2000), 176, 193–94.

59. AAS, dossier Claude Perrault.

60. This could have been one of the purposes of the anticipated visit of the Perraults to the Netherlands, which Huygens planned. See chapter 4.

61. Nathalie Heinich, *Du peintre à l'artiste: Artisans et académiciens à l'âge classique* (Paris: Minuit, 1993), 92–94.

62. Mark Motley, *Becoming a French Aristocrat: The Education of the Court Nobility, 1580–1715* (Princeton: Princeton University Press, 1990), 123–68.

63. Quoted ibid., 134.

64. Erwin Panofsky, "Artist, Scientist, Genius: Notes on the Renaissance-Dämmerung," in *The Renaissance: Six Essays* (New York: Harper & Row, 1962), 121–82, esp. 131–40. The importance of visual and drawing skills for early modern scientific endeavors has been gaining wider recognition; see, for example, Horst Bredekamp, "Gazing Hands and Blind Spots: Galileo as Draftsman," in *Galileo in Context*, ed. Jürgen Renn (Cambridge: Cambridge University Press, 2001), 153–92.

65. Charles Perrault, preface to *Recueil de plusieurs machines de nouvelle invention, ouvrage posthume de M. Perrault*, by Claude Perrault (Paris: J.-B. Coignard, 1700), n.p.

66. On Blondel's career, see Sturdy, *Science and Social Status*, 171–81; Anthony Gerbino, *François Blondel: Architecture, Erudition, and the Scientific Revolution* (London: Routledge, 2010).

67. On the collection and Niquet's involvement with it, see Mallon, "Science and Government," 92–99.

68. Clément, *Lettres, instructions, et mémoires*, 5:xvi, also quoted in Sturdy, *Science and Social Status*, 129n13.

69. Jed Z. Buchwald, "Discrepant Measurements and Experimental Knowledge in the Early Modern Era," *Archive for History of Exact Sciences* 60, no. 6 (2006): 565–649, esp. 606–13.

70. Adrien Baillet, *La vie de Monsieur Descartes* (Paris: Daniel Horthemels, 1691), 1:196–97.

71. Wolfgang Herrmann, *The Theory of Claude Perrault* (London: A. Zwemmer, 1973), 3–5.

72. For the Vesalian challenge to this tradition, see Andrea Carlino, *Books of the Body: Anatomical Ritual and Renaissance Learning* (Chicago: University of Chicago Press, 1999).

73. Sturdy, *Science and Social Status*, 263.

74. ASS, PV, vol. 8, fols. 211r–212r.

75. *Journal des sçavans*, August 12, 1680, 221. For their descriptions in the *Natural History of Animals*, see *Mémoires pour servir à l'histoire naturelle des animaux*, 13–27, 113–19.

76. Brockliss and Jones, *Medical World*, 208.

77. On the artistic collaborations between Charles and Claude, see Marianne Cojannot-Le Blanc, "Les artistes privés de l'invention? Réflexions sur les 'desseins' de Charles et Claude Perrault pour les Bâtiments du roi dans les années 1660," *XVIIe siècle* 66 (2014): 467–79.

78. Claude Perrault, "Voyage à Bordeaux (1669)," in *Mémoires de ma vie, par Charles Perrault. Voyage à Bordeaux (1669) par Claude Perrault*, ed. Paul Bonnefon (Paris: Renouard, 1909).

79. Ibid., 141, 151.

80. Ibid., 199, 209.

81. Gerbino, *François Blondel*, 8–40.

82. Ibid., 118–19.

83. Ibid., 27.

84. Sturdy, *Science and Social Status*, 113, 182–84; Jean-Dominique Cassini, *Mémoires pour servir à l'histoire des sciences . . .* (Paris: Bleuet, 1810); and entries on the Cassini family: René Taton, "Cassini, Gian Domenico (Jean-Dominique) (Cassini I)"; "Cassini, Jacques (Cassini II)"; "Cassini De Thury, César-François (Cassini III)"; "Cassini, Jean-Dominique (Cassini IV)," all in *Complete Dictionary of Scientific Biography*, ed. Charles C. Gillispie, Frederic L. Holmes, and Noretta Koertge (Detroit: Charles Scribner's Sons, 2008), 100–109.

Epilogue

1. Perrault, *Contes*, 908.

2. Jal, *Dictionnaire critique*, 1321.

3. AN, MC, C 471, 19 January 1708. In fact, it is probable that Charles and Charles-Samuel were one and the same person. In this document, Charles is identified as "Charles-Samuel," though in all the other documents cited below he is identified simply as "Charles." If Charles died when Charles-Samuel was young, the latter probably began to use the shorter form "Charles," a relatively common practice. In 2018, Volker Schröder published on his blog *Anecdota* further evidence supporting this hypothesis and added details on Marie-Madeleine Perrault.

4. AN, MC, C 471, 19 January 1708. Charles owed this sum to Joseph le Peintre, described as "ecuier de quartier de Madame la Duchesse de Bourgogne."

5. Le Roy Ladurie, *Saint-Simon*, chap. 4; Gary B. McCollim, *Louis XIV's Assault on Privilege: Nicolas Desmaretz and the Tax on Wealth* (Rochester, NY: University of Rochester Press, 2012), 118–20.

6. For the sale of the house see AN, MC, C 497 Rés, 16 November 1714; see further, lease between Charles Perrault and Pierre de Playes, AN, MC, C 531, 16 August 1728; three leases signed by Charles Perrault, AN, MC, C 499, 16 July 1715; 1 September 1715; and 10 December 1715.

7. AN, MC, C 497, 17 November 1714 (just one day after the sale of the house).

8. *Catalogue des livres de Monsieur Charles Perrault, l'un des quarante de l'Academie Françoise, et de Monsieur C. Perrault son fils, dont la vente à l'amiable commencera le lundy*

30 May 1729 & jours suivans, depuis huit heures du matin jusqu'au soir (Paris: Les Freres Osmont, 1729). The date in the title is corrected by hand.

9. It is hard to connect the title to the name of an actual place: Soriano, *Dossier Charles Perrault*, 287, 379–80.

10. AN, MC, XLIII 233, 18 November 1697 and 30 April 1698. In the fall of 1699 Charles tried to sell a decorated "cabinet d'orgues," perhaps to raise this sum. Nicodème Tessin le Jeune and Daniel Cronström, *Les Relations artistiques entre la France et la Suède*, ed. Carl Hernmarck and Roger-Armand Weigert (Stockholm: Egnellska boktryck, 1964), 243. See also Soriano, *Dossier Charles Perrault*, 324–29.

11. *Mercure galant*, March 1700, 105–6.

12. Rowlands, *Dynastic State*, 169.

13. The importance of this phenomenon was noticed in Denis Richet, "Élite et noblesse: La formation des grands serviteurs de l'État (fin XVIᵉ–début XVIIᵉ siècle)," in *De la Réforme à la Révolution: Études sur la France moderne* (Paris: Aubier, 1991), 151–52; and see Élie Haddad, "Les Mesgrigny ou le coût social et moral des prétentions à l'épée," in *Épreuves de noblesse: Les expériences nobiliaires de la haute robe parisienne (XVIᵉ–XVIIIᵉ siècle)*, ed. Robert Descimon and Élie Haddad (Paris: Belles lettres, 2010), 211–31.

14. André Burguière, "La mémoire familiale du bourgeois gentilhomme: Généalogies domestiques en France aux XVIIᵉ et XVIIIᵉ siècles," *Annales: E.S.C.* 46, no. 4 (1991): 771–88; Giora Sternberg, "Manipulating Information in the Ancien Régime: Ceremonial Records, Aristocratic Strategies, and the Limits of the State Perspective," *Journal of Modern History* 85, no. 2 (2013): 239–79.

15. Soriano, *Dossier Charles Perrault*, 14–17.

16. Perrault, *Mémoires*, 133.

17. Ibid., 201.

18. For the different categories, see, respectively, ibid., 113–14; 133, 174–75; 148, 186, 188, 201, 210; 201. The architectural drawings by Claude Perrault were bound as two volumes, which eventually made their way to the Royal Library, where they were probably destroyed in the commune fire of 1871. The architect Jacques-François Blondel saw them in the eighteenth century; they convinced him that Claude was indeed the author of the Louvre façade. See Jacques-François Blondel, *Architecture française* (Paris: Charles-Antoine Jombert, 1752–56), 4:4–5, 57.

19. Perrault, *Mémoires*, 186, 232. On the monarchy's changing attitudes toward manuscript collections, see Soll, *Information Master*.

20. Perrault, *Mémoires*, 162–63.

21. Perrault, *Parallèle*, 4:265.

22. Ibid., 1:152.

23. Ibid., 4:297–310. This is attributed to the manuscript source in BN, MS FF 23467, fol. 105–7, by Namer, *L'Abbé Le Roy*, 44.

24. *Recueil de plusieurs machines de nouvelle invention, ouvrage posthume de M. Perrault* (Paris: J.-B. Coignard, 1700).

25. *Lettres de M. Antoine Arnauld* (Nancy: Nicolai, 1727), 7:508.

26. Charles Perrault, *Le cabinet des beaux-arts; ou, Recueil d'estampes gravées d'après les tableaux d'un plafond où les beaux-arts sont représentés* (Paris: G. Edelinck, 1690), 26, and prints following pages 35 and 39. Charles was not hostile toward rivals like Bernini when the reputation of his brothers was not on the line. Jeanne Morgan Zarucchi,

"Perrault's Memoirs and Bernini: A Reconsideration," *Renaissance Studies* 27, no. 3 (2013): 356–70.

27. Tessin and Cronström, *Relations artistiques*, 15–16, 44–45; Berger, *Palace of the Sun*.

28. Beyond the work of Christian Jouhaud, see Robert A. Schneider, "Self-Censorship and Men of Letters: Tocqueville's Critique of the Enlightenment in Historical Perspective," in *Tocqueville and Beyond: Essays on the Old Regime in Honor of David D. Bien*, ed. Robert M. Schwartz and Robert A. Schneider (Newark: University of Delaware Press, 2003), 192–225.

29. Françoise Waquet, *"Puer Doctus*, les enfants savants de la république des lettres," in *Le printemps des génies. Les enfants prodiges*, ed. Michèle Sacquin (Paris: Bibliothèque nationale, Robert Laffont, 1993), 87–99.

30. Perrault, *Mémoires*, 110.

31. Ibid., 138.

32. So claimed the king's confessor, Father de la Chaize, quoted in Robin Briggs, *Communities of Belief: Cultural and Social Tension in Early Modern France* (Oxford: Clarendon Press, 1989), 349.

33. Perrault, *Mémoires*, 116.

34. Marcel Mauss, *The Gift* (London: Routledge, 2002), 3.

35. A point made long ago by Jack Goody, "The Evolution of the Family," in *Household and Family in Past Time*, ed. Peter Laslett (Cambridge: Cambridge University Press, 1972), 103–24, esp. 119.

36. Wilding, *Galileo's Idol*, 3.

37. E.g., Simon Werrett, "The Schumacher Affair: Reconfiguring Academic Expertise across Dynasties in Eighteenth-Century Russia," *Osiris*, 2nd ser., 25 (2010): 104–26.

38. Sharon Kettering, "Patronage and Kinship in Early Modern France," *French Historical Studies* 16, no. 2 (1989): 432. Determining the relation between patronage and kinship ties remains an important desideratum. Haddad, "Noble Clienteles," 109.

39. Richet, "Élite et noblesse," and on the de Thou family, Philippe Hamon, "La chute de la maison de Thou: La fin d'une dynastie robine," *Revue d'histoire moderne et contemporaine* 46, no. 1 (1999): 53–85.

40. Daniel Dessert and Jean-Louis Journet, "Le lobby Colbert: Un royaume ou une affaire de famille?," *Annales: E.S.C.* 30, no. 6 (1975): 1303–36.

41. Robert A. Schneider, "Political Power"; Robert Descimon, "Conclusion: Nobles de lignage et noblesse de service"; and Jonathan Dewald, "Les élites de l'ancien régime" (unpublished manuscript, 2010).

42. Sherman, "Genealogy of Knowledge."

43. Charles Perrault, *Le Génie, épistre à M. de Fontenelle* (Paris: Jean-Baptiste Coignard, 1688). Charles also attributed notions of "genius" to La Quintinie's work on gardens in a poem he dedicated to him. Charles Perrault, *A Monsieur de la Quintiniye, sur son livre de l'instruction des jardins fruitiers & potagers* (N.p., c. 1690).

❦ Bibliography

Manuscript and Archival Sources

Archives de l'Académie des Sciences
  Dossier J. G. Duverney
  Dossier Claude Perrault
  Pochettes des séances, 1667–1676
  Registre des procès-verbaux des séances, vols. 4, 7, 8, 10, 11

Archives nationales
  144AP62, dossier 24
  144AP65, dossier 3
  Série E 371b
  Série O^1 19, 25
  Série P 2374

Archives nationales, Minutier central des notaires de Paris
  Étude III 720, 729, 730
  Étude VI 236
  Étude X 97
  Étude XV 232, 267
  Étude XVI 119
  Étude XVIII 186, 187, 189
  Étude XX 341
  Étude XXI 124
  Étude XXIV 447
  Étude XLII 152 (Rés [reserve] 386)
  Étude XLIII 233
  Étude XLVI 70
  Étude XLIX 344
  Étude LI 154, 190, 226, 529, 535, 537, 538, 539, 540, 541, 601
  Étude LII 107, 119
  Étude LXIV 93 (Rés 495)
  Étude LXV 32, 97
  Étude LXIX 102, 110
  Étude LXXIII 195
  Étude LXXVI 62 (Rés 447)
  Étude LXXVIII 493
  Étude LXXXVIII 224, 239, 267, 291
  Étude XC 227

Étude XCI 408
Étude XCIV 47
Étude XCV 49
Étude C 260, 471, 497, 499, 531
Étude CII 142
Étude CX 100
Étude CXII 367

Bibliothèque de l'Arsenal
    MS 5131, 5418, 5422

Bibliothèque du château de Chantilly
    MS 442

Bibliothèque Mazarine
    MS 2475, 3933, 4534

Bibliothèque nationale de France
    500 Colbert 234
    Cabinet d'Hozier 266
    Fond Français 390, 7723, 9297, 15125, 15189, 21725, 22081, 23467, 24346, 24350,
        24714, 25575
    Mélanges Colbert 120bis, 121, 130, 153bis, 176bis

British Library
    Additional Manuscripts, 20087, 24210

Printed Primary Sources

Early modern journals

Histoire des ouvrages des savans
Journal des sçavans
Mercure galant

Alembert, Jean le Rond d'. "Éloge de Charles Perrault." In *Œuvres de d'Alembert*. 5 vols.
    Paris: A. Belin, Bossange père et fils, Bossange frères, 1821.
Ancillon, Charles. *Mémoires concernant les vies et les ouvrages de plusieurs modernes célèbres
    dans la République des Lettres*. Amsterdam: Les Wetsteins, 1709.
Arnauld, Antoine. *Lettres de M. Antoine Arnauld*. 9 vols. Nancy: Nicolai, 1727.
Baillet, Adrien. *Jugemens des savans sur les principaux ouvrages des auteurs*. 7 vols. Paris: Charles
    Moette, Charles Le Clerc, Pierre Morisset, Pierre Prault, Jacques Chardon, 1722.
——. *La vie de Monsieur Descartes*. 2 vols. Paris: Daniel Horthemels, 1691.
Barchilon, Jacques, ed. *Perrault's Tales of Mother Goose, the Dedication Manuscript of 1695
    Reproduced in Collotype Facsimile with Introduction and Critical Text*. New York:
    Pierpont Morgan Library, 1956.
Bayle, Pierre. *Dictionnaire historique et critique*. 4 vols. Rotterdam: R. Leers, 1697.
Bernier, François. *Abrégé de la philosophie de Gassendi*. 8 vols. Lyon: Anyson and Posuel,
    1678.

Blondel, Jacques-François. *Architecture françoise*. 4 vols. Paris: Charles-Antoine Jombert, 1752–56.

Boileau-Despréaux, Nicolas. *Œuvres complètes*. Edited by Antoine Adam. Paris: Gallimard, 1966.

Brice, Germain. *Description nouvelle de la ville de Paris*... Paris: Nicolas Le Gras, Nicolas Le Clerc, and Barthelemy Girin, 1698.

Callières, François de. "Éloges de sept dames illustres françoises." In *De la Science du monde, et des connoisances utiles à la conduite de la vie*, 304–10. Paris: Étienne Ganeau, 1717.

Cassini, Jean-Dominique. *Mémoires pour servir à l'histoire des sciences*... Paris: Bleuet, 1810.

Catalogue des livres de Monsieur Charles Perrault, l'un des quarante de l'Academie Françoise, et de Monsieur C. Perrault son fils, Dont la vente à l'amiable commencera le Lundy 30. May 1729. & jours suivans, depuis huit heures du matin jusqu'au soir. Paris: Les Freres Osmont, 1729 (date corrected by hand).

Catalogue des partisans contre lesquels on doit agir pour la contribution aux dépenses de la Guerre. N.p., 1649.

Cerveau, René. *Nécrologe de plus célebres defenseurs et confesseurs de la verité du dix-huitieme siecle... première partie*. N.p., 1760.

——. *Supplément au nécrologe de plus célebres defenseurs et confesseurs de la verité des dix-septieme et dix-huitieme siecles... N.p., 1763*.

Chapelain, Jean. *Les lettres authentiques à Nicolas Heinsius (1649–1672): Une amitié érudite entre France et Hollande*. Edited by Bernard Bray. Paris: Champion, 2005.

——. *Lettres de Jean Chapelain, de l'Académie française*. Edited by Philippe Tamizey de Larroque. 2 vols. Paris: Imprimerie nationale, 1880.

——. *Opuscules critiques*. Paris: E. Droz, 1936.

Clément, Pierre, ed. *Lettres, instructions et mémoires de Colbert*. 7 vols. Paris: Imprimerie impériale, 1861–73.

Daniel, Gabriel. *Voyage du monde de Descartes*. Paris: Nicolas Pepie, 1702.

Descartes, René. *L'Homme et un traité de la formation de fœtus*. Paris: Charles Angot, 1664.

Dodart, Denis. *Mémoires pour servir à l'histoire des plantes*. Paris: Imprimerie royale, 1676.

Du Verney, Joseph. *Traité de l'organe de l'ouïe*... Paris: Estienne Michallet, 1683.

Elogia Julii Mazarini cardinalis. Paris: Antoine Vitré, 1666.

Faret, Nicolas. *L'Honneste-homme, ou l'art de plaire a la court*. Paris: Toussaincts du Bray, 1630.

Fontenelle, Bernard Le Bovier de. *Conversations on the Plurality of Worlds*. Translated by H. A. Hargreaves. Berkeley: University of California Press, 1990.

——. "Digression sur les Anciens et les Modernes." In *La Querelle des Anciens et des Modernes, XVIIᵉ–XVIIIᵉ Siècles*, edited by Anne-Marie Lecoq, 294–313. Paris: Gallimard, 2001.

——. *Œuvres completes*. Edited by Alain Niderst. Paris: Fayard, 1989–.

Forge, Jean de la. *Le cercle des femmes sçavantes*. Paris: J.-B. Loyson, 1663.

Fortin de la Hoguette, Philippe. *Testament ou conseils fidèles d'un bon père à ses enfants*. Paris: P. Le Petit, 1656.

Furetière, Antoine. *Le Roman bourgeois*. Edited by Jacques Prévot. Paris: Gallimard, 1981.

Gallois, Pierre le. *Traitté des plus belles bibliothèques de l'Europe*. Paris: E. Michallet, 1680.

Guiffrey, Julles, ed. *Comptes des bâtiments du roi sous le règne de Louis XIV*. 5 vols. Paris: Imprimerie Nationale, 1881–1901.

Héritier de Villandon, Marie-Jeanne, l'. *Œuvres meslées*. Paris: Jean Guignard, 1696.

Huet, Pierre-Daniel. *Mémoires (1718)*. Edited by Philippe Joseph Salazar. Toulouse: Société de Littératures Classiques, 1993.

Huygens, Christiaan. *Œuvres complètes*. 22 vols. The Hague: M. Nijhoff, 1888–1950.

——. *Le séjour de Christian Huygens à Paris et ses relations avec les milieux scientifiques français; suivi de son journal de voyage à Paris et à Londres*. Edited by Henri Brugmans. Paris: E. Droz, 1935.

Jombert, Charles-Antoine. *Catalogue raisonnée de l'œuvre de Sébastien Le Clerc, chevalier romain, dessinateur et graveur du cabinet du Roi...2* vols. Paris: Chez l'auteur, 1774.

Lachèvre, Frédéric, ed. *La Chronique des chapons et des gélinottes du Mans d'Étienne Martin de Pinchesne*. Paris: H. Leclerc, 1907.

La Fontaine, Jean de. *L'Amour de Psyché et de Cupidon*. In *Œuvres de J. de La Fontaine*. Edited by Henri Regnier. 12 vols. Paris: Hachette, 1892.

La Rochefoucauld, *Maxims*. Translated by Leonard Tancock. Harmondsworth, UK: Penguin, 1959.

Leibniz, Gottfried Wilhelm. "Note de Leibniz sur l'achèvement du Louvre." *Revue des sociétés savantes* 3 (1857): 592–97.

Le Muet, Pierre. *Manière de bien bastir pour toutes sortes de personnes...* Paris: François Jollain, 1681.

Lettres Patentes pour la décharge des comptes des exercices & maniemens faits tant par le sieur Housset, Tresorier des Parties Casuelles, que par Maistre Pierre Perrault, commis par le Roy à l'exercice de ladite Charge en l'année 1654. & à la reddition & appuremens de ses comptes.

Loyseau, Charles. *Traité des ordres et simples dignitez*. Paris: N.p., 1620.

Mariette, Pierre-Jean. *Abecedario et autres notes inédites sur les arts et les artists*. Edited by Ph. de Chennevières and A. de Montaiglon. 6 vols. Paris: J.-B. Dumoulin, 1856.

Marolles, Michel de. *Le livre des peintres et graveurs*. Edited by Georges DuPlessis. Paris: Paul Daffis, 1872.

Molière. *Œuvres complètes*. Edited by Maurice Rat. Paris: Gallimard, 1956.

Moréri, Louis. *Le grand dictionnaire historique...* Paris: J. Vincent, 1732.

——. *Le grand dictionnaire historique...* Paris: Les libraires associés, 1759.

Nemeitz, Joachim-Christoph. *Séjour de Paris...* Leiden, Neth.: Jean van Abcoude, 1727.

Oldenburg, Henry. *Correspondence*. Edited by A. Rupert and Marie Boas Hall. 13 vols. Madison: University of Wisconsin Press, 1965.

Pasquier, Étienne. "Epigrammata." In *Œuvres d'Estienne Pasquier...2* vols., 1:1125–1222. Amsterdam: Aux depens de la Compagnie des libraires associez, 1723.

Périer, Gilberte. "La vie de Monsieur Pascal, écrite par Madame Périer, sa sœur." In Blaise Pascal, *Œuvres complètes*, 3–34. Edited by Jacques Chevalier. Paris: Gallimard, 1954.

Périer, Marguerite. "Mémoire sur la vie de M. Pascal, écrit par mademoiselle Marguerite Périer, sa nièce." In Pascal, *Œuvres complètes*, 35–41.

Perrault, Charles. *À Mgr le Dauphin sur la prise de Philisbourg, ode*. Paris: J.-B. Coignard, 1688.

———. *À M. le président Rose. Épître.* Paris: J.-B. Coignard, 1691.

———. *À monsieur de La Quintinye, sur son livre De l'instruction des jardins fruitiers & potagers* [1690?].

———. *Le Banquet des Dieux, pour la Naissance de Monseigneur le Duc de Bourgogne.* Paris: J.-B. Coignard, 1682.

———. *Le cabinet des beaux-arts, ou Recueil d'estampes gravées d'après les tableaux d'un plafond où les beaux-arts sont représentés.* Paris: G. Edelinck, 1690.

———. *La Chasse. A Monsieur de Rosieres.* Paris: La Veuve de Jean Bapt. Coignard and Jean Baptiste Coignard Fils, 1692.

———. *Les Contes de Perrault dans tous leurs états.* Edited by Annie Collognat and Marie-Charlotte Delmas. Paris: Omnibus, 2007.

———. *Critique de l'opéra, ou Examen de la tragédie intitulée Alceste, ou le Triomphe d'Alcide.* Paris: Claude Barbin, 1674.

———. *Le Génie, épistre à M. de Fontenelle.* Paris: J.-B. Coignard, 1688.

———. *Les Hommes illustres. Avec leurs portraits au naturel.* Edited by D. J. Culpin Tübingen, Ger.: Gunter Narr, 2003.

———. *Leo aeger, vulpes et lupus, fabula. Le Lion malade, le renard et le loup, fable traduite du latin de M. Du Périer.* Paris: A. Cramoisy, 1686.

———. *Mémoires de ma vie.* Edited by Antoine Picon. Paris: Macula, 1993.

———. *Ode sur la Paix.* Paris: Charles de Sercy, 1660.

———. *Parallèle des Anciens et des Modernes en ce qui regarde les Arts et les Sciences.* 4 vols. Paris: Jean Baptiste Coignard, 1688–97.

———. *La Peinture.* Edited by Jean-Luc Gautier-Gentès. Geneva: Droz, 1992.

———. *Portrait de Messire Benigne Bossuet, evêque de Meaux, au Serenissime Prince Cosme III, Grand Duc de Toscane.* Paris: Jean-Baptiste Coignard, 1698.

———. *Pour le roi de Suède, ode.* Paris: J.-B. Coignard, 1702.

———. *Recueil des divers ouvrages en prose et en vers.* Paris: Jean Baptiste Coignard, Guillaume de Luyne et Jean Guignard, 1675.

———. *Saint Paulin, Evesque de Nole. Poëme.* Paris: Jean Baptiste Coignard, 1686.

———. *Traduction des fables de Faerne.* Paris: J.-B. Coignard, 1699.

Perrault, Charles, and François Boutard. *Au Roy Philippe V allant en Espagne, ode.* Paris: J.-B. Coignard, 1701.

———. *Sur L'embrasement de l'Eglise de Troyes. Ode.* Troyes: Chés Edme Prevost, 1692.

Perrault, Charles, and Claude Perrault. *Mémoires de ma vie, par Charles Perrault. Voyage à Bordeaux (1669) par Claude Perrault.* Edited by Paul Bonnefon. Paris: Renouard, 1909.

Perrault, Charles et al. *Courses de testes et de bagues faites par le roy et par les princes et seigneurs de sa cour en l'année 1662.* Paris: Imprimerie royale, 1670.

Perrault, Claude. *Abregé des dix livres d'architecture de Vitruve.* Paris: Jean Baptiste Coignard, 1674.

———. *Description anatomique d'un Caméléon, d'un Castor, d'un Dromadaire, d'un Ours et d'une Gazelle.* Paris: Léonard, 1669.

———. *Essais de physique.* 4 vols. Paris: Jean-Baptiste Coignard, 1680–88.

———. *Mémoires pour servir à l'histoire naturelle des animaux.* Paris: Imprimerie royale, 1671.

———. *Mémoires pour servir à l'histoire naturelle des animaux.* Paris: Imprimerie royale, 1676.

———. *Recueil de plusieurs machines de nouvelle invention, ouvrage posthume de M. Perrault.* Paris: J.-B. Coignard, 1700.

Perrault, Nicolas. *La morale des Jésuites, extraite fidèlement de leurs livres imprimez avec la permission et l'approbation des supérieurs de leur compagnie, par un docteur de Sorbonne.* Mons: La veuve Waudret, 1667.

Perrault, Pierre. *De l'origine des fontaines.* Paris: Jean and Laurent d'Houry, 1678.

Pinchesne, Étienne Martin de. *Poesies meslées du Sieur de Pinchesne, dediées à Monseigneur le Duc de Montausier.* Paris: André Cramoisy, 1672.

Plaise à Monsieur . . . avoir pour recommandé en justice le bon droit pour maître Pierre Perault, ci-devant receveur général des finances à Paris, . . . contre François Maillot, ci-devant son commis . . .

Plaise au Roi et à Nosseigneurs de son conseil, en jugeant le procès pour René Souchu, . . . demandeur, contre maître Pierre Perrault et Claude Coquille, . . . défendeurs, avoir la bonté de prendre lecture du placet qui est présenté en forme d'état sommaire, servant d'instruction, et de conserver en justice le bon droit dudit Souchu.

Quintinie, Jean de la. *Instruction pour les jardins fruitiers et potagers . . .* Paris: C. Barbin, 1690.

Racine, Jean. *Œuvres complètes.* Edited by Raymond Picard. 2 vols. Paris: Gallimard, 1966.

Scarron, Paul. *La relation véritable de tout ce qui s'est passé en l'autre monde . . .* Paris: Toussaint Quinet, 1648.

Scudéry, Madeleine de. *Clélie, histoire romaine.* 10 vols. Paris: Augustin Courbé, 1654–1660.

Somaize, Antoine Beaudeau, sieur de. *Grand dictionnaire des précieuses.* Reprinted by Roger Duchêne, in *Les précieuses ou comment l'esprit vint aux femmes.* Paris: Fayard, 2001.

Tallement, Abbé François. "Éloge funèbre de Mr. Perrault." In *Recueil des harangues prononcées par messieurs de l'Académie française dans leurs réceptions, & en d'autres occasions différentes, depuis l'establissement de l'Académie jusqu'à présent,* 2:591–602. Amsterdam: Aux dépens de la Compagnie, 1709.

Tallemant des Réaux, Gédéon. *Historiettes.* Edited by Antoine Adam. 2 vols. Paris: Gallimard, 1967.

Teissier, Antoine. *Éloges des hommes savans, tirez de l'histoire de M. de Thou, avec des additions contenans l'Abrégé de leur vie, le jugement, & le Catalogue de leurs Ouvrages.* 2 vols. Geneva: Jean-Herman Widerhold, 1683.

Tessin le Jeune, Nicodème, and Daniel Cronström. *Les Relations artistiques entre la France et la Suède.* Edited by Carl Hernmarck and Roger-Armand Weigert. Stockholm: Egnellska boktryck, 1964.

Thevet, André. *Les vrais pourtraits et vies des hommes illustres grecz, latins et payens, recueilliz de leurs tableaux, livres, médalles antiques et modernes.* Paris: La Veuve Kervert et Guillaume Chaudière, 1584.

Titon du Tillet, Evrard. *Le Parnasse françois, dedié au roi.* 2 vols. Paris: Jean-Baptiste Coignard fils, 1732–34.

Varet, Alexandre. "Avertissement sur la publication de cet ouvrage." In Nicolas Perrault, *La Morale des Jésuites, extraite fidèlement de leurs livres imprimez avec la permission et l'approbation des supérieurs de leur compagnie, par un docteur de Sorbonne.* Mons: La veuve Waudret, 1667.

Villiers, Pierre de. *Entretiens sur les contes de fées et sur quelques autres ouvrages du temps, pour servir de préservatif contre le mauvais gout.* Paris: Jacques Collombat, 1699.

Visconti, Primi. *Mémoires sur la Cour de Louis XIV, 1673–1681.* Introduction and notes by Jean-François Solnon. Paris: Perrin, 1988.

Vitruvius. *Le dix livres d'architecture de Vitruve, corrigez et traduits nouvellement en François, avec des notes et des figures.* Paris: Jean-Baptiste Coignard, 1673.

Voiture, Vincent. *Les œuvres de Monsieur de Voiture.* Paris: A. Courbé, 1650.

Walckenaer, Charles-Athanase. *Lettres sur les contes de fées. Mémoires sur les abeilles solitaires. Notices biographiques.* Paris: Firmin Didot frères, fils et Cie, 1862.

Printed Secondary Works

Abraham, Claude K. "The French Royal Family: Patrons of Science in the Age of Louis XIII." *French Review* 37, no. 2 (1963): 206–12.

Ackerman, James S. *The Villa: Form and Ideology of Country Houses.* Princeton: Princeton University Press, 1990.

Alcover, Madeleine. "Furetière et la stratification sociale: Le 'tariffe des mariages.'" *Papers on French Seventeenth Century Literature* 8 (1981): 75–93.

Algazi, Gadi. "At the Study: Notes on the Production of the Scholarly Self." In *Space and Self in Early Modern European Cultures*, edited by David Warren Sabean and Malina Stefanovska, 12–50. Toronto: University of Toronto Press, 2012.

——. "Bringing Kinship (Back) In." *Mediterranean Historical Review* 25, no. 1 (2010): 83–92.

——. "Eine gelernte Lebensweise: Figurationen des Gelehrtenlebens zwischen Mittelalter und Früher Neuzeit." *Berichte zur Wissenschaftsgeschichte* 30 (2007): 107–18.

——. "*Exemplum* and *Wundertier*: Three Concepts of the Scholarly Persona," *BMGN—Low Countries Historical Review* 131, no. 4 (2016): 8–32.

——. "Food for Thought: Hieronymus Wolf grapples with the Scholarly Habitus." In *Egodocuments in History: Autobiographical Writing in Its Social Context since the Middle Ages*, edited by Rudolf Dekker, 21–44. Hilversum, Neth.: Verloren, 2002.

——. "'For This Boy I Prayed': The Making of Scholarly Families in Northern Europe." *Historia* 14 (2004): 7–48 (in Hebrew).

——. "Scholars in Households: Refiguring the Learned Habitus, 1480–1550." *Science in Context* 16, no. 1–2 (2003): 9–42.

Andersen, Casper, Jakob Bek-Thomsen, and Peter C. Kjærgaard. "The Money Trail: A New Historiography for Networks, Patronage, and Scientific Careers." *Isis* 103, no. 2 (2012): 310–15.

Andriesse, Cornelis Dirk. *Huygens: The Man behind the Principle.* Cambridge: Cambridge University Press, 2005.

Apostolidès, Jean-Marie. *Le Roi-Machine: Spectacle et politique au temps de Louis XIV.* Paris: Éditions de Minuit, 1981.

Azouvi, François. "Entre Descartes et Leibniz: L'Animisme dans les *Essais de physique* de Claude Perrault." *Recherches sur le XVIIᵉ siècle* 5 (1982): 9–19.

Bachrach, A. G. H. "The Role of the Huygens Family in Seventeenth-Century Dutch Culture." In *Studies on Christiaan Huygens*, edited by H. J. M. Bos et al., 27–52. Lisse, Neth.: Swets & Zeitlinger, 1980.

Balayé, Simone. "La Bibliothèque du Roi, première bibliothèque du monde, 1664–1789." In *Histoire des bibliothèques françaises*, vol. 2, *Les bibliothèques sous l'Ancien Régime,*

1530–1789, edited by Claude Jolly, 209–33. Paris: Promodis-Éditions du Cercle du librairie, 1988.

———. *La Bibliothèque nationale, des origines à 1800*. Geneva: Droz, 1988.

Baldwin, Geoff. "Individual and Self in the Late Renaissance." *Historical Journal* 44, no. 2 (2001): 341–64.

Bannister, Mark. "The Crisis of Literary Patronage in France, 1643–1655." *French Studies* 39, no. 1 (1985): 18–30.

Barchilon, Jacques. "Charles Perrault à travers les documents du Minutier Central des Archives Nationales. L'inventaire de ses meubles en 1672." *XVIIᵉ siècle* 65 (1964): 3–15.

———. "Les frères Perrault à travers la correspondance de Christian Huygens." *XVIIᵉ siècle* 56 (1962): 19–36.

Barchilon, Jacques, and Peter Flinders. *Charles Perrault*. Boston: Twayne Publishers, 1981.

Bardon, Maurice. *Critique du livre de Dom Quichotte de la Manche*. Paris: Les Presses Modernes, 1930.

Barnavi, Élie, and Robert Descimon. *La Sainte Ligue, le juge et la potence: L'Assassinat du Président Brisson (15 novembre 1591)*. Paris: Hachette, 1985.

Bayard, Françoise. "Manière d'habiter des financiers de la première moitié du XVIIᵉ siècle." *XVIIᵉ Siècle* 41 (1989): 53–65.

———. *Le monde des financiers au XVIIᵉ siècle*. Paris: Flammarion, 1988.

Bayly, C. A. "'Archaic' and 'Modern' Globalization in the Eurasian and African Arena, ca. 1750–1850." In *Globalization in World History*, edited by A. G. Hopkins, 45–72. New York: Norton, 2002.

Beasley, Faith. *Salons, History, and the Creation of Seventeenth-Century France: Mastering Memory*. Aldershot, UK: Ashgate, 2006.

Beauvalet, Scarlett, and Vincent Gourdon. "Les liens sociaux à Paris au XVIIᵉ siècle: Une analyse des contrats de mariage de 1660, 1665 et 1670." *Histoire, économie et société* 17, no. 4 (1998): 583–612.

Beauvalet, Scarlett, François-Joseph Ruggiu, and Vincent Gourdon. "Réseaux et mobilités à Paris au milieu du XVIIᵉ siècle." *Histoire, économie et société* 17, no. 4 (1998): 547–60.

Beauvalet-Boutouyrie, Scarlett. *La population française à l'époque moderne (XVIᵉ–XVIIIᵉ siècle): Démographie et comportements*. 2nd ed. Paris: Belin, 2008.

Béguin, Katia. *Financer la guerre au XVIIᵉ siècle: La dette publique et les rentiers de l'absolutisme*. Seyssel: Champ Vallon, 2012.

———. *Les princes de Condé: Rebelles, courtisans et mécènes dans la France du Grand Siècle*. Seyssel: Champ Vallon, 1999.

Benedict, Philip. "Toward the Comparative Study of the Popular Market for Art: The Ownership of Paintings in Seventeenth-Century Metz." In *The Faith and Fortunes of France's Huguenots, 1600–85*, 191–207. Aldershot, UK: Ashgate, 2001.

Beik, William. "The Absolutism of Louis XIV as Social Collaboration." *Past & Present* 188 (2005): 195–224.

———. "A Social Interpretation of the Reign of Louis XIV." In *L'État ou le Roi: Les fondations de la modernité monarchique en France (XIVᵉ–XVIIᵉ siècles)*, edited by Neithard Bulst, Robert Descimon, and Alain Guerreau, 145–60. Paris: Éditions de la Maison des Sciences de l'Homme, 1996.

Bell, David A. *The Cult of the Nation in France: Inventing Nationalism, 1680–1800.* Cambridge, MA: Harvard University Press, 2001.

Bennett, Michael. "Note-Taking and Data-Sharing: Edward Jenner and the Global Vaccination Network." *Intellectual History Review* 20, no. 3 (2010): 415–32.

Bennini, Martine. *Les conseillers à la cour des aides (1604–1697): Étude sociale.* Paris: H. Champion, 2010.

Berger, Robert W. *The Palace of the Sun: The Louvre of Louis XIV.* University Park: Penn State University Press, 1993.

Bernard, Birgit. *"Les Hommes illustres*: Charles Perraults Kompendium der 100 berühmtesten Männer des 17. Jahrhunderts als Reflex der Colbertschen Wissenschaftspolitik." *Francia* 18, no. 2 (1991): 23–46.

Bertoloni Meli, Domenico. *Mechanism, Experiment, Disease: Marcello Malpighi and Seventeenth-Century Anatomy.* Baltimore: Johns Hopkins University Press, 2011.

———. *Thinking with Objects: The Transformation of Mechanics in the Seventeenth Century.* Baltimore: Johns Hopkins University Press, 2006.

Bettelheim, Bruno. *The Uses of Enchantment: The Meaning and Importance of Fairy Tales.* New York: Vintage Books, 1989.

Beugnot, Bernard. *Le discours de la retraite au XVIIe siècle: Loin du monde et du bruit.* Paris: Presses universitaires de France, 1996.

Bézard, Yvonne. "Autour d'un éloge de Pascal: Une affaire de censure tranchée par Louis XIV en 1696." *Revue d'histoire littéraire de la France* 33 (1926): 215–24.

Biagioli, Mario. *Galileo, Courtier: The Practice of Science in the Culture of Absolutism.* Chicago: University of Chicago Press, 1993.

———. "Plagiarism, Kinship, and Slavery." *Theory, Culture & Society* 31, no. 2–3 (2014): 65–91.

Bien, David D. "Manufacturing Nobles: The Chancelleries in France to 1789." *Journal of Modern History* 61, no. 3 (1989): 446–86.

———. "Offices, Corps, and a System of State Credit: The Uses of Privilege under the Ancien Regime." In *The French Revolution and the Creation of Modern Political Culture,* vol. 1, *The Political Culture of the Old Regime,* edited by Keith Michael Baker, 89–114. Oxford: Pergamon Press, 1987.

Blair, Ann. *Too Much to Know: Managing Scholarly Information before the Modern Age.* New Haven: Yale University Press, 2010.

Blocker, Déborah, and Élie Haddad. "Protections et statut d'auteur à l'époque moderne: Formes et enjeux des pratiques de patronage dans la querelle du Cid (1637)." *French Historical Studies* 31, no. 3 (2008): 381–416.

Bonnefon, Paul. "Charles Perrault, commis de Colbert, et l'administration des arts sous Louis XIV d'après les documents inédits." *Gazette des Beaux-Arts* 40 (1908): 198–214, 340–52, 426–33.

———. "Charles Perrault. Essai sur sa vie et ses ouvrages." *Revue d'histoire littéraire de la France* 11 (1904): 365–420.

———. "Claude Perrault. Architecte et voyageur." *Gazette des Beaux-Arts* 26 (1901): 209–22, 425–40.

———. "Les dernières années de Charles Perrault." *Revue d'histoire littéraire de la France* 13 (1906): 606–57.

———. "Un poème inédit de Claude Perrault." *Revue d'histoire littéraire de la France* 7 (1900): 449–72.

Bonney, Richard. "The Fouquet-Colbert Rivalry and the 'Revolution' of 1661." In *Ethics and Politics in Seventeenth-Century France*, edited by Keith Cameron and E. Woodrough, 107–18. Exeter: University of Exeter Press, 1996.

——. "Vindication of the Fronde? The Cost of Louis XIV's Versailles Building Programme." *French History* 21, no. 2 (2007): 205–25.

Bosher, John F. "'Chambres de Justice' in the French Monarchy." In *French Government and Society 1500–1850: Essays in Memory of Alfred Cobban*, edited by John Bosher, 19–40. London: Athlone, 1973.

Bossenga, Gail. "Markets, the Patrimonial State, and the Origins of the French Revolution." *1650–1850: Ideas, Aesthetics, and Inquiries in the Early Modern Era* 11 (2005): 443–509.

Bossy, John. "Godparenthood: The Fortunes of a Social Institution in Early Modern Christianity." In *Religion and Society in Early Modern Europe, 1500–1800*, edited by Kaspar von Greyerz, 194–201. Boston: Allen & Unwin, 1984.

Bott, Elizabeth. *Family and Social Network: Roles, Norms, and External Relationships in Ordinary Urban Families*. 2nd ed. New York: Free Press, 1971.

Bourdieu, Pierre. "Le champ littéraire." *Actes de la recherche en sciences sociales* 89 (1991): 3–46.

——. *The Rules of Art: Genesis and Structure of the Literary Field*. Translated by Susan Emanuel. Stanford: Stanford University Press, 1996.

Bredekamp, Horst. "Gazing Hands and Blind Spots: Galileo as Draftsman." In *Galileo in Context*, edited by Jürgen Renn, 153–92. Cambridge: Cambridge University Press, 2001.

Briggs, Robin. "The Académie Royale des Sciences and the Pursuit of Utility." *Past & Present* 131 (1991): 38–88.

——. *Communities of Belief: Cultural and Social Tension in Early Modern France*. Oxford: Clarendon Press, 1989.

Brockliss, L.W. B. *French Higher Education in the Seventeenth and Eighteenth Centuries: A Cultural History*. Oxford: Clarendon Press, 1987.

——. "Patterns of Attendance at the University of Paris, 1400–1800." *Historical Journal* 21, no. 3 (1978): 503–44.

Brockliss, L. W. B., and Colin Jones. *The Medical World of Early Modern France*. Oxford: Clarendon Press, 1997.

Brosseau, Monique, with the contribution of Gérard Gélinas. "Du nouveau dans le dossier Perrault." *Papers on French Seventeenth Century Literature* 36, no. 70 (2009): 267–76.

Brown, Elizabeth A. R. "Authority, the Family, and the Dead in Late Medieval France." *French Historical Studies* 16, no. 4 (1990): 803–32.

Brown, Gregory S. "Am 'I' a 'Post-Revolutionary Self'? Historiography of the Self in the Age of Enlightenment and Revolution." *History and Theory* 47, no. 2 (2008): 229–48.

Bryant, Mark. "Partner, Matriarch and Minister: The Unofficial Consort, Mme de Maintenon of France, 1669–1715." In *Queenship in Europe 1660–1815: The Role of the Consort*, edited by Clarissa Campbell Orr, 77–106. Cambridge: Cambridge University Press, 2004.

Buchwald, Jed. "Discrepant Measurements and Experimental Knowledge in the Early Modern Era." *Archive for History of Exact Sciences* 60, no. 6 (2006): 565–649.

Burguière, André. "La mémoire familiale du bourgeois gentilhomme: Généalogies domestiques en France aux XVIIᵉ et XVIIIᵉ siècles." *Annales: E.S.C.* 46, no. 4 (1991): 771–88.

Burke, Peter. *The Fabrication of Louis XIV.* New Haven: Yale University Press, 1992.

——. "Translations into Latin in Early Modern Europe." In *Cultural Translation in Early Modern Europe*, edited by R. Po-chia Hsia and Peter Burke, 65–80. Cambridge: Cambridge University Press, 2007.

Bury, Emmanuel. *Littérature et politesse: L'Invention de l'honnête homme, 1580–1750.* Paris: Presses universitaires de France, 1996.

——. "Théorie et pratique de la traduction chez les frères Perrault." *XVIIᵉ siècle* 66 (2014): 447–66.

Calvi, Giulia, and Carolina Blutrach-Jelín. "Sibling Relations in Family History: Conflicts, Co-Operation and Gender Roles in the Sixteenth to Nineteenth Centuries: An Introduction." *European Review of History/Revue europeenne d'histoire* 17, no. 5 (2010): 695–704.

Campbell, Julie. *Literary Circles and Gender in Early Modern Europe: A Cross-Cultural Approach.* Aldershot, UK: Ashgate, 2006.

Carlino, Andrea. *Books of the Body: Anatomical Ritual and Renaissance Learning.* Translated by John Tedeschi and Anne C. Tedeschi. Chicago: University of Chicago Press, 1999.

Cavaillé, Jean-Pierre. "'Le plus éloquent philosophe des derniers temps': Les stratégies d'auteur de René Descartes." *Annales: Histoire, sciences sociales* 49, no. 2 (1994): 349–67.

Certeau, Michel de. *The Practice of Everyday Life.* Translated by Steven Rendall. Berkeley: University of California Press, 1984.

Chabaud, Gilles. "Images de la ville et pratiques du livre: Le genre des guides de Paris (XVIIᵉ–XVIIIᵉ siècles)." *Revue d'histoire moderne et contemporaine* 45, no. 2 (1998): 323–45.

Chapman, Sara E. *Private Ambition and Political Alliances: The Phélypeaux de Pontchartrain Family and Louis XIV's Government, 1650–1715.* Rochester, NY: University of Rochester Press, 2004.

Chappey, Jean-Luc. *Ordres et désordres biographiques: Dictionnaires, listes de noms, réputation des Lumières à Wikipedia.* Seyssel: Champ Vallon, 2013.

Chartier, Roger. "Foucault's Chiasmus: Authorship between Science and Literature in the Seventeenth and Eighteenth Centuries." In *Scientific Authorship: Credit and Intellectual Property in Science*, edited by Mario Biagioli and Peter Galison, 13–31. New York: Routledge, 2003.

——. "From Court Festivity to City Spectators." In *Forms and Meanings: Texts, Performances, and Audiences from Codex to Computer*, 43–81. Philadelphia: University of Pennsylvania Press, 1995.

——. "The Man of Letters." In *Enlightenment Portraits*, edited by Michel Vovelle, translated by Lydia G. Cochrane, 142–89. Chicago: University of Chicago Press, 1997.

——. "Le Prince, la bibliothèque et la dédicace." In *Le Pouvoir des bibliothèques: La mémoire des livres en Occident*, edited by Marc Baratin and Christian Jacob, 204–23. Paris: A. Michel, 1996.

——. "Time to Understand: The Frustrated Intellectuals." In *Cultural History: Between Practices and Representations*, translated by Lydia G. Cochrane, 127–150. Ithaca: Cornell University Press, 1988.

Cleary, Richard Louis. *The Place Royale and Urban Design in the Ancien Régime.* Cambridge: Cambridge University Press, 1999.

Cojannot-Le Blanc, Marianne. "Les artistes privés de l'invention? Réflextions sur les 'desseins' de Charles et Claude Perrault pour les Bâtiments du roi dans les années 1660." *XVIIᵉ siècle* 66 (2014): 467–79.

Cole, Charles W. *Colbert and a Century of French Mercantilism.* 2 vols. New York: Columbia University Press, 1939.

Cole, F. J. *A History of Comparative Anatomy, from Aristotle to the Eighteenth Century.* London: Macmillan, 1944.

Coleman, Charly. *The Virtues of Abandon: An Anti-Individualist History of the French Enlightenment.* Stanford: Stanford University Press, 2014.

Collins, James. *The State in Early Modern France.* 2nd ed. Cambridge: Cambridge University Press, 2009.

Cooper, Alix. "Homes and Households." In *The Cambridge History of Science,* vol. 3, *Early Modern Science,* edited by Katharine Park and Lorraine Daston, 224–37. Cambridge: Cambridge University Press, 2006.

——. "Picturing Nature: Gender and the Politics of Natural-Historical Description in Eighteenth-Century Gdańsnk/Danzig." *Journal for Eighteenth-Century Studies* 36, no. 4 (2013): 519–29.

Corcia, Joseph di. "*Bourg, Bourgeois, Bourgeois de Paris* from the Eleventh to the Eighteenth Century." *Journal of Modern History* 50, no. 2 (1978): 208–33.

Couton, Georges. "Effort publicitaire et organisation de la recherche: Les gratifications aux gens de lettres sous Louis XIV." In *Le XVIIᵉ siècle et la recherche: Actes du 6ème Colloque de Marseille,* 41–55. Marseille: A. Robert, 1976.

Cowart, Georgia. *The Triumph of Pleasure: Louis XIV and the Politics of Spectacle.* Chicago: University of Chicago Press, 2008.

Craveri, Benedetta. *The Age of Conversation.* Translated by Teresa Waugh. New York: New York Review Books, 2005.

Croq, Laurence. "Des titulaires à l'évaluation sociale des qualités: Hiérarchie et mobilité collective dans la société parisienne du XVIIᵉ siècle." In *Dire et vivre l'ordre sociale en France sous l'Ancien Régime,* edited by Fanny Cosandey, 125–68. Paris: Éditions de l'École des hautes études en sciences sociales, 2005.

Crowston, Clare. *Credit, Fashion, Sex: Economies of Regard in Old Regime France.* Durham, NC: Duke University Press, 2013.

Darnton, Robert. "The Devil in Holy Water: Political Libel in Eighteenth-Century France." *Proceedings of the British Academy* 151 (2007): 387–422.

——. "The High Enlightenment and the Low-Life of Literature in Pre-Revolutionary France." *Past & Present* 51 (1971): 81–115.

Dasgupta, Sukanya. "'Of Polish'd Pillars, or a Roofe of Gold': Authority and Affluence in the English Country-House Poem." In *Contested Spaces of Nobility in Early Modern Europe,* edited by Matthew P. Romaniello and Charles Lipp, 189–212. Farnham, UK: Ashgate, 2011.

Davis, Natalie Zemon. "Ghosts, Kin, and Progeny: Some Features of Family Life in Early Modern France." *Daedalus* 106, no. 2 (1977): 87–114.

Dear, Peter Robert. "Historiography of Not-So-Recent Science." *History of Science* 50, no. 2 (2012): 197–211.

DeJean, Joan. "Lafayette's Ellipses: The Privileges of Anonymity." *PMLA* 99, no. 5 (1984): 884–902.

——. "The Salons, 'Preciosity,' and the Sphere of Women's Influence." In *A New History of French Literature*, edited by Denis Hollier, 297–303. Cambridge, MA: Harvard University Press, 1989.

——. *Tender Geographies: Women and the Origins of the Novel in France*. New York: Columbia University Press, 1991.

Denis, Delphine. *Le Parnasse galant: Institution d'une catégorie littéraire au XVIIᵉ siècle*. Paris: Champion, 2001.

Desan, Suzanne, and Jeffrey Merrick. Introduction to *Family, Gender, and Law in Early Modern France*, edited by Suzanne Desan and Jeffrey Merrick, xii–xxvi. University Park: Penn State University Press, 2009.

Des Chene, Dennis. "Mechanisms of Life in the Seventeenth Century: Borelli, Perrault, Régis." *Studies in History and Philosophy of Biological and Biomedical Sciences* 26, no. 2 (2005): 245–60.

Descimon, Robert. "The Birth of the Nobility of the Robe: Dignity versus Privilege in the Parlement of Paris, 1500–1700." In *Changing Identities in Early Modern France*, edited by Michael Wolfe, 95–123. Durham, NC: Duke University Press, 1996.

——. "The 'Bourgeoisie Seconde': Social Differentiation in the Parisian Municipal Oligarchy in the Sixteenth Century, 1500–1610." *French History* 17, no. 4 (2003): 388–424.

——. "Chercher de nouvelles voies pour interpréter les phénomènes nobiliaires dans la France moderne. La noblesse, 'essence' ou rapport social?" *Revue d'histoire moderne et contemporaine* 46, no. 1 (1999): 5–21.

——. "Conclusion: Nobles de lignage et noblesse de service: Sociogenèses comparées de l'épée et de la robe (XVᵉ–XVIIIᵉ siècle)." In *Épreuves de noblesse: Les expériences nobiliaires de la robe parisienne (XVIᵉ–XVIIIᵉ siècle)*, edited by Robert Descimon and Élie Haddad, 277–302. Paris: Belles lettres, 2010.

——. "Élites parisiennes entre XVᵉ et XVIIᵉ siècle: Du bon usage du Cabinet des titres." *Bibliothèque de l'École des chartes* 155 (1997): 607–44.

——. "L'exemplarité sociale des *Historiettes* de Tallemant des Réaux." In *Construire l'exemplarité: Pratiques littéraires et discours historiens, XVIᵉ–XVIIIᵉ siècles*, edited by Laurence Giavarini, 181–95. Dijon: Éditions universitaires de Dijon, 2008.

——. "Un langage de la dignité. La qualification des personnes dans la société parisienne à l'époque moderne." In *Dire et vivre l'ordre sociale en France sous l'Ancien Régime*, edited by Fanny Cosandey, 69–123. Paris: Éditions de l'École des hautes études en sciences sociales, 2005.

——. "La vénalité des offices et la construction de l'État dans la France moderne: Des problèmes de la représentation symbolique aux problèmes du coût social du pouvoir." In *Les figures de l'administrateur: Institutions, réseaux, pouvoirs en Espagne, en France, et au Portugal, 16ᵉ–19ᵉ siècle*, edited by Robert Descimon, Jean-Frédéric Schaub, and Bernard Vincent, 77–93. Paris: Éditions de l'École des hautes études en sciences sociales, 1997.

Dessert, Daniel. *Argent, pouvoir et société au Grand Siècle*. Paris: Fayard, 1984.

——. *L'Argent du sel, le sel de l'argent*. Paris: Fayard, 2012.

——. "Finances et société au XVIIe siècle: À propos de la chambre de justice de 1661." *Annales: E.S.C.*24, no. 4 (1974): 847–81.

——. "The Financier." In *Baroque Personae*, edited by Rosario Villari, translated by Lydia G. Cochrane, 57–81. Chicago: University of Chicago Press, 1995.

Dessert, Daniel, and Jean-Louis Journet. "Le lobby Colbert: Un royaume ou une affaire de famille?" *Annales: E.S.C.* 30, no. 6 (1975): 1303–36.

De Vries, Jan. *The Industrious Revolution: Consumer Behavior and the Household Economy, 1650 to the Present.* Cambridge: Cambridge University Press, 2008.

Dew, Nicholas. "Scientific Travel in the Atlantic World: The French Expedition to Gorée and the Antilles, 1681–1683." *British Journal for the History of Science* 43, no. 1 (2010): 1–17.

——. "Species as Specimens: Louis XIV's Menagerie and the *Académie des Sciences.*" Unpublished manuscript, 1998.

——. "*Vers la ligne*: Circulating Measurements around the French Atlantic." In *Science and Empire in the Atlantic World*, edited by James Delbourgo and Nicholas Dew, 53–72. New York: Routledge, 2008.

Dewald, Jonathan. "Les élites de l'ancien régime." Unpublished manuscript, 2010.

——. *Status, Power, and Identity in Early Modern France: The Rohan Family, 1550–1715.* University Park: Penn State University Press, 2015.

Diefendorf, Barbara. "The Catholic League: Social Crisis or Apocalypse Now?" *French Historical Studies* 15, no. 2 (1987): 332–44.

Dijksterhuis, E. J. *The Mechanization of the World Picture.* Translated by C. Dikshoorn. Princeton: Princeton University Press, 1986.

Dijksterhuis, Fokko Jan. *Lenses and Waves: Christiaan Huygens and the Mathematical Science of Optics in the Seventeenth Century.* Dordrecht, Neth.: Kluwer Academic Publishers, 2004.

Dolan, Claire. "Anachronisms or Failures? Family Strategies in the Sixteenth Century, as Drawn from Collective Biographies of Solicitors in Aix-En-Provence." *Journal of Family History* 33, no. 3 (2008): 291–303.

Doyle, William. *Jansenism: Catholic Resistance to Authority from the Reformation to the French Revolution.* New York: St. Martin's, 2000.

Drévillon, Hervé. *L'Impôt du sang: Le métier des armes sous Louis XIV.* Paris: Tallandier, 2006.

Duggan, Anne E. *Salonnières, Furies, and Fairies: The Politics of Gender and Cultural Change in Absolutist France.* Newark: University of Delaware Press, 2005.

Duhamelle, Christophe. "The Making of Stability: Kinship, Church, and Power among the Rhenish Imperial Knighthood, Seventeenth and Eighteenth Centuries." In *Kinship in Europe: Approaches to Long-Term Development (1300–1900)*, edited by David Warren Sabean, Simon Teuscher, and Jon Mathieu, 125–44. New York: Berghahn Books, 2007.

Duindam, Jeroen. "Early Modern Court Studies: An Overview and a Proposal." In *Historiographie an europäischen Höfen (16.–18. Jahrhundert)*, edited by Markus Völkel and Arno Strohmeyer, 37–60. Berlin: Duncker & Humblot, 2009.

——. *Myths of Power: Norbert Elias and the Early Modern European Court.* Translated by Lorri S. Granger and Gerard T. Moran. Amsterdam: Amsterdam University Press, 1994.

——. *Vienna and Versailles: The Courts of Europe's Major Dynastic Rivals, 1550–1780.* Cambridge: Cambridge University Press, 2003.

Eichel-Lojkine, Patricia. "Les Vies d'hommes illustres." *Nouvelle revue du XVIe siècle* 12, no. 1 (1994): 63–77.

Elias, Norbert. *The Civilizing Process.* Translated by Edmund Jephcott. Oxford: Blackwell, 1994.

——. *The Court Society.* Translated by Edmund Jephcott. Oxford: Blackwell, 1983.

Elster, Jon. *Explaining Social Behavior: More Nuts and Bolts for the Social Sciences.* Cambridge: Cambridge University Press, 2007.

Emirbayer, Mustafa, and Jeff Goodwin. "Networks Analysis, Culture and the Problem of Agency." *American Journal of Sociology* 99, no. 6 (1994): 1411–54.

Erlmann, Veit. *Reason and Resonance: A History of Modern Aurality.* New York: Zone Books, 2010.

Findlen, Paula. "Ereditare un museo. Collezionismo, strategie familiari e pratiche culturali nell'Italia del XVI secolo." *Quaderni Storici* 115, no. 1 (2004): 45–81.

——. "Masculine Prerogatives: Gender, Space, and Knowledge in the Early Modern Museum." In *The Architecture of Science*, edited by Peter Galison and Emily Thompson, 29–57. Cambridge, MA: MIT Press, 1999.

Foucault, Michel. "What Is an Author?" In *Language, Counter-Memory, Practice: Selected Essays and Interviews*, edited by Donald F Bouchard, 113–38. Ithaca: Cornell University Press, 1977.

Fumaroli, Marc. "Les abeilles et les araignées." In *La Querelle des Anciens et des Modernes, XVIIe–XVIIIe siècles*, edited by Anne-Marie Lecoq, 7–220. Paris: Gallimard, 2001.

——. *L'Âge de l'éloquence: Rhétorique et "res literaria" de la Renaissance au seuil de l'époque classique.* Paris: A. Michel, 1994.

——. *Trois institutions littéraires.* Paris: Gallimard, 1994.

Gady, Alexandre. "Les maisons de Claude et Charles Perrault, à l'Estrapade (5e arr. actuel)." *Commion du vieux Paris: Procès-verbaux* (1997): 11–22.

Gady, Bénédicte. *L'Ascension de Charles Le Brun: Liens sociaux et production artistique.* Paris: Éditions de la Maison des sciences de l'Homme, 2010.

Garber, Daniel. "On the Frontlines of the Scientific Revolution: How Mersenne Learned to Love Galileo." *Perspectives on Science* 12, no. 2 (2004): 135–63.

Garrioch, David. *The Formation of the Parisian Bourgeoisie, 1690–1830.* Cambridge, MA: Harvard University Press, 1996.

——. *The Making of Revolutionary Paris.* Berkeley: University of California Press, 2002.

Gautier, Jean-Luc. "Charles Perrault, premières œuvres, 1649–1675." Thèse de 3e cycle, Paris-X, 1978.

Gélinas, Gérard. *Enquête sur les Contes de Perrault.* Paris: Imago, 2004.

Genet, Jean-Philippe. "La mesure et les champs culturels." *Histoire & Mesure* 2, no. 1 (1987): 137–53.

Génetiot, Alain. *Le Classicisme.* Paris: Presses universitaires de France, 2005.

Gerbino, Anthony. *François Blondel: Architecture, Erudition, and the Scientific Revolution.* London: Routledge, 2010.

Giesey, Ralph E. "Rules of Inheritance and Strategies of Mobility in Prerevolutionary France." *American Historical Review* 82, no. 2 (1977): 271–89.

Gigerenzer, Gerd. "Where Do New Ideas Come From?" In *Dimensions of Creativity*, edited by Margaret A. Boden, 53–74. Cambridge, MA: MIT Press, 1994.

Gillispie, Charles C., Frederic L. Holmes, and Noretta Koertge, eds. *Complete Dictionary of Scientific Biography*. Detroit: Charles Scribner's Sons, 2008.

Goldgar, Anne. *Impolite Learning: Conduct and Community in the Republic of Letters, 1680–1750*. New Haven: Yale University Press, 1995.

Goldstein, Claire. *Vaux and Versailles: The Appropriations, Erasures, and Accidents That Made Modern France*. Philadelphia: University of Pennsylvania Press, 2008.

Goody, Jack. "The Evolution of the Family." In *Household and Family in Past Time*, edited by Peter Laslett, 103–24. Cambridge: Cambridge University Press, 1972.

Gordon, Daniel. "'Public Opinion' and the Civilizing Process in France: The Example of Morellet." *Eighteenth-Century Studies* 22, no. 3 (1989): 302–28.

Grafton, Anthony. *Joseph Scaliger: A Study in the History of Classical Scholarship*. 2 vols. Oxford: Clarendon, 1983–93.

——. "The World of the Polyhistors: Humanism and Encyclopedism." In *Bring Out Your Dead: The Past as Revelation*, 166–180. Cambridge, MA: Harvard University Press, 2001.

Grafton, Anthony, Elizabeth L. Eisenstein, and Adrian Johns. "How Revolutionary Was the Print Revolution?" *American Historical Review* 107, no. 1 (2002): 84–128.

Gregory, Brad S. "Is Small Beautiful? Microhistory and the History of Everyday Life." *History and Theory* 38, no. 1 (1999): 100–110.

GRIHL (Groupe de Recherches Interdisciplinaires sur l'Histoire du Littéraire). *Écriture et action: XVIIᵉ–XIXᵉ siècle, une enquête collective*. Paris: Éditions de l'École des hautes études en sciences sociales, 2016.

Grivel, Marianne. "Le Cabinet du Roi." *Revue de la Bibliothèque nationale* 18 (1985): 36–57.

Gruber, Howard E. "The Evolving Systems Approach to Creative Work." In *Creative People at Work: Twelve Cognitive Case Studies*, edited by Doris B. Wallace and Howard E. Gruber, 3–24. New York: Oxford University Press, 1989.

Guerrini, Anita. *The Courtiers' Anatomists: Animals and Humans in Louis XIV's Paris*. Chicago: University of Chicago Press, 2015.

Haddad, Élie. *Fondation et ruine d'une maison: Histoire sociale des comtes de Belin, 1582–1706*. Limoges: Presses universitaires de Limoges, 2009.

——. "Les Mesgrigny ou le coût social et moral des prétentions à l'épée." In *Épreuves de noblesse. Les expériences nobiliaires de la haute robe parisienne (XVIᵉ–XVIIIᵉ siècle)*, edited by Robert Descimon and Élie Haddad, 211–31. Paris: Belles lettres, 2010.

——. "Noble Clienteles in France in the Sixteenth and Seventeenth Centuries: A Historiographical Approach." *French History* 20, no. 1 (2006): 75–109.

Hahn, Roger. *The Anatomy of a Scientific Institution: The Paris Academy of Sciences, 1666–1803*. Berkeley: University of California Press, 1971.

——. "Huygens and France." In *Studies on Christiaan Huygens*, edited by H. J. M. Bos et al., 53–65. Lisse, Neth.: Swets & Zeitlinger, 1980.

——. "Louis XIV and Science Policy." In *Sun King: The Ascendancy of French Culture during the Reign of Louis XIV*, edited by David L. Rubin, 195–206. Washington, DC: Folger Shakespeare Library, 1992.

Hallays, André. *Les Perrault*. Paris: Perrin et cie, 1926.

Hamon, Philippe. "La chute de la maison de Thou: La fin d'une dynastie robine." *Revue d'histoire moderne et contemporaine* 46, no. 1 (1999): 53–85.

Hanley, Sarah. "Engendering the State: Family Formation and State Building in Early Modern France." *French Historical Studies* 16, no. 1 (1989): 4–27.

Hardwick, Julie. *Family Business: Litigation and the Political Economies of Daily Life in Early Modern France.* Oxford: Oxford University Press, 2009.

——. *The Practice of Patriarchy: Gender and the Politics of Household Authority in Early Modern France.* University Park: Penn State University Press, 1998.

Harkness, Deborah E. "Managing an Experimental Household: The Dees of Mortlake and the Practice of Natural Philosophy." *Isis* 88, no. 2 (1997): 247–62.

——. "Maps, Spiders, and Tulips: The Cole-Ortelius-L'Obel Family and the Practice of Science in Early Modern London." In *From Strangers to Citizens: The Integration of Immigrant Communities in Britain, Ireland, and Colonial America, 1550–1750,* edited by Randolph Vigne and Charles Littleton, 184–96. London: Huguenot Society of Great Britain and Ireland and Sussex Academic Press, 2001.

Harth, Erica. *Ideology and Culture in Seventeenth-Century France.* Ithaca: Cornell University Press, 1983.

Haynes, Christine. "Reassessing 'Genius' in Studies of Authorship." *Book History* 8 (2005): 287–320.

Heinich, Nathalie. *Du peintre à l'artiste: Artisans et académiciens à l'âge classique.* Paris: Minuit, 1993.

Herrmann, Wolfgang. *The Theory of Claude Perrault.* London: A. Zwemmer, 1973.

Hoffman, Philip T., Gilles Postel-Vinay, and Jean-Laurent Rosenthal, *Priceless Markets: The Political Economy of Credit in Paris, 1660–1870.* Chicago: University of Chicago Press, 2000.

Holmes, Frederic L. *Investigative Pathways: Patterns and Stages in the Careers of Experimental Scientists.* New Haven: Yale University Press, 2004.

Horowski, Leonhard. "'Such a Great Advantage for My Son': Office-holding and Career Mechanisms at the Court of France, 1661 to 1789." *Court Historian* 8 (2003): 125–75.

Howard, Nicole. "Marketing Longitude: Clocks, Kings, Courtiers, and Christiaan Huygens." *Book History* 11 (2008): 59–88.

Howells, R. J. "The Uses of Versailles in the 'Parallèle des anciens et des modernes.'" *Newsletter of the Society for Seventeenth-Century French Studies* 5 (1983): 70–77.

Hsia, Florence. "Mathematical Martyrs, Mandarin Missionaries, and Apostolic Academicians: Telling Institutional Lives." In *Institutional Culture in Early Modern Society,* edited by Anne Goldgar and Robert I. Frost, 3–34. Leiden, Neth.: Brill, 2004.

——. *Sojourners in a Strange Land: Jesuits and Their Scientific Missions in Late Imperial China.* Chicago: University of Chicago Press, 2009.

Hyde, Elizabeth. *Cultivated Power: Flowers, Culture, and Politics in the Reign of Louis XIV.* Philadelphia: University of Pennsylvania Press, 2005.

Jal, Augustin. *Dictionnaire critique de biographie et d'histoire; errata et supplément pour tous les dictionnaires historiques, d'après des documents authentiques inédits.* 2nd ed. Paris: H. Plon, 1872.

Janczukiewicz, Jérôme. "La prise du pouvoir par Louis XIV: La construction du mythe." *XVIIᵉ siècle* 57 (2005): 243–64.

Johns, Adrian. *The Nature of the Book: Print and Knowledge in the Making.* Chicago: University of Chicago Press, 1998.

Johnson, Christopher H. *Becoming Bourgeois: Love, Kinship, and Power in Provincial France, 1670–1880.* Ithaca: Cornell University Press, 2015.

Johnson, Christopher H., and David Warren Sabean, eds. *Sibling Relations and the Transformations of European Kinship, 1300–1900.* New York: Berghahn, 2011.

Jones, Colin. *Paris: Biography of a City.* New York: Viking, 2005.

Jouhaud, Christian. "Histoire et histoire littéraire: Naissance de l'écrivain." *Annales: E.S.C.* 43, no. 4 (1988): 849–66.

———. *Les pouvoirs de la littérature: Histoire d'un paradoxe.* Paris: Gallimard, 2000.

Jouhaud, Christian, and Alain Viala, eds. *De la publication: Entre Renaissance et Lumières.* Paris: Fayard, 2002.

Jurgens, Madeleine, and Pierre Couperie. "Le logement à Paris au XVIe et XVIIe siècles: Une source, les inventaires après décès." *Annales: E.S.C.* 17, no. 3 (1962): 488–500.

Kettering, Sharon. "Patronage and Kinship in Early Modern France." *French Historical Studies* 16, no. 2 (1989): 408–35.

Klapisch-Zuber, Christiane. *Women, Family, and Ritual in Renaissance Italy.* Translated by Lydia Cochrane. Chicago: University of Chicago Press, 1985.

Kostroun, Daniella J. *Feminism, Absolutism, and Jansenism: Louis XIV and the Port-Royal Nuns.* New York: Cambridge University Press, 2011.

Lahire, Bernard. "De la théorie de l'habitus à une sociologie psychologique." In *Le Travail sociologique de Pierre Bourdieu: Dettes et critiques,* edited by Bernard Lahire, 121–52. Paris: La Découverte, 2001.

Lavallée, Théophile. *Histoire de Paris depuis les temps des Gaulois jusqu'à nos jours.* 2nd ed. Paris: Michel Lévy frères, 1857.

Legay, Marie-Laure. *La banqueroute de l'État royal: La gestion des finances publiques de Colbert à la Révolution.* Paris: Éditions de l'École des hautes études en sciences sociales, 2011.

Leiner, Wolfgang. *Der Widmungsbrief in der französischen Literatur (1580–1715).* Heidelberg, Ger.: Winter, 1965.

Lemercier, Claire. "Analyse de réseaux et histoire de la famille: Une rencontre encore à venir?" *Annales de démographie historique* 109, no. 1 (2005): 7–31.

Lesaulnier, Jean. "Nicolas Perrault, théologien de Port-Royal 1624–1661." *XVIIe siècle* 66 (2014): 417–27.

Leveel, Pierre. *Histoire de la Touraine.* 2nd ed. Paris: Presses universitaires de France, 1967.

Lévi-Strauss, Claude. *The View from Afar.* Translated by Joachim Neugroschel and Phoebe Hoss. New York: Basic Books, 1985.

Lilti, Antoine. *Le monde des salons: Sociabilité et mondanité à Paris au XVIIIe siècle.* Paris: Fayard, 2005.

Loisel, Gustave. *Histoire des ménageries de l'antiquité à nos jours.* 3 vols. Paris: Ocatve Doin et fils, 1912.

Loriga, Sabina. *Soldats: Un laboratoire disciplinaire: L'armée piémontaise au XVIIIe siècle.* 2nd ed. Paris: Belles lettres, 2007.

Lougee, Carolyn C. *Le paradis des femmes: Women, Salons, and Social Stratification in Seventeenth-Century France.* Princeton: Princeton University Press, 1976.

Lough, John. *Writer and Public in France: From the Middle Ages to the Present Day.* Oxford: Clarendon, 1978.

Love, Harold. *Scribal Publication in Seventeenth-Century England*. Oxford: Clarendon Press, 1993.

Lüthy, Christoph. "Where Logical Necessity Becomes Visual Persuasion: Descartes's Clear and Distinct Illustrations." In *Transmitting Knowledge: Words, Images, and Instruments in Early Modern Europe*, edited by Sachiko Kusukawa and Ian Maclean, 97–133. Oxford: Oxford University Press, 2006.

Lynch, Katherine A. "The Family and the History of Public Life." *Journal of Interdisciplinary History* 24, no. 4 (1994): 665–84.

Maber, Richard. "Colbert and the Scholars: Menage, Huet and the Royal Pensions of 1663." *Seventeenth-Century French Studies* 7 (1985): 106–14.

Maître, Myriam. *Les Précieuses: Naissance des femmes de lettres en France au XVIIᵉ siècle*. Paris: H. Champion, 1999.

Mallon, Adrian. "Science and Government in France, 1661–1699: Changing Patterns of Scientific Research and Development." PhD diss., Queen's University Belfast, 1983.

Margócsy, Dániel. *Commercial Visions: Science, Trade, and Visual Culture in the Dutch Golden Age*. Chicago: University of Chicago Press, 2014.

Martin, Henri-Jean. *Livre, pouvoirs et société à Paris au 17ᵉ siècle (1598–1701)*, 2 vols. 3rd ed. Geneva: Droz, 1999.

Martin, John. "Inventing Sincerity, Refashioning Prudence: The Discovery of the Individual in Renaissance Europe." *American Historical Review* 102, no. 5 (1997): 1309–42.

Mauss, Marcel. *The Gift*. Translated by W. D. Halls. London: Routledge, 2002.

McClellan, James E. III. "L'Académie royale des sciences (1666–1793)." In *Lieux de savoir*, vol. 1, *Espaces et communautés*, edited by Christian Jacob, 716–36. Paris: A. Michel, 2007.

McCollim, Gary B. *Louis XIV's Assault on Privilege: Nicolas Desmaretz and the Tax on Wealth*. Rochester, NY: University of Rochester Press, 2012.

McMahon, Darrin M. *Divine Fury: A History of Genius*. New York: Basic Books, 2013.

Meynell, Guy. "The Académie des sciences at the rue Vivienne, 1666–1699." *Archives internationales d'histoire des sciences* 44 (1994): 22–37.

Miller, Peter N. "The 'Man of Learning' Defended: Seventeenth-Century Biographies of Scholars and an Early Modern Ideal of Excellence." In *Representations of the Self from the Renaissance to Romanticism*, edited by Patrick Coleman, Jayne Lewis, and Jill Kowalik, 39–62. Cambridge: Cambridge University Press, 2000.

——. *Peiresc's Europe: Learning and Virtue in the Seventeenth Century*. New Haven: Yale University Press, 2000.

Minard, Philippe. *La fortune du colbertisme: État et industrie dans la France des Lumières*. Paris: Fayard, 1998.

Moch, Leslie Page, Nancy Folbre, Daniel Scott Smith, Laurel L. Cornell, and Louise A. Tilly. "Family Strategy: A Dialogue." *Historical Methods* 20, no. 3 (1987): 113–25.

Mohr, John, and Harrison White. "How to Model an Institution." *Theory and Society* 37, no. 5 (2008): 485–512.

Montbas, Vᵗᵉ de. "Un manuscrit inédit de Claude Perrault." *Revue de l'art ancien et moderne* 51 (1927): 331–33.

Motley, Mark. *Becoming a French Aristocrat: The Education of the Court Nobility, 1580–1715*. Princeton: Princeton University Press, 1990.

Moyes, Craig. "Juste(s) titre(s): L'économie liminaire du Roman bourgeois." *Études françaises* 45, no. 2 (2009): 25–45.

Mukerji, Chandra. *Impossible Engineering: Technology and Territoriality on the Canal du Midi*. Princeton: Princeton University Press, 2009.

——. *Territorial Ambitions and the Gardens of Versailles*. Cambridge: Cambridge University Press, 1997.

Mulsow, Martin. "Practices of Unmasking: Polyhistors, Correspondence, and the Birth of Dictionaries of Pseudonymity in Seventeenth-Century Germany." *Journal of the History of Ideas* 67, no. 2 (2006): 219–50.

Namer, Gérard. *L'Abbé Le Roy et ses amis: Essai sur le Jansénisme extrémiste intramondain*. Paris: S.E.V.P.E.N, 1964.

Nédelec, Claudine, and Jean Leclerc. "Pierre Perrault critique littéraire." *XVIIᵉ siècle* 66 (2014): 429–45.

Neuschel, Kristen. *Word of Honor: Interpreting Noble Culture in Sixteenth-Century France*. Ithaca: Cornell University Press, 1989.

Noguès, Boris. *Une archéologie du corps enseignant: Les professeurs des collèges parisiens aux XVIIᵉ et XVIIIᵉ siècles*. Paris: Belin, 2006.

Nolhac, Pierre de. *Les bibliothèques du château de Versailles*. Paris: Le Livre contemporain, 1906.

Norman, Larry. "La pensée esthétique de Charles Perrault." *XVIIᵉ siècle* 66 (2014): 481–92.

——. *The Shock of the Ancient: Literature and History in Early Modern France*. Chicago: University of Chicago Press, 2011.

Noro, Yasushi. "Un littérateur face aux événements du 17e siècle: Amable Bourzeis et les événements dans sa biographie." PhD diss., Université Blaise Pascal—Clermont-Ferrand II, 2006.

Nummedal, Tara, and Paula Findlen. "Words of Nature: Scientific Books in the Seventeenth Century." In *Thornton and Tully's Scientific Books, Libraries, and Collectors: A Study of Bibliography and the Book Trade in Relation to the History of Science*. 4th ed., edited by Andrew Hunter, 164–215. Brookfield, VT: Ashgate, 2000.

Orcibal, Jean. "Descartes et sa philosophie jugés à l'hôtel Liancourt." In *Descartes et la cartésianisme hollandaise. Études et documents*, edited by E. J. Dijksterhuis, 87–107. Paris: Presses universitaires de France, 1950.

Padgett, John F., and Christopher K. Ansell. "Robust Action and the Rise of the Medici, 1400–1434." *American Journal of Sociology* 98, no. 6 (1993): 1259–1319.

Pal, Carol. *Republic of Women: Rethinking the Republic of Letters in the Seventeenth Century*. Cambridge: Cambridge University Press, 2012.

Pallares-Burke, Maria Lúcia. "*The Spectator*, or the Metamorphoses of the Periodical: A Study in Cultural Translation." In *Cultural Translation in Early Modern Europe*, edited by Peter Burke and R. Po-chia Hsia, 142–59. Cambridge: Cambridge University Press, 2007.

Panofsky, Erwin. "Artist, Scientist, Genius: Notes on the Renaissance-Dämmerung." In *The Renaissance: Six Essays*, 121–82. New York: Harper & Row, 1962.

Pardailhé-Galabrun, Annik. *The Birth of Intimacy: Privacy and Domestic Life in Early Modern Paris*. Translated by Jocelyn Phelps. Philadelphia: University of Pennsylvania Press, 1991.

Paul, Charles B. *Science and Immortality: The Éloges of the Paris Academy of Sciences (1699–1791)*. Berkeley: University of California Press, 1980.

Petzet, Michael. *Claude Perrault und die Architektur des Sonnenkönigs: Der Louvre König Ludwigs XIV. und das Werk Claude Perraults*. Munich: Deutscher Kunstverlag, 2000.

Picon, Antoine. *Claude Perrault, 1613–1688, ou, la curiosité d'un classique*. Paris: Picard, 1988.

Pillorget, René. *Paris sous les premiers Bourbons, 1594–1661*. Paris: Association pour la publication d'une histoire de Paris, 1988.

Pomian, Krzysztof. *Collectors and Curiosities: Paris and Venice 1500–1800*. Translated by Elizabeth Wiles-Portier. Cambridge: Polity Press, 1990.

Rabinovitch, Oded. "Anonymat et institutions littéraires au XVIIᵉ siècle: La revendication des œuvres anonymes dans la carrière de Charles Perrault." *Littératures classiques* 80 (2013): 87–104.

———. "Chameleons between Science and Literature: Observation, Writing, and the Early Parisian Academy of Sciences in the Literary Field." *History of Science* 51, no. 1 (2013): 33–62.

———. "A Learned Artisan Debates the System of the World: Le Clerc versus Mallemant de Messange." *British Journal for the History of Science* 50, no. 4 (2017): 603–36.

———. "Rethinking the Center-Periphery Nexus in the Early Modern Period: The Paris-Province Relation in Villiers's *Entretiens sur les contes de fées*." *Proceedings of the Western Society for French History* 38 (2010): 61–79.

Ranum, Orest. *The Fronde: A French Revolution, 1648–1652*. New York: Norton, 1993.

———. *Paris in the Age of Absolutism: An Essay*. Rev. and expanded ed. University Park: Penn State University Press, 2002.

Ribard, Dinah. *Raconter, vivre, penser: Histoire(s) de philosophes, 1650–1766*. Paris: Éditions de l'École des hautes études en sciences sociales–Vrin, 2003.

Richet, Denis. *De la Réforme à la Révolution: Études sur la France moderne*. Paris: Aubier, 1991.

———. *La France moderne: L'esprit des institutions*. Paris: Flammarion, 1973.

Riou, Daniel. "Naissance du roman moderne au XVIIᵉ siècle—idéologie, institution, réception." In *Histoire de la France littéraire*, vol. 2, *Classicismes, XVIIᵉ–XVIIIᵉ siècle*, edited by Jean-Charles Darmon and Michel Delon, 663–682. Paris: Quadrige/PUF, 2006.

Robbins, Louise. *Elephant Slaves and Pampered Parrots: Exotic Animals in Eighteenth-Century Paris*. Baltimore: Johns Hopkins University Press, 2002.

Roberts, Meghan K. *Sentimental Savants: Philosophical Families in Enlightenment France*. Chicago: University of Chicago Press, 2016.

Rosental, Paul-André, "Les liens familiaux, forme historique?" *Annales de démographie historique* 100, no. 2 (2000): 49–81.

Ross, Sarah. *The Birth of Feminism: Woman as Intellect in Renaissance Italy and England*. Cambridge, MA: Harvard University Press, 2009.

Rowlands, Guy. *The Dynastic State and the Army under Louis XIV: Royal Service and Private Interest, 1661–1701*. Cambridge: Cambridge University Press, 2002.

Rule, John C., and Ben S. Trotter. *A World of Paper: Louis XIV, Colbert de Torcy, and the Rise of the Information State*. Montreal: McGill-Queen's University Press, 2014.

Sabatier, Gérard. *Versailles, ou la figure du roi.* Paris: Albin Michel, 1999.

Sabean, David Warren. *Kinship in Neckarhausen, 1700–1870.* Cambridge: Cambridge University Press, 1998.

Sabean, David Warren, and Simon Teuscher. "Kinship in Europe: A New Approach to Long-Term Development." In *Kinship in Europe: Approaches to Long-Term Development (1300–1900),* edited by David Warren Sabean, Simon Teuscher, and Jon Mathieu, 1–32. New York: Berghahn, 2007.

Sahlins, Peter. "The Beast Within: Animals in the First Xenotransfusion Experiments in France, ca. 1667–68." *Representations* 129 (2015): 25–55.

——. "The Royal Menageries of Louis XIV and the Civilizing Process Revisited." *French Historical Studies* 35, no. 2 (2012): 237–67.

Salomon-Bayet, Claire. *L'Institution de la science et l'expérience du vivant: Méthode et expérience à l'Académie royale des sciences, 1666–1793.* Paris: Flammarion, 1978.

Sarmant, Thierry, and Mathieu Stoll. *Régner et gouverner: Louis XIV et ses ministres.* Paris: Perrin, 2010.

Saunders, David, and Ian Hunter. "Lessons from the 'Literatory': How to Historicise Authorship." *Critical Inquiry* 17, no. 3 (1991): 479–509.

Schalk, Ellery. "Ennoblement in France from 1350 to 1660." *Journal of Social History* 16, no. 2 (1982): 101–10.

Schapira, Nicolas. "Ecrivains et élites urbaines au XVIIᵉ siècle: Peut-on se passer du modèle du salon ?" In *La Ville et l'esprit de société, Actes de la journée d'études du 27 mai 2002 organisée par le CEVHI,* edited by Katia Béguin and Olivier Dautresme, 17–32. Tours: Presses universitaires François Rabelais, 2004.

——. *Un professionnel des lettres au XVIIᵉ siècle: Valentin Conrart, une histoire sociale.* Seyssel: Champ Vallon, 2003.

——. "Le 'Salon' écrit par les professionnels des Lettres (France, XVIIᵉ siècle)." *Papers on French Seventeenth Century Literature* 38, no. 75 (2011): 315–28.

Schmitt, Stéphane. "Studies on Animals and the Rise of Comparative Anatomy at and around the Parisian Royal Academy of Sciences in the Eighteenth Century." *Science in Context* 29, no. 1 (2016): 11–54.

Schnapper, Antoine. *Curieux du Grand Siècle.* Vol. 2 of *Collections et collectionneurs dans la France du XVIIᵉ siècle.* Paris: Flammarion, 1994.

——. "Probate Inventories, Public Sales and the Parisian Art Market in the Seventeenth Century." In *Art Markets in Europe, 1400–1800,* edited by Michael North and David Ormrod, 131–41. Aldershot, UK: Ashgate, 1998.

Schneider, Robert A. "Friends of Friends: Intellectual and Literary Sociability in the Age of Richelieu." In *Men and Women Making Friends in Early Modern France,* edited by Lewis C. Seifert and Rebecca M. Wilkin, 135–159. Farnham, UK: Ashgate, 2015.

——. "Political Power and the Emergence of Literature: Christian Jouhaud's Age of Richelieu." *French Historical Studies* 25, no. 2 (2002): 357–80.

——. "Self-Censorship and Men of Letters: Tocqueville's Critique of the Enlightenment in Historical Perspective." In *Tocqueville and Beyond: Essays on the Old Regime in Honor of David D. Bien,* edited by Robert M. Schwartz and Robert A. Schneider, 192–225. Newark: University of Delaware Press, 2003.

Seifert, Lewis. *Fairy Tales, Sexuality, and Gender in France, 1690–1715: Nostalgic Utopias.* Cambridge: Cambridge University Press, 1996.

———. *Manning the Margins: Masculinity and Writing in Seventeenth-Century France.* Ann Arbor: University of Michigan Press, 2009.

Sewell, William H. "The Concept(s) of Culture." In *Logics of History: Social Theory and Social Transformation,* 152–74. Chicago: University of Chicago Press, 2005.

Shank, J. B. "Making Science and State (Or the Other Way Around) in Louis XIV's France." Unpublished manuscript, 2012.

———. *The Newton Wars and the Beginning of the French Enlightenment.* Chicago: University of Chicago Press, 2008.

Shelford, April G. *Transforming the Republic of Letters: Pierre-Daniel Huet and European Intellectual Life, 1650–1720.* Rochester, NY: University of Rochester Press, 2007.

Sherman, Caroline R. "The Ancestral Library as an Immortal Educator." *Proceedings of the Western Society for French History* 35 (2007): 41–54.

———. "The Genealogy of Knowledge: The Godefroy Family, Erudition, and Legal-Historical Service to the State." PhD diss., Princeton University, 2008.

Shoemaker, Peter. *Powerful Connections: The Poetics of Patronage in the Age of Louis XIII.* Newark: University of Delaware Press, 2007.

Sircoulon, Jacques. "Pierre Perrault, précurseur de l'hydrologie moderne." *Europe* 68, no. 739–40 (1990): 40–47.

Sluhovsky, Moshe. "Discernment of Difference, the Introspective Subject, and the Birth of Modernity." *Journal of Medieval & Early Modern Studies* 36, no. 1 (2006): 169–99.

Smith, Jay M. *The Culture of Merit: Nobility, Royal Service, and the Making of Absolute Monarchy in France, 1600–1789.* Ann Arbor: University of Michigan Press, 1996.

Soll, Jacob. *The Information Master: Jean-Baptiste Colbert's Secret State Intelligence System.* Ann Arbor: University of Michigan Press, 2009.

Solnon, Jean François. *La Cour de France.* Paris: Fayard, 1987.

Soriano, Marc. "Burlesque et langage populaire de 1647 à 1653: Sur deux poèmes de jeunesse des frères Perrault." *Annales: E.S.C.* 24, no. 4 (1969): 949–75.

———. *Les Contes de Perrault, culture savante et traditions populaires.* Paris: Gallimard, 1968.

———. *Le dossier Charles Perrault.* Paris: Hachette, 1972.

Soullard, Éric. "Les eaux de Versailles sous Louis XIV." *Hypothèses,* no. 1 (1997): 105–12.

Sternberg, Giora. "Manipulating Information in the Ancien Régime: Ceremonial Records, Aristocratic Strategies, and the Limits of the State Perspective." *Journal of Modern History* 85, no. 2 (2013): 239–79.

———. *Status Interaction during the Reign of Louis XIV.* Oxford: Oxford University Press, 2014.

Stroup, Alice. *A Company of Scientists: Botany, Patronage, and Community at the Seventeenth-Century Parisian Royal Academy of Sciences.* Berkeley: University of California Press, 1990.

Sturdy, D. J. *Science and Social Status: The Members of the Academie Des Sciences 1666–1750.* Woodbridge, Suffolk, UK: Boydell Press, 1995.

Surrault, Jean-Pierre. "La Touraine des temps modernes (1515–1789)." In *L'Indre-et-Loire: La Touraine des origines à nos jours,* edited by Claude Crubois, 195–285. Saint-Jean-d'Angély: Editions Bordessoules, 1982.

Sutton, Geoffrey V. *Science for a Polite Society: Gender, Culture, and the Demonstration of Enlightenment.* Boulder: Westview Press, 1995.

Taton, René. "Cassini, Gian Domenico (Jean-Dominique) (Cassini I)." In *Complete Dictionary of Scientific Biography*, edited by Charles C. Gillispie, Frederic L. Holmes, and Noretta Koertge, 100–104. Detroit: Charles Scribner's Sons, 2008.

———. "Cassini, Jacques (Cassini II)." In Gillispie, Holms, and Koertge, *Complete Dictionary of Scientific Biography*, 104–6.

———. "Cassini, Jean-Dominique (Cassini IV)." In Gillispie, Holmes, and Koertge, *Complete Dictionary of Scientific Biography*, 106–7.

———. "Cassini De Thury, César-François (Cassini III)." In Gillispie, Holmes, and Koertge, *Complete Dictionary of Scientific Biography*, 107–9.

Taylor, George V. "Noncapitalist Wealth and the Origins of the French Revolution." *American Historical Review* 72, no. 2 (1967): 469–96.

———. "Types of Capitalism in Eighteenth-Century France." *English Historical Review* 79 (1964): 478–97.

Tenenti, Alberto. "Claude Perrault et la pensée scientifique française dans la seconde moitié du XVIIe siècle." In *Éventail de l'histoire vivante, hommage à Lucien Febvre offert par l'amité d'historiens, linguistes, géographes, économistes, sociologues, ethnologues*, 2:303–16. Paris: A. Colin, 1953.

Tiberghien, Frédéric. *Versailles: Le chantier de Louis XIV, 1662–1715*. Paris: Perrin, 2002.

Trout, Andrew. *City on the Seine: Paris in the Time of Richelieu and Louis XIV*. New York: St. Martin's, 1996.

Turnovsky, Geoffrey. *The Literary Market: Authorship and Modernity in the Old Regime*. Philadelphia: University of Pennsylvania Press, 2010.

Tuttle, Lesley. *Conceiving the Old Regime: Pronatalism and the Politics of Reproduction in Early Modern France*. New York: Oxford University Press, 2010.

Van Damme, Stéphane. *Descartes: Essai d'histoire culturelle d'une grandeur philosophique*. Paris: Presses de sciences Po, 2002.

———. *L'Épreuve libertine: Morale, soupçon et pouvoirs dans la France baroque*. Paris: CNRS Editions, 2008.

———. "La sociabilité intellectuelle. Les usages historiographiques d'une notion." *Hypothèses* (1997): 121–32.

Velay-Vallantin, Catherine. "Tales as a Mirror: Perrault in the *Bibliothèque bleue*." In *The Culture of Print: Power and the Uses of Print in Early Modern Europe*, edited by Roger Chartier, translated by Lydia G. Cochrane, 92–135. Princeton: Princeton University Press, 1989.

Véron, Jacques. "L'Académie Française et la circulation des élites: Une approche démographique." *Population* 40, no. 3 (1985): 455–71.

Viala, Alain. *La France galante: Essai historique sur une catégorie culturelle, de ses origines jusqu'à la Révolution*. Paris: Presses Universitaires de France, 2008.

———. *Naissance de l'écrivain: Sociologie de la littérature à l'âge classique*. Paris: Minuit, 1985.

———. *La naissance des institutions de la vie littéraire en France au XVIIe siècle (1643–1665): Essai de sociopoétique*. Lille: A.N.R.T., 1983,

Viazzo, Pier Paolo, and Katherine A. Lynch. "Anthropology, Family History, and the Concept of Strategy." *International Review of Social History* 47, no. 3 (2002): 423–52.

Vittu, Jean-Pierre. "Du *Journal des savants* aux *Mémoires pour l'histoire des sciences et des beaux-arts*: L'esquisse d'un système européen des périodiques savants." *XVIIe siècle* 57 (2005): 527–45.

Vivo, Filippo de. *Information and Communication in Venice: Rethinking Early Modern Politics.* Oxford: Oxford University Press, 2007.

Waquet, Françoise. "Conserver et transmettre le savoir à l'époque classique." In *Tisser le lien social*, edited by Alain Supiot, 275–85. Paris: Éditions de la Maison des sciences de l'homme, 2004.

———. *Les Enfants de Socrate: Filiation intellectuelle et transmission du savoir, XVIIᵉ–XXIᵉ siècle.* Paris: Albin Michel, 2008.

———. "*Puer Doctus*, les enfants savants de la république des lettres." In *Le printemps des génies. Les enfants prodiges*, edited by Michèle Sacquin, 87–99. Paris: Bibliothèque nationale, Robert Laffont, 1993.

Watson, E. C. "The Early Days of the *Académie des Sciences* as Portrayed in the Engravings of Sébastien Le Clerc." *Osiris* 7 (1939): 556–87.

Werrett, Simon. *Fireworks: Pyrotechnic Arts and Sciences in European History.* Chicago: University of Chicago Press, 2010.

———. "The Schumacher Affair: Reconfiguring Academic Expertise across Dynasties in Eighteenth-Century Russia." *Osiris*, n.s., 25 (2010): 104–26.

Wetherell, Charles. "Historical Social Network Analysis." Supplement, *International Review of Social History* 43 (1998): 125–44.

Whitehead, A. N. *Science and the Modern World.* New York: Free Press, 1967.

Wild, Francine. *Naissance du genre des ana (1574–1712).* Paris: Honoré Champion, 2001.

Wilding, Nick. *Galileo's Idol: Gianfrancesco Sagredo and the Politics of Knowledge.* Chicago: University of Chicago Press, 2014.

Woodmansee, Martha. "The Genius and the Copyright: Economic and Legal Conditions of the Emergence of the 'Author.'" *Eighteenth-Century Studies* 17, no. 4 (1984): 425–48.

Yardeni, Myriam. "L'Ordre des avocats et la grève du barreau parisien en 1602." *Revue d'histoire économique et sociale* 44, no. 4 (1966): 481–507.

Yeo, Richard. "Alphabetical Lives: Scientific Biography in Historical Dictionaries and Encyclopaedias." In *Telling Lives in Science: Essays on Scientific Biography*, edited by Michael Shortland and Richard Yeo, 139–69. Cambridge: Cambridge University Press, 1996.

Zanger, Abby E. *Scenes from the Marriage of Louis XIV: Nuptial Fictions and the Making of Absolutist Power.* Stanford: Stanford University Press, 1997.

Zarucchi, Jeanne Morgan. "Perrault's Memoirs and Bernini: A Reconsideration." *Renaissance Studies* 27, no. 3 (2013): 356–70.

❧ INDEX

Note: Page numbers in italics indicate illustrations.

CPSIA information can be obtained
at www.ICGtesting.com
Printed in the USA
LVHW111124031118
595846LV00016B/721/P